CW00675063

THE GEOPOLITICS OF SHAMII

Princeton Studies in International History and Politics

Tanisha M. Fazal, G. John Ikenberry, William C. Wohlforth, and Keren Yarhi-Milo, Series Editors

For a full list of titles in the series, go to https://press.princeton.edu/series /princeton-studies-in-international-history-and-politics

The Geopolitics of Shaming

When Human Rights Pressure Works—and When It Backfires

Rochelle Terman

PRINCETON UNIVERSITY PRESS

PRINCETON AND OXFORD

Copyright © 2023 by Princeton University Press

Princeton University Press is committed to the protection of copyright and the intellectual property our authors entrust to us. Copyright promotes the progress and integrity of knowledge. Thank you for supporting free speech and the global exchange of ideas by purchasing an authorized edition of this book. If you wish to reproduce or distribute any part of it in any form, please obtain permission.

Requests for permission to reproduce material from this work should be sent to permissions@press.princeton.edu

Published by Princeton University Press
41 William Street, Princeton, New Jersey 08540
99 Banbury Road, Oxford OX2 6JX

press.princeton.edu

All Rights Reserved

Library of Congress Cataloging-in-Publication Data

Names: Terman, Rochelle, 1986– author.
Title: The geopolitics of shaming: when human rights pressure works—and when it
    backfires / Rochelle Terman.
Description: Princeton: Princeton University Press, 2023. | Series: Princeton studies
    in international history and politics | Includes bibliographical references and index.
Identifiers: LCCN 2022056651 (print) | LCCN 2022056652 (ebook) | ISBN 9780691250489
    (paperback) | ISBN 9780691250472 (hardback) | ISBN 9780691250496 (ebook)
Subjects: LCSH: Human rights—International cooperation. | Human rights advocacy—Political
    aspects. | International relations—Moral and ethical aspects. | BISAC: POLITICAL SCIENCE /
    Human Rights | POLITICAL SCIENCE / Political Process / Political Advocacy
Classification: LCC JC571.T43 2023 (print) | LCC JC571 (ebook) | DDC 323—dc23/eng/20230123
LC record available at https://lccn.loc.gov/2022056651
LC ebook record available at https://lccn.loc.gov/2022056652

British Library Cataloging-in-Publication Data is available

Editorial: Bridget Flannery-McCoy and Alena Chekanov
Production Editorial: Theresa Liu
Jacket/Cover Design: Karl Spurzem
Production: Lauren Reese
Publicity: William Pagdatoon
Copyeditor: Cynthia Buck

This book has been composed in Adobe Text and Gotham

10 9 8 7 6 5 4 3 2 1

To Terry

CONTENTS

LIST OF FIGURES AND TABLES

Figures

Tables

ACKNOWLEDGMENTS

I have incurred so many debts in writing this book, from so many mentors, colleagues, and friends, that I am afraid any attempt to recognize them all will be inadequate. As with many of life's challenges, it is worth a try.

This book germinated from my PhD dissertation at the University of California at Berkeley. I am grateful to my committee—Ron Hassner, Steve Weber, Jason Wittenberg, and Raka Ray—for their guidance, both on the dissertation and throughout the perilous transition from dissertation to book. I am especially indebted to Ron Hassner for introducing me to constructivism and encouraging me to pursue a shoddy term paper containing a half-baked idea about backlash to human rights shaming. His infectious excitement for ambitious, creative projects was a great inspiration to me, and I will forever appreciate his faith in my abilities. I owe much to Erik Voeten, who—perhaps foolishly—took a chance on a random graduate student outside his department and eventually coauthored the article on which chapter 4 is based. Through his exemplary scholarship and patient mentoring, Erik profoundly shaped my intellectual trajectory. I can only hope to extend to my own students the same generosity afforded to me.

Throughout the research and writing, I was blessed with an incredible community of talented scholars who provided support of all stripes. This book benefited enormously from a manuscript workshop held in May 2020, and I am thankful to Rebecca Adler-Nissen, Karen Alter, Clifford Bob, Martha Finnemore, and Beth Simmons for their thoughtful and constructive comments. My colleagues at the University of Chicago have sustained me throughout most of the writing process, nurturing an environment that has been in equal measure intellectually rigorous, methodologically diverse, and unfailingly collegial. I am especially lucky to have been welcomed into a stellar IR group, joining Austin Carson, Robert Gulotty, John Mearsheimer, Robert Pape, Paul Poast, Paul Staniland, and Anton Strezhnev. I thank them for the many productive comments they have offered over the years, alongside unwavering encouragement. Before coming to Chicago, I had the good fortune to spend two years as a postdoctoral fellow at Stanford University's Center for International Security and Conflict, where I benefited from the inspiring mentorship of Lisa Blaydes, Harold Trinkunas, and Amy Zegart. Even as I struggled with impasses in my research, the community at CISAC enlivened my intellectual curiosity and motivation.

I am also grateful to the many interlocuters who offered feedback or advice on various portions of this project, including Lisa Argyle, Lotem Bassan, Zoltán Búzás, Valentina Carraro, Stephen Chaudoin, Miles Evers, Jamie Gruffydd-Jones, Homa Hoodfar, Amoz Hor, Eric Min, Scott Sagan, Kenneth Schultz, Omer Solodoch, William Spaniel, Michael Tomz, Joseph Torigian, Andrea Vilan, Steven Michael Ward, Anna Weichselbraun, and Ayşe Zarakol, among many others. This project improved each time I work-shopped my ideas at various venues, and I am indebted to the many hosts and participants for providing excellent commentary and sharpening my thinking. I feel a special sense of gratitude toward Nina Hagel and Ryan Philips; if not for their continual help and encouragement over the last eight years, I would have never finished this project.

I want to recognize the industrious research assistants who contributed their many talents to this project. Grace Carlebach lent her expertise on China, locating several sources and examples. Pete Cuppernull wrangled and analyzed data for chapter 4. Jenna Gibson and Casey Mallon coded survey responses in chapter 5. Among many other contributions, Giácomo Ramos read nearly every page of this manuscript and offered detailed copy-edits, corrections, and suggestions. Joshua Byun was indispensable during the book manuscript workshop, where he organized and distilled heaps of feedback while providing his own detailed comments. I also have Josh to thank for several examples, diagrams, and sources found in the book, as well as for helping me clarify the book's "big picture."

It is a privilege to publish this book with Princeton University Press, where I have the luxury of working with Bridget Flannery-McCoy, Alena Chekanov, Theresa Liu, Cynthia Buck, and their exemplary team. I am also grateful to the three readers for Princeton University Press, whose incisive comments greatly improved the manuscript. Financial support for this book was generously provided by Stanford University's Center for International Security and Cooperation, Time-Sharing Experiments for the Social Sciences, and the University of Chicago's Center for International Social Science Research.

Writing this book has been an emotionally trying process, and I would not have made it without my friends and loved ones. I am especially grateful to my "pod," whose immeasurable care and joy ushered me through the darkest pandemic days. Thank you to my family—David, Effat, Sarah, Jeff, William, and Nora—for their unending love and support. Above all, I owe a profound debt to Terry Johnson, who suffered all the trials of this process with little of the acclaim. Terry often sustained a kind of confidence in me and this project that far surpassed my own; this book would not exist without his relentless patience and nourishment. As we celebrate the birth of this project and prepare the next, I could not imagine a better coauthor.

THE GEOPOLITICS OF SHAMING

1

Introduction

Human rights are a moral concern, but also a geopolitical one. As a set of normative principles and ideals, the global human rights project has achieved unparalleled success, attaining nearly universal endorsement from around the world. As a set of practices, however, human rights are routinely and ubiquitously violated. Today an international framework has emerged to define, promote, and monitor human rights, encompassing numerous institutions, organizations, and mechanisms. And yet, in an inescapably anarchic world, there remains no centralized authority to enforce compliance with human rights agreements. Instead, the punishment of violations largely depends on the discretion of other actors in the international system—most importantly, other states.

States enforce compliance with human rights norms in multiple ways. The most common tool in this regard is "naming and shaming"—publicly condemning governments for abusing human rights. By shaming violators, states attempt to enforce a norm by imposing social and political costs on violations. While some states occasionally supplement verbal criticism with other kinds of pressure, such as economic sanctions or military intervention, shaming is by far the most common mode of enforcement, practiced by virtually every state since the inception of the human rights regime.[1]

International enforcement is certainly not the only way to promote compliance with human rights norms; other processes such as learning, persuasion, and technical assistance can also be important. But scholars and

1. Donnelly 1986, 608.

1

activists alike place special emphasis on enforcement as an essential, if not *the* most essential mechanism to protect human dignity around the globe. A long research tradition in the social sciences demonstrates that strong enforcement is critical for the maintenance of normative orders, including the international human rights regime.[2] As discussed in the next section, the international relations (IR) literature provides several important theories on the impact of international shaming and other forms of normative pressure on states' domestic practices. Several quantitative studies suggest that shaming leads to an improvement in human rights conditions.[3] Moreover, a plethora of case studies document "success stories" of governments reforming their behavior following global pressure.[4]

Yet to be effective, international human rights enforcement must overcome two substantial obstacles. First, foreign policymakers must voluntarily choose to punish other countries for human rights violations, but they often hesitate to do so. Enforcing human rights requires some amount of effort and resources, the beneficiaries of which are citizens of other countries. While some leaders may genuinely support the human rights project, they must balance these principles against their own national interests, such as security and trade. Even when punishment is purely rhetorical, criticizing other governments can generate serious political risks by upsetting a valuable strategic relationship. For example, China's allies—including many Muslim nations—have refused to condemn China's alleged abuse of Uyghurs in Xinjiang because they fear undermining a profitable partnership. "Few countries are willing to put the economic benefits of good relations with China at risk," observed Daniel Russel, former assistant secretary of State for East Asian and Pacific Affairs, "let alone find themselves on the receiving end of Chinese retaliation."[5] And yet, despite these disincentives, we still see leaders shaming other countries quite often—even where there appear to be few direct benefits from doing so. Why, and under what conditions, do states punish human rights violations in other countries?

Second, even when leaders manage to condemn human rights violations abroad, their efforts are not always effective. International shaming often fails to produce any meaningful change in the target country. In some cases, it can even backfire by provoking resistance and worsening human rights

2. Axelrod 1986; Bendor and Swistak 2001; Carraro 2019; Coleman 1994; Ellickson 1994; Moravcsik 2000.

3. Cole 2012; Hendrix and Wong 2013; Krain 2012; Murdie 2009; Murdie and Davis 2012b.

4. Franklin 2008; Risse, Ropp, and Sikkink 1999.

5. Perlez 2019.

practices. For example, after Western countries condemned Uganda and Nigeria for attempting to criminalize homosexuality in 2014, some observers reported a spike in human rights violations of LGBT people.[6] Early scholarship on international norm dynamics recognized the potential for shaming to be counterproductive but did not plumb the depths of this phenomenon. In the last few years, global events have sparked renewed scholarly interest in norm resistance and backlash, generating a number of valuable studies on the topic. And yet a robust theoretical account of these myriad effects remains to be made. When does shaming lead to an improvement in human rights conditions, and when does it backfire? And in cases when shaming *is* counterproductive, why do actors continue to do it?

The Argument in Brief

In this book, I address these questions by developing a *relational approach* to the study of international human rights shaming. Instead of treating norms like human rights as the moral consensus of a singular, amorphous "international community," I propose that we obtain better analytic leverage by thinking of shaming as a strategic interaction between discrete actors. As a form of social sanctioning, shaming occurs in and through preexisting relationships, particularly the relationship between shamer and target. The key insight of a relational approach is that we cannot understand human rights shaming—including its likely effects—without appreciating the relational context in which it occurs.

Starting from this approach, I construct a theory of interstate shaming that accounts for both its causes and consequences in world politics. I start by explaining why states condemn other countries for human rights violations. Despite its reputation as a tool to deter abuse, shaming is not always designed to secure compliance with human rights norms. Rather, leaders wield shaming as a weapon in geopolitical struggles for power, status, and legitimacy. When it comes to human rights violations, leaders seeking to protect their strategic interests may hesitate to shame friends and allies. To reproach a partner requires strong preferences for norm-compliant behavior—a rarity given the nature of human rights norms. In contrast, leaders will condemn rivals, regardless of genuine normative beliefs, to inflict political damage and gain a strategic advantage on the world stage. As a result, countries shame their rivals in particularly stigmatizing, sensationalist, and

6. Onishi 2015.

inflammatory ways. Critically, it is rational for leaders to continue shaming adversaries even if their efforts fail to change the target's behavior and even if those efforts backfire and exacerbate violations.

Understanding when and how countries shame is important because different kinds of normative pressure lead to different outcomes. The key insight is that shaming transmits vastly different signals depending on the relationship between source and target. The threat to a valued political relationship gives criticism exchanged between friends and allies greater leverage. Moreover, because there are few *strategic* incentives to reproach a friend, shaming in such cases serves as a credible signal to third-party observers that a genuine violation took place, damaging the target's reputation. Shaming from rivals, on the other hand, is easier to ignore. Because there is no valued relationship to protect, target states have fewer incentives to acquiesce to the shamer's demands. Such accusations are also less credible; they are widely seen as a cynical attempt to attack the target for political reasons. Governments can safely reject and deny such accusations without damaging their international reputation or domestic legitimacy.

Importantly, shaming from adversaries not only fails to secure compliance but can backfire by stimulating *defiance* in the target country. That is, it can be rational for leaders to react to foreign criticism by doubling down and ramping up norm violations. Why? Because when governments are shamed by adversaries, their domestic audiences can plausibly assume that the shamers, motivated by hostile intentions, are attempting to weaponize norms in order to degrade the status of their country. For these domestic publics, foreign shaming transforms local policy issues into an international battle over status and submission, driving defensive reactions that delegitimize outside criticism and place higher value on norm violation as a symbol of national identity and resistance. A popular defensive reaction generates incentives for rulers to resist international shaming, not out of an intrinsic desire to violate norms but rather to reap the political rewards generated at home. In such cases, shaming is not merely irrelevant but counterproductive by encouraging further offenses and even retaliatory actions.

In short, human rights enforcement is a deeply political process that operates in and through geopolitical relationships, is deployed and resisted for strategic purposes, and is interwoven in the nexus of global conflict. Adversaries are quick to condemn human rights abuses but often provoke a counterproductive response. Allies are the most effective shamers, but they are reluctant to impose social sanctions. Thus, shaming is most common in situations where it is least likely to be effective. This is not to say that such efforts are *always* counterproductive. In my theory, shaming can produce compliance, defiance, or deflection, depending on the relational conditions in which it unfolds. By combining these causal logics into a single framework, this book aims to develop a theory of international norm enforcement that accounts in equal measure for conflict and conformity.

The findings have important implications for both practitioners and scholars. For human rights promoters, this study provides not only a warning on the potential risks of shaming but also guidance on how to use this tool more effectively. The key insight is that, when it comes to enforcing human rights, the *critic* matters as much as (and perhaps more than) the *criticism*. Shaming associated with a geopolitical adversary is likely to backfire owing to the presumption of hostile motives, regardless of content. Shaming from an ally is more credible, and thus more effective, but also more difficult to mobilize. By delineating these mechanisms, this study provides practical guidance for governments and civil society actors who want to promote human rights abroad.

For scholars, the book extends and amends our understanding of international norms and their effect on state behavior. I argue that shaming exerts heterogeneous effects—a spectrum from compliance to defiance—depending on certain conditions. Importantly, the theory looks for these conditions in the shaming process itself, namely, the strategic interaction between shamer and target. This approach departs from many existing explanations for norm adoption and resistance, which emphasize the causal role of autonomous state attributes such as domestic political structure, material interests, or local culture. My theory, in contrast, shows how reactions to compliance pressures are generated through a process that is *endogenous* to international human rights enforcement. In pursuing this argument, this book expands our understanding of the ways in which norms shape the identity and interests of states even as they resist their governance.

More broadly, a deeper understanding of the strategic logic of norm enforcement opens new avenues for thinking productively about the relationship between norms and power politics in IR theory. Human rights shaming is often disparaged as hopelessly "politicized": states punish violations selectively, attending more to their geopolitical interests than universal moral principles. Indeed, my findings confirm that selective enforcement is rampant in the human rights arena. This does not mean, however, that such efforts amount to meaningless "cheap talk," or that the norms undergirding them are weak or irrelevant to political outcomes. On the contrary, states instrumentalize and manipulate human rights precisely *because* of their normative power, not their lack thereof. Insofar as enforcement is an inherently relational process, politicization is integral to—not a corruption of—the global human rights project.

The purpose of this introductory chapter is to set the conceptual foundation for the rest of the book. I first situate the study in the scholarly debate on international norms and shaming, elaborating both the conventional wisdom and the lingering questions concerning shaming's variegated effects. The next section clarifies some conceptual issues and describes my approach to shaming as a form of social sanctions that occur in and through relationships. I then introduce my empirical strategy and preview the evidence. The chapter concludes with a discussion of limitations and disclaimers.

The Topic

This book contributes to a large literature on norm enforcement in international politics. The general propositions I develop should offer insights for the causes and outcomes of interstate normative pressure in a wide array of cases, including those involving political-economic sanctions or even military force. That said, my discussion in this book focuses on a specific mode of international norm enforcement: "shaming," or the public expression of disapproval by states of specific actors—typically other states—for perceived violations of appropriate conduct (for example, protecting human rights).

My reasoning for this focus is twofold. First, shaming has emerged as the chief tool of norm enforcement in international politics. Shaming is practiced routinely by virtually every state in the modern era, whereas only the most powerful states are able to wield economic or military resources to coerce compliance. Moreover, economic or military tools in international human rights enforcement are typically mobilized only *after* the application of rhetorical punishment. Given its ubiquity and substantive importance, shaming offers ideal grounds for testing general theories of norm enforcement.

Second, shaming provides strong inferential leverage for a theory that views norm enforcement as a fundamentally political process, as mine does. Some scholars have dismissed shaming as toothless "cheap talk": too weak and frivolous to impose a meaningful coercive effect.[7] But if it is shown that this relatively "low-cost" form of norm enforcement is the domain of fierce geopolitical struggle over power, status, and legitimacy, it would stand to

---

7. Krasner 1999; Simmons 2009, chap. 4.

reason that the same dynamics should go a long way toward explaining more costly cases of norm enforcement as well. Simply put, shaming represents a "least-likely case" for a theory of norm enforcement that focuses on geopolitical relationships. Therefore, throughout this book I use the terms "shaming," "enforcement," and "pressure" interchangeably, with the understanding that shaming is an especially important *subset* of the broader phenomenon of norm enforcement and international pressure in world politics. The next section elaborates my conceptualization of shaming.

Shaming is performed by numerous actors, including, among others, nongovernmental organizations (NGOs), intergovernmental organizations (IOs), and media outlets.[8] Without denying the importance of other actors, this book devotes special attention to shaming between *states*. When it comes to international norm dynamics, states play an outsized role in several respects. First, while they vary in power, states generally wield greater power than human rights organizations or other nonstate actors, power that extends beyond military power or economic coercion. Even if countries fail to back up their rhetoric with material force, official statements often yield considerable symbolic importance—for example, by signaling future consequences.

Moreover, states exert considerable influence over the activities of nonstate actors. For example, they shape the work of NGOs by enabling or restricting financing.[9] Likewise, powerful countries direct the activities of IOs through institutional power (such as the veto), donor support, or ideological influence.[10] This is not to say that nonstate actors are unimportant, only that they must work in an inescapably state-centric environment in which governments hold a unique position of influence. Indeed, it is for good reason that activists and civil society typically direct their work at securing *state* support for the condemnation of human rights violations abroad.[11]

8. Amanda Murdie produced groundbreaking work on shaming by NGOs; see, for example, Murdie 2014; Murdie and Davis 2012a, 2012b; Murdie and Peksen 2014, 2015. On IOs, see Carraro, Conzelmann, and Jongen 2019; Koliev 2020; Koliev and Lebovic 2018; Lebovic and Voeten 2006; Squatrito, Lundgren, and Sommerer 2019. For other actors, see Hafner-Burton and Ron 2013; Ramos, Ron, and Thoms 2007.

9. Chaudhry 2022; Dupuy, Ron, and Prakash 2015.

10. Johnson 2011.

11. For example, Stephen Ropp and Kathryn Sikkink (1999, 23) explain how transnational advocacy networks lobby Western governments and publics. "Moral persuasion," they write, "involves networks persuading Western states to join network attempts to change human rights practices in target states."

Finally, while the shaming literature devotes considerable attention to nonstate actors, the activities of states are surprisingly neglected relative to their importance. Focusing too much on nonstate actors could bias our understanding of the nature of international shaming and generate misleading conclusions. For these reasons, I put states at the center of my inquiry.

Existing Approaches

Shaming has attracted significant attention in IR. Early research on international norms revealed the power of shaming to improve states' human rights behavior, contrary to realist expectations. Subsequent research has complicated this view by highlighting the myriad outcomes of international normative pressure, including resistance and backlash. Today the literature has culminated in a key question for which we lack satisfying answers: Why does international shaming result in compliance in some cases and resistance in others?

THE POWER OF SHAME

Modern scholarship on international norms emerged in the 1990s as a response to materialist approaches that dominated the field of IR. Much of this research sought to explain how principled norms such as human rights influence states' behavior in the absence of centralized, material enforcement. One influential paradigm emphasized the role of social inducements and shaming in advancing compliance.[12] Broadly speaking, shaming was thought to promote compliance by increasing the social and political costs associated with norm violation. In many ways, this argument still commands the conventional wisdom and so warrants further unpacking.

According to influential theories, international shaming promotes compliance with human rights via two broad channels: from "above" and from "below."[13] Shaming exerts pressure on governments "from above" by imposing social and reputational costs that violate international norms. For constructivists, shaming threatens the prestige, status, and identity of those states (or the leaders heading them) that view themselves as members of the

---

12. Other mechanisms have been proposed to explain norm compliance, including learning (Checkel 2001), persuasion (Risse 2000), and general isomorphism (Meyer et al. 1997). Here I focus on theories that emphasize rationalist incentives, wherein social pressure affects the cost-benefit calculations of policymakers regardless of their normative beliefs.

13. The "above" and "below" analogy comes from Alison Brysk (1993).

"international community."[14] For liberal institutionalists, states may not care about social approval per se, and yet shaming may reveal credible information on a country's general reputation for compliance, threatening other kinds of international benefits such as trade agreements or foreign aid.[15]

International normative pressure is thought to influence governments "from below" by empowering pro-compliance constituencies and fueling social mobilization.[16] International actors and institutions can provide credible information to domestic audiences, building consensus about a target state's human rights violations.[17] They can also introduce powerful ideas and discourses that cultivate rights-consciousness and mobilize local stakeholders to claim those rights from their government.[18] Finally, increased international attention can legitimate the activities of local NGOs and human rights advocates, broadening their basis of support and enhancing their political efficacy.[19] Indeed, many scholars believe that foreign shaming greatly empowers local human rights defenders.[20]

These two pathways—from above and below—often work in tandem. Indeed, some of the most influential theories of international shaming— including Margaret Keck and Kathryn Sikkink's "boomerang" and Thomas Risse, Stephen Ropp, and Sikkink's "spiral" models—attribute human rights improvements to the *combined* efforts of domestic civil society and the international community.[21] Both forms of influence adhere to a similar logic: shaming increases the costs associated with norm violation, whether through peer approval, foreign donors, or domestic publics. Governments comply with human rights demands to minimize these costs and salvage their legitimacy.

14. Finnemore and Sikkink 1998; Goodman and Jinks 2013; Greenhill 2010; Johnston 2001; Katzenstein 1996.

15. Lebovic and Voeten 2009.

16. Keck and Sikkink 1998; Ropp and Sikkink 1999, 5; Simmons 2009, chap. 4. A different pathway of influence works through certain branches of domestic policymaking, such as the legislative, executive, or judiciary (Kelley and Simmons 2015; Simmons 2009).

17. Xinyuan Dai (2005) claims that international monitoring provides credible information to pro-compliance constituencies, which they can use to hold their governments accountable. Echoing this logic, Daniela Donno (2013, 39–42) argues that IGO criticism of electoral misconduct encourages domestic protests by validating accusations of norm violations—providing the opposition with much needed credibility—and by reducing the likelihood of repression and retaliation. See also McEntire, Leiby, and Krain 2015.

18. Alter 2014; Merry 2006; Simmons 2009, 140–44.

19. Keck and Sikkink 1998; Simmons 2009.

20. Bob 2005; Carter 2016; Donno 2013; Murdie and Bhasin 2011; Simmons 2009.

21. Keck and Sikkink 1998; Risse, Ropp, and Sikkink 1999.

In formulating these arguments, few of the earlier scholars claimed that international human rights pressure always or inevitably produces compliance. The pioneering works recognized that shaming produces results beyond commitment and internalization and may backfire by inciting counterreactions.[22] Nevertheless, compliance and conformity were the principal themes permeating the first wave of norms research. Against this backdrop, shaming was considered a powerful tool to punish violations and promote human rights.

RECOGNIZING NORM RESISTANCE AND BACKLASH

In many ways, it is unsurprising that the first wave of norms research foregrounded diffusion and compliance. In an intellectual environment dominated by materialist paradigms, simply establishing the causal importance of norms and shaming was an impressive feat. However, this literature quickly came under scrutiny for presenting an overly optimistic view of international shaming. By focusing too heavily on the successful promotion of "good" norms by "good" actors, such work downplayed the central role of politics on both the giving and receiving ends of norm enforcement, while muting the widespread realities of contestation, resistance, and backlash.

A newer wave of research has sought to correct these oversights, elaborating two key insights. First, human rights enforcement is ineluctably political: actors often shame one another in order to promote their own self-interests, not necessarily the universality of human rights. As Clifford Bob highlights, for example, rights are used as tools and instruments to advance strategic agendas, including illiberal agendas.[23] Likewise, work by Rebecca Adler-Nissen, Ayşe Zarakol, and Ann Towns converges on the idea that international norms and shaming constitute a form of social power, (re)producing social hierarchies by establishing relations of insider-outsider or superior-inferior.[24] Meanwhile, large-N empirical work demonstrates the politicized nature of norm enforcement: as with most processes in

---

22. Keck and Sikkink (1998), for example, highlighted cases where transnational advocacy campaigns around traditional gender practices, such as female genital cutting and foot-binding, backfired by provoking the resistance of local actors. Likewise, Risse, Ropp, and Sikkink recognized that international shaming can stimulate counterreactions from autocrats and right-wing social forces that view human rights as a threat to their power—what they call "blocking factors" (1999, 24, 260–62). They revised the "spiral model" in 2013 to expand on the dynamics of denial and resistance and the conditions in which they persist.

23. Bob 2019.

24. Adler-Nissen 2014; Towns 2009; Towns and Rumelili 2017; Zarakol 2014, 2017.

international relations, geopolitics plays a critical role in determining who gets shamed for norm violations and why.[25] As a result, international condemnation is highly uneven and does not always follow the worst behavior.[26] For these reasons, many scholars view shaming as too inconsistent, too unreliable, and too cynical to have a meaningful impact on state behavior.[27]

Second, target countries are not passive objects of international shaming; they can and do resist in creative ways. States translate and adapt norms in order to better fit with local conditions;[28] contest and argue over their meaning;[29] deflect and evade accusations of abuse;[30] implement domestic institutions to immunize themselves from international influences;[31] and craft rhetorical arguments that justify their actions or minimize the perception of noncompliance.[32] While highlighting the agency of "norm takers," this body of work catalogs the myriad outcomes of international normative pressure beyond compliance or *status quo ante*.[33]

In addition to multiple flavors of resistance and contestation, some scholars recognize the potential for norm *backlash*: instances in which shaming not only fails to induce compliance but stimulates further offense, driving change in the opposite direction of the norm advocated.[34] Some posit that shaming one kind of violation can drive an increase in other violations, such as the use of government repression to offset improvements in political rights.[35] Others argue that shaming can provoke adverse reactions or countermobilization in the target state.[36] For example, research on norm "antipreneurs" and rival advocacy networks demonstrates that transnational advocacy can stimulate countermovements that often deploy tactics

25. Donno 2013; Lebovic and Voeten 2006; Zarpli and Zengin 2022.

26. Boockmann and Dreher 2011; Hafner-Burton and Ron 2013; Hill, Moore, and Mukherjee 2013; Hug and Lukács 2014; Lebovic and Voeten 2006; Murdie and Urpelainen 2015; Ramos, Ron, and Thoms 2007; Ron, Ramos, and Rodgers 2005.

27. Johns 2022, chap. 4.

28. Acharya 2004; Cloward 2016; Merry 2006.

29. Wiener 2004.

30. Búzás 2017, 2018; Hurd 2005; McKeown 2009.

31. Nuñez-Mietz and Garcia Iommi 2017.

32. Cardenas 2006, 2011; Dixon 2017; Risse, Ropp, and Sikkink 1999, 2013; Schimmelfennig 2001. The concepts of "tactical concessions," "account making," and "rhetorical adaptations" have been introduced to describe this phenomenon.

33. Bob 2019; Dixon 2017; Hurd 2017; Schimmelfennig 2001.

34. Carothers 2006; Hopgood, Snyder, and Vinjamuri 2017; Nuñez-Mietz and Garcia Iommi 2017, 3–4; Wachman 2001.

35. Hafner-Burton 2008. For further discussion of the "negative spillover" hypothesis and a comparison to other kinds of "backlash," see Strezhnev, Kelley, and Simmons 2021.

36. Hopgood, Snyder, and Vinjamuri 2017; Gruffydd-Jones 2018; Snyder 2020a.

and strategies similar to those of their pro-norm counterparts.[37] A number of experimental studies suggest that international normative pressure incites negative reactions in the domestic audience in the target country (see chapter 5 for a summary of experimental work on backlash and individual attitudes). Some stigmatized states may even choose to embrace their "deviant" status as a virtue, proudly flaunting their rejection and defiance of international norms.[38] Empirically, scholars have observed backlash to international normative pressure in several domains, including whaling,[39] sexuality rights,[40] and apologies for mass atrocities.[41]

OUTSTANDING PUZZLES

If the studies cited here usher in a "third wave" of norms research, this book is very much a part of that movement, building on the insights of this work about the political nature of norms and shaming.[42] It also tackles two outstanding puzzles. For one, existing research recognizes the potential for shaming to incite resistance or backlash but provides little explanation as to why actors would choose to shame despite these risks. Why do states engage in shaming in situations where such efforts are ineffective or counterproductive?

Second—and perhaps most crucially—why do some states redouble their commitment to violations in the face of external pressure while others choose to comply? We now have a better understanding of *how* states react to normative pressures but know less about *why* and *under what conditions* they do so. As Sonia Cardenas puts it in her comprehensive review, the central problem facing scholars is "the continued inability to account for why states sometimes resist international human rights norms, even when the conditions for compliance appear propitious."[43] When does shaming lead to an improvement in human rights conditions, and when does it backfire?

To be sure, many have tackled this question, but their answers typically point to attributes of the target state, such as its international power or

---

37. Ayoub 2014; Bloomfield and Scott 2016; Bob 2012; Chaudoin 2016; Nuñez-Mietz and Garcia Iommi 2017; Sanders 2016; Symons and Altman 2015.

38. Adler-Nissen 2014; Evers 2017.

39. Bailey 2008; Epstein 2012.

40. Nuñez-Mietz and Garcia Iommi 2017; Symons and Altman 2015.

41. Dixon 2018; Lind 2008.

42. Adler-Nissen 2016.

43. Cardenas 2004, 213.

status,[44] its domestic political institutions,[45] or its preexisting societal constituencies that support or oppose compliance.[46] These kinds of explanations fall into what social theorists call *substantialist* arguments.[47] A substantialist approach explains variation in norm dynamics by pointing to the substantive content, intrinsic interests, or fixed properties of a particular norm or actor. The vast majority of existing accounts about why shaming works or backfires—and IR in general—are substantialist in nature.[48]

For example, one popular explanation for why shaming backfires emphasizes the local cultural environment and "the degree to which the norms underpinning the stigma are shared."[49] Jack Snyder, for instance, argues that human rights shaming can backfire by igniting social-psychological processes that empower "traditional power structures" in the target group. This is especially likely to occur, he argues, when shaming is wielded by "*cultural outsiders*" (that is, liberal progressives) "in ways that appear to condemn local social practices."[50] In this view, backlash to international human rights shaming is ultimately rooted in autonomous cultural beliefs that are "illiberal," "retrograde," and implicitly non-Western—even as external shaming activates or energizes those beliefs. Here Snyder joins a host of other scholars in arguing that backlash emerges from a lack of compatibility between foreign and domestic norms.[51]

Snyder and I agree on shaming's potential to backfire, as well as on some of the psycho-sociological dynamics by which backlash unfolds. Where our arguments diverge is on root causes. Snyder takes the substantialist view, emphasizing intrinsic cultural factors, such as traditional norms, that supposedly conflict with liberal rights. My own argument, in contrast, is completely agnostic with regard to the *content* of norms—whether liberal, illiberal, compatible, or incompatible—and instead emphasizes the relational *context* in which norms are promoted or resisted. In my view, backlash is not unique to "traditional"

44. Adler-Nissen 2014; Evers 2017; Krasner 1993; Lebovic and Voeten 2006, 2009; Towns 2012; Towns and Rumelili 2017.

45. Checkel 1997, 2001; Davenport 1999; Gurowitz 1999; Moravcsik 2000; Poe and Tate 1994; Risse, Ropp, and Sikkink 2013; Sikkink 1993; Simmons 2009.

46. Ayoub 2014; Bloomfield and Scott 2016; Bob 2012; Búzás 2018; Cardenas 2011; Chaudoin 2016; Nuñez-Mietz and Garcia Iommi 2017; Risse and Ropp 1999; Risse, Ropp, and Sikkink 2013; Sanders 2016; Symons and Altman 2015.

47. Jackson and Nexon 1999, 2019.

48. For critiques of substantialism in IR, see Adler-Nissen 2015; Jackson and Nexon 1999; McCourt 2016.

49. Adler-Nissen 2014, 154.

50. Snyder 2020a, 110.

51. Cloward 2016; Cortell and Davis 1996; Nuñez-Mietz and Garcia Iommi 2017.

or "illiberal" cultures. Indeed, it may even occur in "liberal" and "modern" (even Western!) societies, as well as among individuals who would otherwise support human rights. This is not to deny that substantive attributes like culture are important, only to say that they are indeterminate. I would suggest that responses to international shaming cannot be adequately explained in terms of attributes of norms or states alone and instead require attention to the social relations mediating their interaction. A story that begins and ends with attributes like culture tells only part of the story.

A Relational Approach to Shaming

This book offers a different way to think about international shaming and its influence on state behavior, one that I believe has several advantages over predominant substantialist approaches. I describe this approach as *relational* because it shifts our attention from the attributes of norms or states to the relations between them. This section elaborates this meta-theoretical framework. I first clarify two central concepts: norms and shaming. I then explain why a study of international shaming demands special attention to social relationships, what kinds of analyses such attention demands, and what insights it might yield.

NORMS AND SHAMING

I define norms as standards of appropriate behavior that are enforced through social sanctions and about which there is some degree of consensus. This formulation builds on the standard definition in IR while incorporating two additional components.[52] First, I foreground *social sanctions* as a constitutive element of norms. "Norms cannot be considered merely as a series of 'oughts,'" write Gary Goertz and Paul Diehl, "but the possibility of sanctions is also an essential component."[53] What distinguishes norms from other patterns of behavior or intersubjective beliefs is their enforcement through social rewards and punishments.[54] Thus, understanding the

52. The oft-used definition in IR is "standard[s] of appropriate behavior for actors with a given identity" (Katzenstein 1996, 5). Prescriptive norms differ from statistical norms by virtue of their moral dimension. As Ann Towns (2010, 45) explains, prescriptive norms "are essentially about *value*, as they validate certain kinds of behavior for specific sorts of actors and devalue other sorts of behavior."

53. Goertz and Diehl 1992, 638.

54. Other scholars who center social sanctions in their discussion of norms include Adler-Nissen 2014; Donno 2010; Horne 2009; Zarakol 2014.

social dynamics through which norms are enforced is key to understanding norms themselves.

Second, the phrase "to some degree of consensus" registers my departure from the notion that normative commitments are necessarily shared, adopted, or expected by all relevant actors.[55] Throughout the book, I try to avoid references to "global norms" in order to avoid casting human rights claims as universal ideals, even if particular actors might present them as such. For similar reasons, I avoid references to "the international community" except when quoting other speakers, a choice that reflects my disagreement with the term's implicit assumptions. In its usage as an actor, "the international community" signifies no actor at all, but rather a disembodied authority that has managed to transcend politics to arrive at a shared moral certitude. Not only does such a consensus not exist, but the notion blinds us to something I find much more interesting: the ways in which particular actors gesture toward or make use of "global norms" or the "international community" in order to serve particular ends.

Earlier, I defined international shaming as the public expression of disapproval of specific actors—typically governments—for perceived violations of appropriate conduct. Following a long tradition in the social sciences, I understand shaming as quintessentially an instance of *social sanctioning*. Generally speaking, social sanctions refer to informal methods of enforcing norms through social rewards (for approved behavior) and costs (for disapproved behavior). Shaming represents a form of negative sanctions by which other actors diffusely punish a norm violator through adverse reactions.[56] In the interpersonal realm, these reactions can take a variety of forms, from subtle ridicule and slights to social exile and severe material deprivation. While they range in severity, social costs share a similar logic: by attaching negative consequences to norm-violating behavior, shaming lowers the expected net benefit of defection and encourages compliance with expected conduct. This broad conceptualization has been used to examine public shaming in a wide range of contexts, from the historic public square to modern-day social media, from corporate boycotts to public health interventions.[57] Regardless of the specific technique, actor, or context, most observers converge on a similar intuition about what

55. As Susan Hyde (2011, 24) observes, "It is not necessary for all states to believe that the norm is legitimate in order for it to be enforced."

56. As Christine Horne (2009, 9) explains, "Informal sanctions are relative—treating people better or worse depending on how they behave."

57. Frye 2021; Jacquet 2016; Maibom 2010; Massaro 1997; Scheff 2000.

shaming is: an informal, diffuse attempt to enforce a norm by imposing social costs on the violator.

In international life, shaming likewise occurs through negative reactions to perceived violations of normative conduct, such as human rights abuses. Much of the time this reaction comes in the form of public criticism, although the criticism is occasionally supplemented with additional measures, such as economic sanctions, the withdrawal of foreign aid, or barring the target state from IOs. Much of this book focuses on rhetorical condemnation, owing to its ubiquity in the international human rights arena. However, the general framework can apply to *any* state-to-state enforcement, whether material, political, or ideational in nature. As I suggested earlier, rhetorical and material sanctions are highly intermingled: the former is almost always a precursor to the latter. Perhaps for this reason, early norms scholarship used a very broad notion of "international pressure" or "socialization" that included both shaming and other kinds of material leverage.[58] The key point is that all such penalties are implemented diffusely, through the discretionary actions and choices of individual states. And like their individual-level counterparts, they claim the same ostensible function, despite differences in severity or effectiveness. As George Downs puts it, "Any threatened action or combination of actions that the designers of an enforcement strategy believe will operate to offset the net benefit that a potential violator could gain from noncompliance qualifies as a punishment strategy."[59]

It is worth pausing here to underscore how these conceptualizations diverge from other, more common approaches in the literature. In the first place, my framework diverges from many of those that theorize shaming as a "socializing" influence instructing states on appropriate conduct. On my view, normative demands do not necessarily represent the principles of any "international community" (or, as we will see, even the shamer itself). Condemnation is the result of specific political relationships, not a reflection of discordance with the international community writ large. Nor should we assume that most states strive for membership in a supposed "civilized community" or necessarily depend on a positive image within this group for their status or esteem.

Relatedly, mine is not a persuasive approach to shaming but a coercive one. The former involves changing hearts and minds through noncoercive

58. For example: "In the context of international politics, socialization involves diplomatic praise or censure, either bilateral or multilateral, which is reinforced by material sanctions and incentives" (Finnemore and Sikkink 1998, 902). Similar usage can be found in Risse, Ropp, and Sikkink (1999, 2013).

59. Downs 1998.

deliberation; the latter hinges on social inducements to elicit desired behavior.[60] Nothing about shaming requires the target to internalize a norm.[61] Indeed, individuals who move between cultures are often shamed for things they never considered unacceptable, and yet they change their behavior to fit in nonetheless.[62] Likewise, states, and the individuals who constitute them, need not share the norms of the stigmatizer in order to be responsive to social sanctions. Rather, because actors depend on the judgment of others for things they care about, they behave strategically to shape that judgment regardless of whether they genuinely believe what they are doing is right or wrong.[63]

Moreover, *shaming* does not require *shame*, a word that denotes a painful, internal emotion experienced by individuals.[64] "Shaming" is a form of external pressure imposed by others that may or may not generate feelings of shame in the target.[65] In other areas of the social sciences, the general consensus is that shame (the feeling) is tangential to shaming (the penalty). When it comes to shaming, as Raffaele Rodogno puts it, "it is sufficient that [observers] understand that disapproval is being conveyed to the offender."[66] Likewise, since I remain agnostic about the extent to which international actors *feel* shame, I focus instead on external social inducements generated by an expression of disapproval.[67] Again, this move is tenable because actors need not experience guilt, shame, or any other emotion in order to feel the costs of social sanctions, which operate primarily through the instrumental logic of costs and benefits.

60. Checkel 2001; Johnston 2001.

61. Schimmelfennig 2000, 2001.

62. Heidi Maibom gives the example of students from traditional working-class areas who go to prestigious universities, where they are shamed for their provincial accents and subsequently lose their accents (2010).

63. The desire for outward conformity, rather than internal drives, is what leads to decoupling policies from practices. For a discussion on decoupling and international human rights, see Hafner-Burton and Tsutsui 2005.

64. While I focus primarily on shaming (the sanction) over shame (the feeling), it is worth noting the social character of the latter as well. George Cooley considered shame and pride the primary "social self-feelings" (Cooley 1992). Shame is often associated with other emotions such as embarrassment, rejection, and humiliation, but as Thomas Scheff (2000, 96–97) points out, what all these terms have in common is that they involve a threat to one's social identity and the social bond. As Maibom (2010, 576) puts it, shame is "essentially about our lives with others, about our identity in a group, and our standing within it."

65. Braithwaite 1989, 100.

66. Rodogno 2009, 447. See also Kahan 1996, 636.

67. For an extended discussion on shame (the emotion) in human rights shaming, see Ilgit and Prakash 2019.

Finally, despite its reputation in some circles as a "weapon of the weak," shaming is not exclusive to those lacking in material power.[68] Nor is shaming always directed toward hypocrisy, meant to expose the discrepancy between stated commitments and actual deeds.[69] It could be the case that shaming is more *effective* when it is wielded by the weak, or if it addresses hypocrisy, but these conditions are not necessary for shaming to take place. As it happens, in the theory I present, these two aspects of shaming play a negligible role in the causes and consequences of human rights enforcement.

Some readers may object to my conceptualization of international shaming as overly capacious. Can we really speak about formal denunciations, informal criticism, and rhetorical threats as manifestations of the same phenomenon? After all, the IR literature features numerous terms for specific behaviors that I lump together under the umbrella category of "shaming." Indeed, it is important to acknowledge the nuances distinguishing these activities, which may provide useful analytic leverage in some studies. It is equally important, however, to recognize what they share: all of these activities are discretionary attempts by one state to denounce another state for perceived violations of human rights norms.

A capacious definition of shaming enables us to see the theoretical commonalities joining seemingly distinct phenomena in world politics, as well as the commonalities between shaming among states and among individuals. Indeed, shaming draws broad interest from across the social sciences: from sociology and economics to criminology and law, all rely on a similar set of conceptual tools to build cumulative theories, despite the tremendous differences across their substantive domains. Using a broad, abstract conceptualization enables us to bring the study of international shaming in line with the study of shaming in the social sciences more broadly and to harness theoretical insights from other fields. Put differently, what we lose in theoretical precision is compensated with theoretical power.

THE SOCIAL IN "SOCIAL SANCTIONS"

To begin to construct a theory about international shaming, we need to dig a little deeper into what shaming really is and how it works at its most basic level. For many writers, what makes shaming distinctive is its ineluctably *social* character—how it operates in and through relationships. Relationships mediate the process in two ways.

68. Cf. Jacquet 2016.
69. Cf. Busby and Greenhill 2015.

First, shaming penalties are imposed "horizontally" through interactions between actors in a group or network, as opposed to "from above" by some centralized authority.[70] Unlike formal or institutionalized enforcement mechanisms, shaming manifests through the voluntary reactions of other actors in a group. Critically, this makes shaming as much about the shamer's behavior as it is about the target's. The clearest formulation of this point can be found in classical works on the sociology of stigma and deviance, which relied on a relational ontology.[71] People do not *have* stigma per se; rather, they are *stigmatized* by others. As the sociologist Howard Becker puts it:

> Deviance is *not* a quality of the act the person commits, but rather a consequence of the application by others of rules and sanctions to an "offender." The deviant is one to whom that label has successfully been applied; deviant behavior is behavior that people so label.[72]

In other words, what is considered a violation of social norms does not follow naturally from individual behavior or attributes but instead reflects a social process by which others interpret, name, and punish certain acts as violations. The actual characteristics of "deviant" behavior are quite arbitrary and can vary considerably across different cultures and contexts. It is always up to others to determine which acts, and which actors, are labeled deviant. For this reason, readers should consider my use of the terms "violation" and "abuse" in this book as shorthand for *"what is considered to be* violation or abuse."

This insight is particularly salient for world politics. Despite a multitude of human rights institutions and mechanisms, the international environment contains no supranational authority to pass laws, monitor compliance, or punish violations in a way that achieves broad legitimacy.[73] To the extent that it happens at all, human rights enforcement *always* occurs diffusely, through the voluntary reactions of other stakeholders—especially states. Countries may work in concert to punish violations—as in multilateral action—but each polity must ultimately decide for itself if and how it wants to address

70. Although shaming is imposed horizontally, I do not presume substantive equality between the relevant actors. Indeed, shaming often involves unequal power relationships and dependencies—a theme throughout the book.

71. For reviews on the sociology of deviance, see Downes, Rock, and McLaughlin 2016; Goode and Ritzer 2007.

72. Becker 2008, 9.

73. This does not mean that international institutions such as courts or treaties command *no* legitimacy or exert *no* independent effect on state behavior. See Alter 2014.

alleged human rights violations. Moreover, unlike the domestic communities studied by Becker and others, the international context is populated by states that frequently diverge in their interpretation of what constitutes norms or deviance. As I detail in the next chapter, the decision to punish human rights violations abroad is a deeply political one, and different states make different decisions on how to proceed.

Second, shaming aims to secure compliance by imposing *social costs*. Unlike other kinds of penalties that deprive the transgressor of material assets (fines, for example) or liberty (such as imprisonment), social costs leverage relationships and relational goods to punish violators.[74] As Dan Kahan and Eric Posner explain, the punitive element in shaming arises from the damage to the target's reputation, which "injures the victim not because reputation is intrinsically valuable" but because it "prevent[s] him from obtaining future gains" through cooperation with others.[75] Shaming imposes a "stigmatizing judgment" that, when successful, alienates the offender both directly— between shamer and target—and indirectly by potentially influencing the reactions of observers.[76] When third-party observers compound the stigmatizing judgment, shaming further degrades the target's overall reputation, resulting in widespread and diffuse social costs. To reiterate, stigmatization can still play a role even when the target fails to share the norms of the stigmatizer or to acknowledge any wrongdoing. To the extent that people rely on others for the things they care about, the costs associated with a degraded reputation clearly have material consequences beyond psychological injury.

In world politics, interstate shaming likewise works by leveraging relationships. Despite its reputation in some circles as "cheap talk," shaming is rarely *just* rhetorical. International expressions of disapproval are meaningful insofar as they threaten underlying geopolitical relationships and the benefits they enable. As I explain in the next chapter, these benefits can be ideational, political, or economic in nature. By shaming other governments, states leverage these relational goods in an attempt to coerce target governments. To clarify, not every instance of public criticism is *successful* in this attempt. For this reason, my use of the term "shaming" can perhaps be more accurately understood as "an attempt at shaming."

---

74. On an interpersonal level, relational goods are those that "either distinctively exist within interpersonal relationships or are themselves constitutive of such relationships" (Cordelli 2015, 86). Chapter 2 provides a fuller discussion of relational goods in the international sphere.

75. Kahan and Posner 1999, 370.

76. Adkins 2019. Some make a distinction between stigmatizing and reintegrative shaming; see, for example, Braithwaite 1989 and Koschut 2022.

ANALYTIC IMPLICATIONS

The fact that shaming occurs in and through relationships has important analytic implications. To paraphrase Erving Goffman, the very nature of shaming requires a language of relationships, not attributes.[77] In placing relationships at the center of my analysis, I am indebted to work in relational sociology (especially that of Christine Horne), as I emphasize relational ties in the process of norm enforcement among individuals, while also building on a diverse body of scholarship constituting the "relational turn" in international relations.[78] "Relationalism" refers to a family of social theories with roots in practice theory, pragmatic philosophy, social-network analysis, and actor-network theory, among other intellectual strands.[79] The diversity and nuances of this tradition notwithstanding, my use of the term mainly reflects Patrick Jackson and Daniel Nexon's understanding of relationalism as "a broad sensibility that emphasizes concrete connections and ties rather than individual characteristics of entities or the general categories to which those entities belong."[80]

When it comes to theory building, this sensibility manifests in three concrete ways. First and foremost, a relational approach requires that we foreground the *relational ties* that mediate norm enforcement.[81] These relationships exist prior to and beyond the normative sphere and are embedded

---

77. Goffman 2009, 3.

78. Horne 2001, 2004, 2007, 2009; Goodliffe et al. 2012. In addition to extending Horne's approach to the international sphere, this book extends her insights in three ways. First, while Horne centers cooperative relationships, I examine norm dynamics in the context of both relational affinity and antagonism, as international relationships are characterized by conflict and enmity as much as by cooperation and trust. Second, I expand the scope from intrasociety to intersociety encounters. States are societies unto themselves, and the interaction between domestic and international politics is an important component of international shaming. Finally, while existing sociological work focuses on the determinants of norm enforcement, I attend to both causes and consequences, examining various outcomes.

79. McCourt 2016; see also Adler-Nissen 2015; Jackson and Nexon 1999, 2019; Pratt 2016, 2019. For an example of a relational approach applied to international status, see Duque 2018.

80. Jackson and Nexon 2019, 2. In addition to a class of explanations, relationalism is sometimes understood as an ontology: relations generate other phenomena like states, which rely on social interactions for their existence (see previous note). Although I use relationalism mainly as a meta-theoretical framework directing explanatory emphasis, nothing in this account is incompatible with a relational ontology as such.

81. Other studies that emphasize the relationship between shamer and target include Esarey and DeMeritt 2017; Flockhart 2006; Goodliffe et al. 2012; Johnston 2001; Schimmelfennig 2000. Although valuable, most of these contributions focus only on the target's behavior, and so a fully fledged relational account of international shaming (addressing both the causes and consequences) remains outside their scope.

in political, economic, historical, and strategic entanglements. The main analytic wager of a relational approach is that much of what we find interesting about international shaming—including its causes and consequences—inheres in these relationships and not just in the autonomous attributes of the parties to those relationships. Changes in the nature and strength of these relationships are likely to change both norm enforcement and compliance decisions.

Second, a relational approach demands attention to both the social and *strategic* nature of shaming. As I alluded to earlier, this strategic element differentiates social sanctions from other mechanisms associated with norms, such as persuasion or learning. At the same time, social sanctions are grounded in *intersubjective* beliefs about appropriate behavior that define normative expectations.[82] In this sense, shaming involves a "logic of appropriateness" as well as a "logic of expected consequences," hinging on sincere ideological beliefs along with strategic behavior that leverages those beliefs to maximize utility.[83] We must presume, as Ian Hurd puts it, that "strategic actors [are] embedded in a socially constructed environment."[84]

Finally, a relational approach centers processes and interactions rather than outcomes. In their reflection on processual relationalism, Jackson and Nexon describe processes as "a causally or functionally linked set of occurrences or events" that take place "in an identifiable temporal series" to produce change.[85] A process approach foregrounds the dialogical nature of social sanctioning: shamers and targets respond to one another, and those responses, in turn, shape their future actions. Importantly, this observation requires that we analyze the causes and consequences of norm enforcement together as a coherent system. Most of the existing empirical work on shaming directs the analytic focus on just one step in this interaction. That is, one stream of research examines shaming as a dependent variable by asking what determines the human rights agenda, which countries are singled out for the global spotlight, and how transnational advocacy networks set their strategic priorities.[86] Another group looks into shaming as an independent

---

82. Johnston 2001, 501–2.
83. Olsen and March 1989.
84. Hurd 2005, 497.
85. Jackson and Nexon 1999, quoting Rescher 1996, 36.
86. Barry et al. 2014; Bob 2005; Carpenter 2007b, 2011; Cole 2010; Hafner-Burton and Ron 2013; Hendrix and Wong 2014; Hertel 2006; Hill, Moore, and Mukherjee 2013; Lebovic and Voeten 2006; Meernik et al. 2012; Murdie 2013; Ovsiovitch 1993; Ramos, Ron, and Thoms 2007; Ron, Ramos, and Rodgers 2005; Terman 2017.

variable, asking what impact, if any, it has on state behavior or other outcomes of interest.[87] These literatures rarely speak explicitly to each other or investigate how the first process informs the second. This book takes a more holistic and dialectical approach, viewing shamer and target in tandem as they interact and influence one another.

These three premises form the analytic bedrock for my substantive theory of international shaming. The next two chapters develop this theory in more detail, showing how the strategic interaction between shamer and target guides both the decision to shame human rights violations and the response. Chapter 2 focuses on the decision-making of the shamer, while Chapter 3 turns to the target. The discussion culminates in a set of predictions about states' reactions to international shaming—including compliance, defiance, and deflection—and when we usually witness these reactions.

Empirical Strategy and Findings

A relational approach raises some thorny methodological challenges. Foremost, because the theory generates observable implications pertaining to different outcomes (the onset and consequences of shaming), the actors (shamer, target, audience), and levels of analysis (international, domestic), testing the entire theory using a single data set or analysis is infeasible. And yet these implications, while analytically distinct, are closely related both theoretically and empirically. Indeed, as I emphasize throughout the book, the same dynamics that give rise to strong shaming efforts are also the ones that incentivize resistance to those efforts.

My empirical approach employs analytic tools aimed at disentangling messy causal relations while respecting the relational and processual nature of international shaming. This involves selecting critical components of the theory and examining them individually, using the appropriate data and methods. Chapter 4 focuses on the *interstate* aspects of my argument, examining the influence of strategic relations on shaming between states. Chapter 5 then concentrates on the *domestic* level, examining how international shaming alters public opinion and political dynamics within target states. Both chapters use quantitative methods—large-N and experimental, respectively—to test specific empirical implications derived from my

---

87. Ausderan 2014; Cole 2012; DeMeritt 2012; Hafner-Burton 2008; Krain 2012; Lebovic and Voeten 2009; Murdie and Davis 2012b; Murdie and Bhasin 2011; Murdie and Peksen 2013, 2014, 2015; Myrick and Weinstein 2021; Tingley and Tomz 2022. See also the literature cited in chapter 5.

theory. Then, in chapter 6, I bring these individual components together using two case studies drawn from real-life episodes of international shaming. In addition to filling in some of the gaps linking the claims tested in the previous two chapters, the case studies illustrate how they fit together to form a cohesive framework that helps to explain human rights enforcement as it occurs in practice.

Chapter 4 provides evidence for the parts of my theory pertaining to interactions between states using data from the UN Universal Periodic Review (UPR), the most elaborate multilateral human rights process in the international system. The UPR is a process conducted by the UN Human Rights Council wherein states "peer-review" one another's human rights records. The forum provides an ideal laboratory to examine interstate shaming for several reasons. For one, by reviewing all 193 UN members, it is the only international human rights mechanism to achieve 100 percent voluntary participation. Further, the fact that the reviewers are the states themselves enables researchers to trace the influence of political relationships in the enforcement of human rights. Importantly, the UPR represents a highly systematic, formalized, and repetitive environment and thus is able to provide a granularity of information (who says what to whom) that is unmatched by other data sources.

I examined over fifty-seven thousand recommendations from the first two cycles of UPR, testing the influence of three kinds of strategic relationships: geopolitical affinity, formal military alliance, and arms trade. Results from the statistical analysis reveal the deep and extensive role of strategic relationships in the shaming process. States condemn norm violations selectively, sparing their strategic partners in the review process. Meanwhile, they condemn geopolitical rivals in more demanding and inflammatory fashion, all else equal. I also show that the target state's sensitivity to normative pressure is conditional on its relationship to the source of that pressure. That is, states will accommodate or reject shaming based on their relationship with the shamer, regardless of the norm in question or the substantive content of the criticism.

In chapter 5, I look at the ways in which international shaming alters domestic politics, using survey experiments that examine public reactions to foreign shaming. Contrary to some received wisdom, I find that international shaming exerts counterproductive effects on public opinion, increasing both nationalist sentiments and hostility toward advocacy efforts. Importantly, these defensive reactions appear to be relational, not ideological, in nature. Identical criticism can evoke very different reactions depending on the source and target. Indeed, the evidence shows that foreign shaming can incite defensive reactions even among those individuals who are sympathetic to human rights causes. This suggests that antagonism toward international shaming is not reducible to preestablished ideological positions opposing human rights and hinges critically on relational context.

The main empirical advantage of both survey experiments and formal processes like the UPR lies in their ability to isolate causal factors in a highly controlled and stylized environment. But to understand how these mechanisms unfold in real life, we need detailed qualitative evidence culled from natural settings. To this end, Chapter 6 applies my relational framework of international shaming to two case studies. I first examine the US position toward Saudi Arabia following the death of *Washington Post* journalist Jamal Khashoggi in 2018. The second case turns to Iran and the 2010–2011 "Save Sakineh" campaign, an international shaming operation concerning a woman who was sentenced to death by stoning for adultery. In each case, I examine both the choice to shame human rights violations and the consequences of that choice, reconstructing the strategic interaction between (potential) shamers, target countries, and relevant audiences. Together, the cases illustrate the mechanisms underlying interstate human rights shaming and its variegated effects.

Scope, Limitations, and Disclaimers

Before proceeding, it is important to clarify what this book is not. For one, it does not provide an exhaustive analysis of human rights shaming or enforcement. International human rights enforcement is a complex phenomenon that involves a cast of state and nonstate characters, formal and informal institutions, and a range of processes occurring on multiple levels of analysis, from interpersonal to international. Clearly it is not possible to do justice to all of these facets, nor do I pretend to.

Rather, as discussed earlier, this book centers states and their role as shaming actors. It is important to keep in mind that states have a distinct set of strategic interests and capabilities that make them qualitatively different from NGOs and other nonstate actors. That said, the insights emerging from this study are not uniquely relevant to states. We know that NGOs and civil society play an important role in human rights enforcement. But to do so, they must navigate the ineluctably state-centric nature of the international environment. Put differently, the strategic interaction between states inevitably shapes the work of NGOs and vice versa. Therefore, although the activities of nonstate actors lie outside my immediate focus, a study of inter-state shaming yields important implications for nonstate actors as well. In the concluding chapter, I highlight these implications by attending to other kinds of shamers—including NGOs, activists, and media outlets—and the interaction between them.

Importantly, this book does not offer a normative judgment of shaming as a political device. The history of human rights has demonstrated the power of moral criticism to mobilize political movements, articulate claims to equality and dignity, and even tame the most egregious abuses of power. These are undeniable feats. Beyond its utility as a political device, human rights shaming may thwart instrumentalist logic altogether, reflecting a deontological imperative to bear witness and speak up in the face of injustice.

While we should acknowledge the good that human rights pressure has done to uplift the human condition, it is equally important to recognize that shaming exerts myriad effects that may or may not align with the noble intentions of advocates. As a social process, it entails actions and reactions that may alter the political environment in ways that are unforeseen and often unintended by the agents involved. An empirical inquiry into this process should not be confused with a rejection or condemnation of international shaming or human rights ideals. To the extent that the arguments herein have normative implications, they urge a richer empirical investigation into the consequences of human rights enforcement—both intended and unintended—as a requirement of any responsible policy or action.

I provide additional information on the empirical analyses conducted in chapters 4 and 5 in online appendixes, which can be accessed at www.rochelleterman.com.

2

A Relational Theory of International Shaming

THE SHAMER

This chapter and the next one present a relational theory of shaming that accounts for both its causes and consequences in world politics. In the last chapter, I described shaming as a relational phenomenon that is about the shamer as much as the target. Understanding the drivers of social sanctioning is critical to apprehending its effects because, as I intend to demonstrate, states shame their friends and rivals in systematically different ways, leading to different effects. Thus, my explanation for the various reactions to normative pressure requires examining the origins of such pressure.

The theory is presented in two parts, each tackling the perspective and motives of one party in this iterative process. After introducing the main theoretical building blocks of the argument, this chapter focuses on the decision-making of the shamer. Why and how do governments accuse and shame other governments for human rights violations? The next chapter shifts the analytic focus to the target, explaining why states respond in various ways to international human rights pressure. When does shaming lead to an improvement in human rights conditions and when does it backfire?

The rest of this chapter proceeds as follows. The first section introduces the relevant actors and the sequence of events that fall within the scope of the theory. The next section establishes some foundational assumptions about the international environment and the role of strategic relationships, relational goods, and relational costs in this environment. I then proceed to the question of why and how states shame other states for perceived human rights violations. After identifying the main costs and benefits factoring into this decision, I explain that such inducements shift depending on the political relationship between shamer and target. The discussion culminates in two main insights. First, shaming can be rational even when it fails to promote compliance. Second, states will shame their geopolitical rivals more often, and more harshly, than their strategic partners.

Relevant Actors and Events

My theory focuses on interactions between shamers, targets, and audiences. Shamers are those who identify and condemn specific actors for perceived human rights violations. In the previous chapter, I explained that shaming can be deployed by different actors, including states, NGOs, IOs, and media outlets. Because of their outsized influence in world politics, the following theory focuses on states. I also acknowledge, however, the role of civil society and other nonstate actors in influencing the behavior of state decision-makers, a point I develop later.

Shaming can target individuals, corporate actors such as firms or countries, or classes of people, such as political parties or religious sects. When it comes to human rights, governments are the most common targets for shame, largely owing to the historical legacy of the human rights regime, which specifies states as having human rights obligations. Although the human rights regime has expanded in recent years to include violations committed by nonstate actors (for example, domestic abusers and armed militias), governments remain principally responsible for protecting human rights within their territory (and potentially outside their territory as well). To clarify, targets are those who are *accused* of violations, regardless of whether they have actually violated human rights in any objective sense.

Finally, shaming, as a public expression of criticism, occurs in front of an *audience* of observers. Although audiences are the most amorphous actors in the story, they are central to its logic.[1] Audiences observe leaders

---

1. Nearly all writers on shame and shaming emphasize the importance of audiences. See Adkins 2019.

making decisions vis-à-vis human rights enforcement and maintain some interest or stake in the controversy. Multiple kinds of audiences—foreign and domestic—are relevant in shaming dynamics. Throughout this volume, I place special focus on domestic publics in both the shaming and target countries, but other audiences are likely to be relevant, such as specific constituencies, the factions of a ruling coalition, or foreign actors that affiliate with a sanctioned regime and have some leverage over it.[2]

Figure 2.1 maps the actors and events that fall within the scope of the theory. As shown, I do not intend to explain the initial apparent violation of human rights.[3] The large literature devoted to this question elaborates the numerous factors and contexts associated with abuse.[4] It is worth noting that, logically speaking, the fact that a government has violated human rights is neither necessary nor sufficient for shaming to occur. Many actions that we would classify as abuses go unnoticed, and international pressure is unevenly distributed across similar problems.[5] False allegations also occur, as when Cambodian anti-sex-trafficking activist Somaly Mam was revealed to have fabricated some claims of mistreatment.[6] To make matters more complicated, an act of violation is unobservable—perhaps even unintelligible—absent its designation as such, which typically manifests as condemnation. In other words, the two events—a government violating a norm and a government being shamed for violating a norm—are epistemologically intertwined. We rarely observe one without the other.

For these reasons, I bracket the question of why governments abuse human rights in the first place—or even whether a bona fide violation occurred—and focus instead on *reactions* to an apparent violation and the interactions that follow.[7] Nor do I systematically address the process by

2. For conceptualizations of "audience" in IR that move beyond the mass public of a democratic regime, see Dai 2005; Weeks 2008.

3. I use the phrase "apparent violation" to include contested allegations (for example, some see the behavior in question as a violation of human rights while others do not) as well as false or misleading allegations (such as propaganda or rumor). As I emphasized in chapter 1, my use of "violation" is almost always shorthand for "what some consider a violation."

4. Hafner-Burton 2014; Poe, Tate, and Keith 1999.

5. Donno 2010; Hafner-Burton and Ron 2013; Hill, Moore, and Mukherjee 2013; Lebovic and Voeten 2006; Ramos, Ron, and Thoms 2007; Ron, Ramos, and Rodgers 2005; Terman and Voeten 2018.

6. Joseph 2014.

7. This move is not without precedent in the social sciences. Many sociologists, for example, focus their attention on "secondary deviance." Unlike primary deviance, which can arise from any number of factors and has only marginal impact on the status and life course of the perpetrator, secondary deviance reflects "deviant behavior, or social roles based upon it, which becomes a means of defense, attack, or adaptation to the overt and covert problems created by the societal

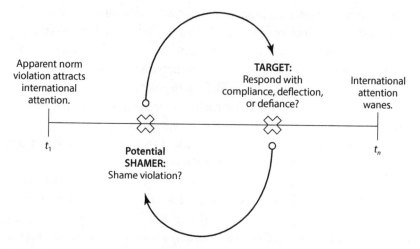

FIGURE 2.1. Theoretical Scope: Timeline of Events and Choices
The figure visualizes the timeline of events and choices that fall within the scope of the theory. Arrows denote an interaction between the shamer and the target.

which perceived violations initially capture the interest or attention of international actors. On this subject, I refer readers to the ample research on transnational advocacy, social movements, and human rights monitoring.[8] My main concern is with the onset of international attention to an alleged offense and the events that follow.

Once a perceived violation attracts international attention, the observing states (potential shamers) must choose whether and how to respond. It is the deeply *political* decision to condemn a human rights violation that I explore in the rest of this chapter. Different actors settle on different choices about whether and how to condemn a perceived violation, and these decisions are important for the question of shaming's effects.

If observing states do decide to shame, leaders in the target country are prompted to respond. Sometimes leaders in the target state simply ignore foreign shaming, but they do often react in some way. The next chapter outlines a scheme cataloging potential responses to international human rights shaming, including *compliance, defiance,* and *deflection*. After the target state reacts, international actors counter by, for example, ramping up

reaction to primary deviation" (Lemert 1972, 17). In effect, society's reaction to the original offense becomes the engine propelling future offenses.

8. Bob 2005; Bush 2017; Carpenter 2007a; Hafner-Burton and Ron 2013; Keck and Sikkink 1998; Ramos, Ron, and Thoms 2007; Ron, Ramos, and Rodgers 2005.

their shaming efforts, switching to private diplomacy or another strategy, or backing down on their criticisms. Shamers and targets continue to interact in an iterative fashion. I am interested in both short- and long-term outcomes of international shaming, including the target state's immediate response, as well as more structural shifts in the normative environment at the domestic and international levels.

Relational Goods and Relational Costs

My theory assumes that states are egoists, concerned primarily with advancing their own interests. Crucially, however, states also rely on others in the international system for things they care about. This set of strategic relationships provides the foundation for my argument.

Because states behave primarily to further their interests, they strive to avoid offending other states on which those interests depend. Jay Goodliffe and Darren Hawkins call this set of relationships the state's "dependence network": "those with whom a state regularly engages in exchanges of valued goods, where those exchanges would be costly to break."[9] These "relational goods" are diverse and encompass both material and nonmaterial assets, including those related to security (formal alliances, arms agreements) and wealth (preferential trade agreements, direct foreign investment), political objectives (membership in IOs, foreign policy coordination), and even identity (legitimacy, prestige). States exchange such goods in the context of a strategic partnership in which each party cooperates as a means to further its own interests.

For example, the United States provides Saudi Arabia with aid, arms, and some degree of legitimacy in exchange for oil production and security cooperation. As this example makes clear, strategic partnerships are not necessarily equal. The Saudi regime would probably have more to lose than the United States if their relationship went sour. Likewise, China depends on several African nations for energy, but probably not as much as those countries depend on China for investment. In this regard, the United States and China enjoy an asymmetric position of power in their relationships. That said, strategic partnerships are rarely entirely one-sided. The United States exports arms to Saudi Arabia not just for financial gain but also because it values its strategic partnership. China invests in African countries because it profits from their cooperation. More generally, countries provide foreign

9. Goodliffe and Hawkins 2009a, 978.

aid and arms selectively, with their own geopolitical interests in mind.[10] Even powerful states benefit from such relationships and depend on the cooperation of their partners to some extent.

Leaders vary in the type of relational goods they value. As Susan Hyde writes in her volume on democracy-contingent benefits, some governments prioritize military alliance or foreign aid, while others strive for greater status and recognition.[11] In Hyde's theory—as in mine—it is unnecessary to assume that leaders prioritize material goods over intangible benefits or vice versa.[12] What is important is that such goods are exchanged in and through a relationship. Generally speaking, the more an actor values a particular set of goods, the more it values the *relationship* on which those goods depend.[13]

This is not to say that strategic relationships are all that states care about. Leaders typically hold multiple interests simultaneously, and these goals often conflict. For example, a government's interest in maintaining a strategic partnership may conflict with a preference for a robust human rights regime. All else equal, however, states would rather avoid provoking a negative reaction from their partners owing to the relational costs involved.

Throughout this book, I use the terms "friends" or "partners" to describe a pair of states with a mutually beneficial relationship that reflects broad and deep dependence ties. We naturally refer to the United States and Canada, for example, as friends. Because leaders value these relationships, they strive to maintain them to ensure future benefits. Leaders anticipate the potential reactions of partners and choose actions that provoke a positive, rather than negative, response. In other words, states engage in *strategic acquiescence*: they behave in ways that elicit positive reactions and avoid negative ones, with the goal of sustaining relationships. As Goodliffe and Hawkins note, these reactions need not involve explicit rewards or punishments that are contingent on behavior. Rather, states merely anticipate the *potential* costs (or benefits) to a valued relationship and factor these into their decision calculus.[14]

"Adversaries" or "rivals" describe those states that not only lack significant dependence ties but share negative dependencies. Unlike friends, who

10. Donor countries often provide aid in exchange for some politically relevant benefit, such as military cooperation, access to important resources, or special rights to transit or territory. See Alesina and Dollar 2000; Blanton 2005; Lebovic 1988, 2005; Perkins and Neumayer 2010.

11. Hyde 2011, 36.

12. Ibid.

13. "People cannot generally enjoy [relational] goods without participating in the relationships and networks that produce and reproduce them" (Cordelli 2015, 90).

14. Goodliffe and Hawkins 2009a, 978.

tend to cooperate for mutual benefit, rivals engage with the expectation of zero-sum outcomes. And because they tend to anticipate future conflict, they prioritize concerns about relative gains.[15] Thus, states that share negative dependencies are typically pulled apart by the forces of conflict and competition. Because of their anticipation of future conflict, they have no incentive to evoke a positive reaction. Indeed, leaders often interpret a benefit to their rival as a disadvantage to themselves.

It is important to emphasize that the constructs of "friends" and "adversaries" are heuristics reflecting two poles on a *spectrum*, not a literal binary. The multiplex dynamics permeating the international environment leave few interstate dyads standing fully at one end or the other. The United States and Saudi Arabia, for instance, are cooperative on some dimensions (security) and hostile on others (ideology). American citizens and elites alike consider China a rival, even though there are clear economic ties between the two nations. Later empirical chapters take these nuances into account by using multiple and continuous measures of dyadic relations. For now, these crude abstractions provide useful theoretical leverage to delineate the logic linking political relationships to norm enforcement. Despite the manifest ambiguities characterizing the majority of international relations, the terms "friend," "partner," and "adversary" are ubiquitous—even unavoidable—in discussions of world politics. Fortunately, this language is congruent with everyday speech and the basic intuition it denotes.

The Decision to Shame Human Rights Violations

Why do governments shame other governments for human rights violations? Fundamentally, the decision to enforce norms is problematic because the act of punishing is costly.[16] Not only does sanctioning require some degree of time and effort, but shamers also run the risk of blowback by provoking a negative reaction in the target. I might avoid confronting someone I see littering in a park, for example, because I am scared of how he or she would react. Similar costs may be incurred at the international level, where human rights encroach on sensitive issues surrounding legitimacy and sovereignty, potentially upsetting valuable geopolitical relationships. Saudi Arabia, for instance, threatened to retaliate against the United States economically following criticism over the death of the journalist Jamal

15. Drezner 1999.
16. Axelrod 1986, 1098.

Khashoggi.[17] Likewise, facing "possible retribution," many Muslim nations stayed silent on China's abuse of Uyghurs and other ethnic minorities.[18] For both individuals and states, these "enforcement costs" generate the temptation to free-ride—that is, to ignore violations with the hope that someone else will address the problem.[19]

THE BENEFITS OF SHAMING

And yet we still observe interstate shaming on a regular basis despite these potential costs. Why? I argue that enforcement costs can be overcome by three kinds of "shaming benefits."[20] These benefits reflect different sorts of rewards that actors realize by defending international norms and sanctioning offenders. First, shamers benefit from deterring unwanted behavior and reinforcing compliance with a preferred norm. Second, shamers are rewarded by third-party audiences, such as domestic publics, for promoting human rights abroad. Finally, shaming degrades the target's legitimacy and status, which can be beneficial in an adversarial relationship.

Behavioral Rewards

The first kind of shaming reward arises from the behavior that a given norm is designed to regulate. Simply put, some actors prefer that others conform to particular standards, are negatively impacted by deviations, and benefit from compliance. They shame in order to deter unwanted behavior and defend preferred norms.[21] For example, I have an interest in the anti-littering norm because I do not want to be surrounded by trash. Insofar as my preference for cleanliness outweighs the costs of sanctioning, I might shame those who litter. Such motives can be understood as "behavioral" because they are rooted in preferences for certain behaviors that can be manipulated through

---

17. "The Kingdom also affirms that if it receives any action, it will respond with greater action, and that the Kingdom's economy has an influential and vital role in the global economy" (Salama and Stancati 2018). See chapter 6.

18. Perlez 2019.

19. For more on enforcement costs, see Axelrod 1986; Horne 2009.

20. Some researchers suggest that enforcement costs can be overcome by certain psychological traits (Fehr and Gächter 2002). For instance, some individuals are more inclined to punish than others and achieve psychic satisfaction from doing so (Knutson 2004). By and large, this book brackets individual-level psychological traits that motivate the desire to punish, focusing instead on environmental and social factors.

21. Even when social sanctions fail to induce compliance in the target offender, they may still deter other members of the community from pursuing deviance, thus reaffirming community norms.

shaming. Since people care about others' behavior, they are motivated to enforce norms that regulate others' behavior.[22]

In IR, most of the attention on shaming has focused on behavioral motivations. Research on human rights, for example, centers the work of norm entrepreneurs and transnational advocates who, by definition, prefer that states adopt global human rights norms.[23] These actors hold ideational commitments to certain values or principles, such as gender equality, or the protection of civilians in wartime. They shame violators to defend such principles and engender political change.

Of course, such motives are not limited to activists. Some heads of state shame other countries for human rights violations because, as "true believers," they hold genuine normative beliefs. That said, a preference for compliance need not imply altruism. States may enforce norms if violations undermine their national interests. For example, if a country uses chemical weapons during conflict, others may follow suit, inciting a domino effect. Governments may shame offenders of the chemical weapons ban to avoid having to defend against such attacks in the future. In this sense, the norm prohibiting chemical weapons constitutes a public good that states wish to sustain for mutual benefit.

Thus, behavioral rewards can be value-based (the shamer genuinely believes the norm is good or right), interest-based (the shamer benefits from compliance with the norm), or both.[24] The key point is that actors punish violators out of a preference for the norm itself and a desire that others conform. Shamers will bear enforcement costs if they believe that punishment will deter violations and promote compliance.

While behavioral motives dominate the IR literature on norms, the logic is not wholly satisfying when applied to international human rights enforcement. To begin with, states rarely have a direct interest in other countries' human rights practices. As Beth Simmons points out, the main stakeholders

---

22. This view is strongly influenced by the rationalist-functionalist perspective on norms. In this view, certain behaviors harm the welfare of others. The interest of those who are negatively affected by harmful behavior in regulating that behavior creates a demand for norms. In other words, norms serve as equilibria or public goods that sustain cooperative behavior and maximize collective utility. Some writers challenge this perspective by noting that many norms have no welfare-enhancing benefits (such as fashion trends), while others in fact harm group welfare. See Horne 2009, 4–5.

23. Finnemore and Sikkink 1998; Keck and Sikkink 1998.

24. As Martha Finnemore and Kathryn Sikkink (1998, 899) point out, the distinction between values-based and interest-based motives is somewhat misleading because "many norm entrepreneurs do not so much act against their interest as they act in accordance with a redefined understanding of their interest."

in human rights enforcement are domestic citizens in the target state, not other countries.[25] Some governments may value respect for human dignity for principled reasons, but they are rarely affected *directly* by foreign abuses. For this reason, protecting human rights abroad tends to be lower in priority than other foreign policy goals more salient to national interests, such as security or trade.[26]

In addition, behavioral motives are often stymied by the free-rider problem. Even if states prefer a robust international human rights regime, they may nonetheless avoid punishing violations if they think other countries will bear the costs of enforcement.[27] Thus it is not immediately clear why countries would go through the trouble of shaming abuses abroad, even if they care a great deal about human rights.[28]

Not surprisingly, scholars who focus on behavioral motives tend to be skeptical of international sources for human rights enforcement. As Simmons puts it, "If we are looking for empathic enforcement from other countries, we will be looking in vain for a long time."[29] And yet we still observe states shaming one another for human rights violations under certain conditions. More puzzling, we observe shaming even when such tactics are ineffective in changing behavior. The logic of behavioral preferences cannot easily account for these instances of shaming.

Metanorms

Scholars are right to be skeptical of international human rights enforcement based on behavioral inducements. However, behavioral change is not the only goal that actors pursue when shaming violations. Two other types of benefits come from enforcing norms. Unlike the first type, which is tied

25. Simmons 2009, 126.

26. Other mechanisms ensuring international cooperation—such as reciprocity—are irrelevant to human rights, since the human rights regime involves no reciprocal compliance (Ibid., 123).

27. Olson 1965.

28. The rationalist literature does suggest a number of conditions under which states may circumvent the free-rider problem and engage in costly norm enforcement. For example, Chaim Kaufmann and Robert Pape (1999, 664) argue that "costly moral action" in the international system is more likely to be "pursued unilaterally by a single powerful state." Likewise, Stephen Krasner (1993) posits that human rights enforcement depends on the "capabilities and commitment" of great powers to punish violators. He goes on to recognize, however, that great powers often lack the will to commit substantial resources to the enforcement of human rights abroad, resulting in a weak regime. While acknowledging these important insights, I maintain that human rights enforcement is much more prevalent—that is, the free-rider problem is resolved much more frequently—than this logic would suggest.

29. Simmons 2009, 116.

to behavioral consequences, the motives I discuss here are not behavioral in nature but social. That is, actors shame others not because they think shaming will deter violations but because they expect to accrue some kind of reward for publicly promoting norms.

The first of these social rewards pertains to "metanorms," or social pressure to enforce norms by punishing violators.[30] Here, actors condemn perceived abuses in order to signal their commitment to human rights norms and appease third-party audiences. Metanorms, in effect, are norms that demand the enforcement of norms. A large body of research in economics and sociology suggests that metanorms serve a critical role in the reinforcement and continuity of normative orders.[31] Individuals bear the personal costs of enforcing norms in order to show that they themselves abide by the rules and are thus good, reputable, trustworthy, and so on.[32] I might be more willing to shame litterers if I expect to be applauded for doing so by fellow park-goers. Like an actor on a stage, the shamer is ostensibly speaking to the target, but in reality the performance is directed to an audience that witnesses the display and confers some kind of social reward on those who punish deviance.

Metanorms also operate at the international level. It is sometimes said that human rights define a "new standard of civilization" on which domestic and international legitimacy depends.[33] Even as they quarrel about the specific content and application of human rights, virtually all governments endorse the international human rights project in general, including those harboring little interest in actually complying with human rights obligations. Many countries sign on to human rights treaties, for example, as "window-dressing" with no intention of implementing the provisions.[34] Even outright oppressive regimes are compelled to demonstrate their commitment to human rights ideals.[35] For instance, Goodliffe and his colleagues

30. Christine Horne defines "metanorms" as a "specific type of norm that regulates sanctioning" (2009). Robert Axelrod defines them as norms requiring an actor to "punish those who do not punish defection" (1986, 1101).

31. For a review, see Horne 2009. In his classic paper on the evolution of norms, Axelrod uses computer simulations to show the conditions under which norms emerge and stabilize, emphasizing the necessary role of metanorms in both processes (Axelrod 1986).

32. Jordan et al. 2016; Posner 2000. Some developmental psychologists posit that internalized normative beliefs—intrinsic feelings about right and wrong—arise out of these more primal social considerations that guide our moral development in childhood. See Jordan and Rand 2020; McAuliffe, Jordan, and Warneken 2015.

33. Donnelly 1998.

34. Hafner-Burton and Tsutsui 2005.

35. Hafner-Burton, Tsutsui, and Meyer 2008.

note the rapid and widespread endorsement of the International Criminal Court (ICC), which grants significant authority to foreign actors to enforce human rights norms by prosecuting individual violators. Given the ferocity with which states typically guard their sovereignty, the decision by many governments—including quite repressive governments—to commit to the ICC can be seen as an example of metanorms at work.[36]

Another way countries can signal their commitment to human rights is by shaming other countries for their performance.[37] Criticizing foreign abuses satisfies domestic and international audiences that genuinely believe in human rights and wish to see governments take action to protect them. For instance, in March 2012, the viral distribution of the *Kony 2012* YouTube video prompted a bipartisan US Senate resolution condemning Joseph Kony for his "unconscionable crimes against humanity" in Central Africa.[38] "When you get 100 million Americans looking at something, you will get our attention," said Senator Lindsey Graham, a cosponsor of the resolution. "This YouTube sensation is gonna help the Congress be more aggressive and will do more to lead to his demise than all other action combined."[39]

As this example illustrates, domestic publics play an especially important role in enforcing metanorms. Indeed, Amnesty International and other human rights organizations dedicate most of their strategic activity to arousing metanorm pressures. Raising awareness among ordinary citizens makes it more likely that they will push their government to enforce human rights internationally. For this reason, several studies examine the conditions under which citizens support punishing violations abroad.[40] This question is important because domestic publics are key enforcers of metanorms who push leaders to enforce human rights abroad when they would otherwise not interfere.

Stigma Impositions

A final set of rewards originates in contests over legitimacy and status. At its core, shaming works not merely as a behavioral nudge but also, in Dan Kahan's words, as a "degradation penalty" meant to "lower the offender's social status within [a] community."[41] As Ann Towns explains, norms do

---

36. Goodliffe and Hawkins 2009a; Goodliffe et al. 2012.
37. Horne 2009.
38. Wong 2012.
39. Quoted in ibid.
40. See, for example, Lee and Prather 2016; McEntire, Leiby, and Krain 2015.
41. Kahan 1996, 636–37.

more than homogenize actors to a shared standard; they also stratify actors in a social hierarchy, ranking them as superior or inferior.[42] Shaming, as Martha Nussbaum writes, "targets not a single deed but an entire person."[43] In other words, it *stigmatizes* the violator, imposing a label that distinguishes, devalues, and degrades the actor in the eye of others within the stigmatizer's community.[44] This negative evaluation results in loss of status and, by extension, social resources and privileges.[45]

For norm entrepreneurs and other behaviorally motivated shamers, stigmatizing human rights violators operates primarily as a means to an end, one in service to the ultimate goal of behavioral change. Establishing an "ostracized 'out-group' of norm breakers" helps to deter violations and enforce compliance with international norms.[46] But stigma imposition can also constitute a goal in itself. Because shaming inflicts social costs, it can be weaponized to degrade rivals in global hierarchies. As James Lebovic and Erik Voeten put it, "Governments may talk the talk when it comes to human rights, but their intent is to inflict political damage on foreign adversaries, not to induce them to treat their citizens according to some universally accepted standard."[47] Put differently, leaders may denounce violations not because they genuinely care about human rights but because they have an antagonistic relationship to the target and want to stigmatize them. We can think of this strategy as "weaponized shaming."

There are several reasons why governments would want to stigmatize other countries as human rights abusers, even if they care little about violations per se. For instance, shaming degrades the status of the target, which in turn advances the relative status of the shamer.[48] A large literature on status in IR provides compelling evidence that states not only care about their rank in the global hierarchy but also embark on costly

---

42. Towns 2012.

43. Nussbaum 2005, 283.

44. The successful application of stigma is community-dependent; what is shameful for one group could be a source of pride for another. For more on stigma and stigmatization, see Adler-Nissen 2014; Goffman 2009; Link and Phelan 2001.

45. Duque 2018.

46. Lutz and Sikkink 2000, 657.

47. Lebovic and Voeten 2006, 872.

48. By "status" I mean an actor's position in a social hierarchy, stratified by relative amounts of honor and prestige. Those on the top of a status order enjoy greater recognition, legitimacy, and social privileges than those on the bottom. As Goffman (1951, 294) writes, status is "ranked on a scale of prestige, according to the amount of social value that is placed upon it relative to other statuses in the same sector of social life."

actions to advance their position relative to others.[49] Most of this research highlights military actions, but norms provide another powerful tool to manipulate status. As Steven Ward argues, "Norms, rules, and institutions produce and sustain social hierarchies by generating intersubjective bases for social comparisons between actors, and by constituting actors with different statuses and bundles of rights."[50] By highlighting abuse, actors can degrade the target's status on a relative dimension of comparison, that is, human rights.

Governments also stigmatize other countries as human rights abusers because of the important political and distributional implications of stigma.[51] States that fail to uphold a certain set of norms—human rights chief among them—are labeled "deviant" or "rogue" and become subject to punishment and infringements of their sovereignty.[52] Governments naturally try to stigmatize their rivals in order to increase their own bargaining power and lower the costs of pursuing certain foreign policy goals.[53] Denouncing certain regimes as human rights abusers also helps to persuade domestic audiences to support military action or other foreign policies.[54]

History is replete with examples of weaponized shaming. During the Cold War, for instance, the United States made a concerted effort to stigmatize communist governments as human rights violators in order to cast the "free world" as morally superior.[55] The Soviet Union deployed a similar strategy, broadcasting news of US racial conflicts to audiences in Asia, Africa, and South America in an effort to expose American hypocrisy and turn global public opinion.[56] In both instances, human rights shaming ostensibly tar-

49. In the debate over why states pursue status—whether they value status for its intrinsic benefits or for its distributional effects vis-à-vis power and resources—the current consensus is that actors pursue status for both intrinsic and instrumental reasons, and that the distinction is not particularly helpful for empirical research (Renshon 2016, 521–22).

50. Ward 2017, 13.

51. Duque 2018; Ward 2017.

52. Nincic 2005; Wagner, Werner, and Onderco 2014.

53. For a succinct description of this argument, see Moravcsik 2000, 221–22; Lebovic and Voeten 2006, 871–72. The literatures on hegemonic stability and legitimation show that international struggles for power and domination are partly struggles for relative legitimacy. Legitimate power is a cheaper and more efficient method of control, producing more compliance and less resistance than more direct (that is, economic or military) coercion. For more on the power politics of legitimacy and legitimation, see Goddard 2018; Hurd 1999, 2005, 2007; Reus-Smit 2007; Schimmelfennig 2001.

54. Tomz and Weeks 2020.

55. Belmonte 2013, 141–42.

56. Onion 2013.

geted adversarial governments but in reality was performed for third-party audiences, including mass publics at home and abroad, in an effort to inflict political damage on a geopolitical rival.

More recently, the Trump administration—hardly a principled defender of human rights in many areas of domestic and foreign policy—spoke harshly against alleged human rights violations in Iran. "We should consider human rights as an important issue in regard to US relations with China, Russia, North Korea, and Iran," explained official Brian Hook, not only out of moral concern but also "because pressing those regimes on human rights is one way to impose costs, apply counter-pressure, and regain the initiative from them strategically."[57]

While weaponized shaming is especially germane to states, a similar logic is used by nonstate actors who share an interest in damaging a target's international standing. For example, insurgent groups may have a strong incentive to degrade the legitimacy of a hostile regime, even if they have no interest in human rights compliance per se.[58] Whether performed by state or nonstate actors, status-driven shaming diverges from behavioral or normative logics, even as shamers take advantage of existing moral structures to manipulate the balance of legitimacy.

It is worth emphasizing that weaponized shaming is distinct from metanorms. The former is prompted by a desire to inflict political damage on the target, while the latter reflects a desire to be seen promoting human rights in general, regardless of the impact on the violator. The two logics often function in a mutually complementary fashion: metanorms provide the incentive to engage in *some* form of shaming, while stigma imposition directs the shaming toward the *target*. As the Khashoggi case demonstrates, however, the two sets of concerns are ultimately independent and may conflict.

Implications

Once we consider these two socially grounded motivations—to weaponize shaming and to enforce metanorms—it is no longer puzzling why actors would sometimes choose to enforce human rights despite the costs (figure 2.2). Unlike behavioral rewards, which follow from the consequences of punishment and benefit the entire group, social rewards follow from the act of punishment itself and benefit only those who perform such acts. Shaming

57. Toosi 2017.
58. Bob 2005.

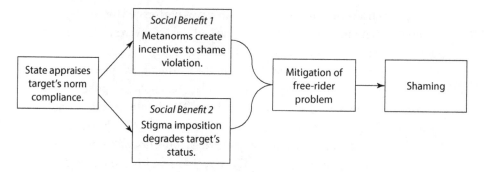

FIGURE 2.2. The Social Logic of Shaming in the Human Rights Regime

would be vastly underproduced if not for these social motivations. Free-riding is less tempting when shamers benefit *directly* from the sanctioning act. Two other important implications derive from this framework.

THE GOAL OF COMPLIANCE

First, shaming can be rational even when it is not expected to result in compliance. As I explained earlier, behaviorally motivated actors choose to punish because they want to deter violations and strengthen the norm. For them, compliance is the explicit goal. In situations where sanctioning is *not* expected to deter violations (by either the target or other potential offenders), enforcement costs render shaming irrational. Socially motivated actors, on the other hand, might continue shaming even when they do not expect it to "work"—that is, when it is unlikely to enforce compliance.

With stigma motives, compliance is emphatically *not* the goal. In fact, compliance might run counter to the main objective, which is to tarnish the target's legitimacy by labeling it deviant. When shaming is weaponized such that the shamer is promoted and the target is degraded, a lack of compliance does little to inhibit further condemnation. As Erving Goffman observed:

> We [normals] may perceive his [the stigmatized] defensive response to his situation as a direct expression of his defect, and then see both defect and response as just retribution for something he or his parents or tribe did, and hence a justification of the way we treat him.[59]

59. Goffman 2009, 6.

From the shamer's perspective, the continuation of perceived violations is a welcome outcome, as it provides additional opportunities to stigmatize the target.[60] Not only are such actors unfazed by the "failure" to produce compliance, but they may also benefit from such failures and are reenergized to continue shaming.

Metanorms are more ambiguous with regard to the value of compliance. Here, compliance might come as a welcome side effect, but it is not the primary goal, which is to appease audiences through performative outrage. If shaming succeeds in securing compliance, leaders benefit from the opportunity to claim credit. A meaningful change in the target's behavior is often unnecessary, however, since leaders benefit merely by *attempting* to enforce human rights abroad. Many domestic constituencies want to see their government take a strong rhetorical stance on international human rights, even if full adherence is unrealistic.[61] Importantly, superficial improvements in the target may be sufficient to project an *image* of compliance and satisfy metanorm demands.[62]

THE ROLE OF STRATEGIC RELATIONSHIPS

The second major implication concerns *who* is likely to be shamed and *how*. The core insight is that shaming involves different strategic considerations based on the political relationship between shamer and target. While behavioral interests and metanorms plausibly remain constant across potential violators, enforcement costs and social benefits vary considerably depending on whether the violator is a geopolitical partner or rival.

Consider the choice to shame a geopolitical partner. Generally speaking, enforcement costs arise because condemning human rights abuses risks provoking a negative reaction and upsetting a potentially valuable relationship. Thus, governments pay higher enforcement costs the more they value their relationship with the violator. As a result, they hesitate to condemn friends, allies, and others with whom they share a strategic partnership.[63]

---

60. Kahan (1996, 636) observes that shaming need not induce feelings of remorse in the offender in order to motivate punishers: "If anything, the perception that the offender is not shamed by what is commonly understood to be shame*ful* would reinforce onlookers' conclusion that he is depraved and worthy of condemnation."

61. There is one exception: if citizens become aware that their government is actively enabling violations abroad through material support of the violating state, they may demand stronger actions.

62. Búzás 2017.

63. This claim is consistent with a body of empirical work showing that strong countries can elude international punishment for norm violations more easily, while weak nations are held to a higher standard (see, for example, Donno 2010; Lebovic and Voeten 2006). While most of these

For instance, in the words of one European diplomat, "There are African countries who are heavily dependent on Chinese assistance, and who would not dare to say one word of criticism against China."[64] Moreover, the benefits of shaming diminish drastically when the target is a strategic partner. Leaders have few incentives to degrade the status and legitimacy of their political allies. Not only does such a move serve no strategic purpose, but it needlessly undermines a valued partnership by provoking hostility and resentment.

Shaming a rival entails a very different strategic calculation. First, rebuking an adversary carries negligible enforcement costs. Because there is no valued relationship to protect, provoking additional hostility is relatively harmless. Moreover, shaming a rival is potentially rewarding, regardless of whether the shamer holds genuine normative commitments. In addition to the metanorm rewards (support from those who genuinely care about human rights), shaming an adversary provides a strategic advantage in contests over legitimacy. Even if such efforts are materially inconsequential, leaders may be rewarded for the *attempt* by nationalist constituencies at home.

As a result of these divergent strategic considerations, states apply social pressure to their geopolitical friends and rivals in dramatically different ways (table 2.1). Although leaders often hesitate to condemn allies, they are sometimes compelled to do so anyway for two reasons: they hold genuine normative beliefs (behavioral rewards), and they are pressured by others who hold genuine normative beliefs (metanorms). For instance, as Rachel Myrick and Jeremy Weinstein show, public pressure surrounding the release of female prisoners pushed US policymakers to overcome their competing interests, engage in "coercive diplomacy," and leverage relational goods to extract concessions from target governments.[65]

But even when governments choose to confront their strategic partners in such cases, the actual shaming tends to be more credible, less demanding, and less offensive to target governments, all else equal. Shaming is more *credible* by virtue of the costs inherent in criticizing an ally, and violations tend to be unambiguous: there is clear and credible information regarding

---

studies focus on absolute capabilities (for example, hegemons and great powers), my argument rests entirely on *relative* power and dependence in the context of a dyadic relationship between shamer and target. For instance, China is more powerful to Singapore than it is to Mexico owing to divergent relations and levels of dependence.

64. Piccone 2018.

65. Myrick and Weinstein 2021.

TABLE 2.1. Shaming Friends and Enemies: A Comparison

	Shaming Friends	Shaming Enemies
ENFORCEMENT COSTS	High	Low
STATUS-DIRECTED REWARDS (STIGMA IMPOSITION)	Low	High
GENERAL INCENTIVES TO SHAME	Low	High
CREDIBILITY OF ACCUSATIONS	More credible	Less credible
SEVERITY OF DEMANDS AND THRESHOLD FOR COMPLIANCE	More lenient; more permissive standards for compliance	More demanding; more severe standards for compliance
RHETORIC	Careful, accurate, respectful	Hyperbolic, inaccurate, inflammatory

abuse.[66] Moreover, leaders tend to be more lenient and less severe in their demands when pressuring a friend; that is, they lower the bar for what constitutes adequate compliance. Generally speaking, leaders have an incentive not to antagonize their strategic partners, so they make an extra effort to mitigate potential blowback. As a result, their rhetorical approach tends to be more careful, accurate, and respectful.

Shaming an adversary looks very different. Unlike criticism between friends, where the credibility threshold is high when it comes to accusations of abuse, adversaries take any opportunity to defame a rival, even if the charges are inaccurate, sensationalist, or hypocritical. They may even have incentives to exaggerate or fabricate accusations of alleged abuse, especially when domestic audiences and other third parties are unmotivated to challenge them. Likewise, states tend to shame their rivals in particularly demanding and inflammatory ways. For example, they might

66. In her study on democratic norms, Daniela Donno argues that international election monitors can push regional IGOs to punish faulty elections—even in geopolitically powerful countries—by providing reputable information and publicity on electoral misconduct (Donno 2013). In effect, election observers generate metanorm pressures on observing states to support enforcement by establishing credible information regarding violations. A similar principle applies to human rights shaming. Human rights violations are often shrouded in secrecy and ambiguity. When faced with an apparent violation committed by a partner, leaders may appeal to such uncertainty in order to avoid rocking the boat. This is less possible, however, when violations are obvious.

agitate around particularly sensitive issues, use derogatory and aspersive language, or issue excessive demands. Importantly, condemnation of this sort provides an abundance of rhetorical resources that can be used to arouse feelings of insult, provocation, and defiance—a dynamic I return to in the next chapter.

Conclusion

To sum up, states shame for three reasons: to change behavior, to please audiences, and to damage the target's social standing. These goals are not mutually exclusive and often co-occur in the same case and are even pursued by the same actor. For this reason, they can be difficult (though not impossible) to distinguish empirically. Crucially, by delineating the three types of incentives driving countries to sanction, this framework provides analytic leverage to explain some puzzling features of international shaming. Specifically, shaming a violator to please audiences and to damage the target's social standing—which I term social rewards—explain why states continue to sanction violations even if their efforts fail to change behavior or are counterproductive to the goal of compliance. Put simply, reforming the violation is rarely the primary goal when it comes to shaming.

I have also explained how enforcement costs and benefits change depending on the political relationship between shamer and target. Punishing a rival is less costly—and more rewarding—than punishing a friend. Typically, leaders criticize their geopolitical partners only when they, or their constituents, hold a strong commitment to human rights norms. But they condemn rivals regardless of genuine normative beliefs, because doing so provides a strategic advantage. As a result, states shame their geopolitical rivals more often, and more harshly, than they do their strategic partners.

Understanding when and how governments shame other countries is important, because different kinds of social pressure lead to different outcomes. The next chapter shifts the spotlight to the *target* to explore the effects of international shaming on state behavior.

3

A Relational Theory of International Shaming

THE TARGET

In the previous chapter, I explained why governments condemn other countries for human rights violations, focusing on three types of motivations: to change behavior, to appease audiences, and to defame the target. Two critical implications followed from this discussion. First, shaming is not always designed to secure compliance with human rights norms. Second, states shame their geopolitical rivals more often, and more harshly, than their allies. Understanding when and how actors shame is important, because different kinds of social pressure engender different responses.

This chapter shifts the analytic focus to the *target* to examine the effects of international shaming on state behavior. When observing states decide to shame them, leaders in the target country must decide how to respond. The first section describes the main options available to governments when reacting to international human rights shaming. I then identify three sets of inducements that inform this choice. First, leaders must consider their preferences and interests in the norm-violating behavior itself, *ex ante* any external criticism. Second, international shaming could sabotage the target government's foreign relations and impose relational costs in the international sphere. Finally, leaders of a targeted government must consider the reactions of domestic audiences; such audiences can exert pressure on the government either to comply *or* to defy international pressure.

Applying the insights established in the last chapter, I argue that the latter two mechanisms are conditioned by the *ex ante* geopolitical relationship between shamer and target. Shaming from geopolitical partners imposes greater relational costs in the international environment while mitigating the potential for adverse reactions in the domestic sphere. In contrast, shaming from rivals fails to secure compliance through international pathways, while energizing defensive reactions *within* the target country that undermine the state's ability to comply and reward overt resistance.

The final section consolidates these insights into a general model of state reactions to international shaming, wherein relational factors interact to produce four possible responses: status quo maintenance, compliance, deflection, and defiance.

Responses to Shaming

States react to compliance pressures in myriad ways, ranging from acquiescence to defiance. Drawing from Erving Goffman, Rebecca Adler-Nissen productively catalogs these options into a tripartite typology of "strategies" for managing stigma in the international environment. Here, I adapt Adler-Nissen's scheme to model the potential outcomes of international human rights shaming, integrating other conceptual contributions where appropriate (see table 3.1).

First, shaming can result in *compliance* (similar to Adler-Nissen's notion of "stigma recognition") whereby representatives affirm the legitimacy of relevant norms, acknowledge their failure to adhere to those norms, and acquiesce to the shamer's demands.[1] Put simply, most observers would consider a target state's shift in behavior toward compliance in a meaningful way a "successful" outcome of naming and shaming.

Alternatively, shamed countries can pursue a strategy of *deflection* (analogous to what Adler-Nissen calls "stigma rejection") whereby they affirm the legitimacy of the norm in question while minimizing perceptions that they violated said norm. Here, governments attempt to appear compliant by denying the veracity of allegations, hiding evidence of abuse, evading accountability, or justifying their actions as acceptable within

---

1. "Compliance refers to a particular kind of response—acquiescence—to a particular kind of communication—a request.... In all cases, the target recognizes that he or she is being urged to respond in a desired way" (Cialdini and Goldstein 2004, 592). In IR, there is some debate over what "compliance" means and how it can be observed. For an illuminating discussion, see Traven and Holmes 2021.

TABLE 3.1. Responses to International Shaming

Compliance	Deflection	Defiance
Target affirms the legitimacy of relevant norms and acquiesces to the shamer's demands.	Target denies committing a norm violation (minimizes the perception of noncompliance) without explicitly challenging the legitimacy of the norm *per se*.	Target overtly rejects global norms and doubles down on violations.
Associated concepts • Stigma recognition (Adler-Nissen 2014)	**Associated concepts** • Stigma rejection (Adler-Nissen 2014) • Evasion (Búzás 2017) • Rhetorical adaptation (Dixon 2017) • Account making (Cardenas 2006) • Denials (Cohen 2013) • Tactical concessions (Risse, Ropp, and Sikkink 1999, 2013)	**Associated concepts** • Counterstigmatization (Adler-Nissen 2014) • Transgression (Evers 2017) • Norm immunization (Nuñez-Mietz and Garcia Iommi 2017)

the terms of international human rights standards.[2] Notwithstanding the nuances differentiating these tactics, the basic idea is to challenge the validity of shaming without explicitly challenging the legitimacy of associated norms.

To clarify, deflection is not equivalent to *status quo ante*. Target states may not ramp up violations, but their deflection entails political change on other dimensions of interest. In their attempt to "manipulate the standards of legitimacy," governments do not merely avoid discussion of international criticism but engage in a rebuttal of the accusations lobbied against them.[3] That is, they construct a political discourse that justifies particular policies, casts certain critics and criticisms as illegitimate, and mobilizes other norms such as national sovereignty and cultural rights to justify their claims.[4] For example, China often deflects human rights criticism in the UN by elevating development as a global priority.[5] Such tactics are not

2. For more on the specific tactics associated with deflection, see Búzás 2017; Cardenas 2006; Dixon 2017; Hurd 2005, 2007; Schimmelfennig 2001; Shannon 2000.

3. Schimmelfennig 2000, 117–18.

4. For a fascinating discussion of these dynamics in China, see Wachman 2001.

5. Piccone 2018, 9, 13–14.

merely matters of short-term strategy. As Bart Bonikowski puts it, "Over time, the terms of particular debates become institutionalized and taken-for-granted and, as a result, play an important causal role in setting the conditions of possibility for subsequent political struggle."[6] Thus, unlike *status quo ante*, deflection inaugurates political dynamics that affect norm adherence in the long term.

Finally, states can respond to shaming with *defiance*, displaying overt disobedience to compliance pressures. Defiance is similar to Adler-Nissen's strategy of "counter-stigmatization," whereby "stigma is turned into a virtue and the deviant value their exclusionary status."[7] Here, states explicitly reject the contested norm and refuse to comply with the shamer's demands.[8] Defiance differs from more general cases of noncompliance in that it entails "knowingly and overtly flaunting [*sic*] a norm when one had the means and ability to conform. . . . Whereas deviance captures a status, defiance captures a stance."[9] Unlike deflecting states, defiant states attack the norm they have supposedly violated and often promote one or more rival norms—for example, attacking the norm of LGBT equality with rival norms of "traditional values" or "protection of the family."[10] From the perspective of those who value norm compliance, defiance is the least desirable outcome because it often ramps up the commitment to or prevalence of norm-offending behavior.[11] In this regard, defiance resembles our intuitive understanding of backlash, in that the target's policies or behavior shift in the *opposite* direction of norm internalization.

As Adler-Nissen notes in her original conceptualization, these strategies are not mutually exclusive and may be used simultaneously by different factions of a government or by the same leaders at different times. Nor are they discrete—compliance, deflection, and defiance should be thought of

6. Bonikowski 2015, 389.

7. Adler-Nissen 2014, 153.

8. Defiance is also similar to the concept of "transgressions" (Evers 2017, 788). Specifically, defiance resembles "rejective transgression," whereby the defiant actor embraces their "out-group" status. The main distinction between defiance and transgression is that the former is a reaction to overt compliance pressures, whereas the latter assumes no such relation. In this sense, defiance can be thought of as a special case of transgression incited by shaming.

9. Monin and O'Connor 2011, 265–66.

10. See Bob 2005 for a discussion of rival norms and advocacy networks.

11. The criminologist Lawrence Sherman (1993, 459) developed the concept of defiance to understand how the administration of criminal sanction produces subsequent offending. He defines defiance as "the net increase in the prevalence, incidence, or seriousness of future offending against a sanctioning community caused by a proud, shameless reaction to the administration of a criminal sanction."

as ideal types representing different points on a spectrum of outcomes. The world is simply too complicated to fit neatly into such a crude scheme. These caveats aside, the framework I have laid out serves as a useful analytical tool for studying the effects of international shaming on state behavior.

Behavioral Interests

Like shamers, target governments must weigh various costs and benefits when choosing how to respond to normative criticism. Three sets of inducements factor into this decision.

First, leaders must consider their interests vis-à-vis the specific behavior that critics find objectionable. Governments prefer to violate norms to the degree that they value practices prohibited by those norms. For example, realists expect a state to abuse human rights when it holds countervailing material interests; rights such as freedom of association or fair trial could undermine such a state's national security, political control, and regime stability. Governments' natural prioritization of such material interests generates incentives to violate human rights norms. Behavioral preferences can also originate in nonmaterial concerns, such as an ideational commitment to certain values or beliefs. For example, some communities may perpetuate "harmful traditional practices" that violate the rights of women or children, like female genital cutting or early marriage, because of sincere beliefs in their rightfulness.[12] In essence, behavioral interests correspond to the value or utility that actors extract from a potentially objectionable law, policy, or practice *per se*. What makes these behavioral preferences distinct is that they are observable *ex ante* any external criticism or interference.

Political scientists have devoted considerable attention to the behavioral interests motivating repression and human rights violations.[13] For the most part, however, I bracket behavioral interests in the following discussion. This is not to say that I find behavioral interests unimportant or disregard their influence, only that I control for this influence in order to analytically distinguish two other sets of incentives that arise *once violations attract outside*

---

12. Winter, Thompson, and Jeffreys 2002. Even if leaders are agnostic about these practices themselves, they must often contend with domestic constituencies—important interest groups, the electorate writ large, and so on—that display a fierce ideological commitment to such practices in their own right and demand that the government respect these commitments. For example, a policymaker may not care for the practice of female genital cutting personally but represents a community that does and therefore holds a behavioral interest in such practices.

13. For a review, see Cardenas 2004.

attention. Unlike behavioral interests, the inducements I describe below are relational in nature; they hinge on the perceptions and reactions of observers and their relationship to the target government. Like other scholars, I find it helpful to organize these incentives in two categories: international and domestic.

International Reactions: Pressures to Comply

SHAMING AND RELATIONAL COSTS

Human rights shaming may influence target behavior by leveraging international relationships. The key insight is that many governments seek relational benefits that are conditional on the approval of other countries. International shaming imposes relational costs that threaten these benefits, incentivizing target governments to comply with the shamer's demands.

In the previous chapter, I explained how countries rely on one another for things they care about, such as security cooperation, economic exchange, membership in international organizations, and prestige. States exchange such goods in the context of a strategic relationship requiring the participation of both parties. Further, a state's ability to collect these benefits depends partly on the approval of its partners. Insofar as leaders prefer that other states respect human rights, they reward such behavior through positive regard, stronger relations, and enhanced cooperation.[14] If a country behaves in ways that others disapprove of, relational goods can be withdrawn or withheld. As a result, leaders are sensitive to the preferences of their strategic partners and are incentivized to act in ways that match these expectations.

For the target government, human rights shaming threatens international relational benefits in two ways. First, it signals disapproval from the shamer *directly*, straining a valued relationship. Again, it is not necessary that the enforcing state actually withhold international benefits or explicitly threaten to do so. For shaming to affect decision-making, leaders in the target country need only to believe that disapproval could undermine future cooperation.[15] All else equal, insofar as the target country values its partnership with the shamer and would suffer if this partnership collapsed, it takes this criticism seriously to avoid relational costs.

14. For an elaboration of this claim, see Hyde 2011, 36–38.
15. Goodliffe and Hawkins 2009a, 978.

Supporting this idea, some research shows that states are able (though not always willing) to influence the human rights practices of their strategic partners by leveraging aid, economic exchange, and other relational benefits. For example, Hafner-Burton finds that preferential trade agreements (PTAs) containing "hard" human rights mandates effectively incentivize members to improve their human rights practices "as a side payment for market gain."[16] There is also some evidence that donor countries condition the allocation of bilateral aid on the human rights practices of recipients, incentivizing reforms.[17]

Second, shaming works indirectly by informing a broader international audience of the target's apparent violations. This information, in turn, can shape the beliefs of other international actors who maintain their own preferences regarding human rights compliance.[18] Assuming that these third-party observers care about human rights, they may add their voice to the criticism, resulting in diffuse relational costs. Put differently, shaming by one state could lead others to join in, damaging the target state's overall reputation for compliance and limiting beneficial forms of cooperation.[19] For example, Lebovic and Voeten find that countries condemned by the UN Commission on Human Rights see a significant reduction in multilateral aid from the World Bank.[20] When a large number of states pass a targeted resolution, they enable third-party actors like the World Bank to execute their own preferences regarding human rights protections, resulting in significant material costs for targeted governments. I refer to this mechanism as *indirect relational costs*.

To clarify, these direct and relational costs vary within and across strategic partnerships. The United States or China, for example, may not be as vulnerable to reputational damage as weak or poor nations. The severity of such costs depends on the relative value that a state places on a particular strategic partnership and is discernible only through empirical investigation. The key point is that, all else equal, states would rather avoid such costs if possible.

16. Hafner-Burton 2005, 606.

17. A large literature examines the relationship between human rights and bilateral foreign aid, generating mixed results. Overall, respect for human rights is not as important as strategic interests in determining foreign aid allocations (Neumayer 2003a, 2003b). Further, donors that derive greater political benefits from an aid relationship are less likely to punish clients accused of human rights violations (Esarey and DeMeritt 2017; Nielsen 2013). Such findings are highly congruent with my theory, which expects that states hesitate to shame aid recipients for alleged human rights violations in order to maintain a mutually beneficial relationship.

18. Lebovic and Voeten 2009.

19. Guzman 2007.

20. Lebovic and Voeten 2009.

CONDITIONS OF INTERNATIONAL INFLUENCE

One straightforward but important implication follows from this discussion. Because shaming threatens international benefits through direct and indirect relational costs, the structure of states' relationships matter. Not all shaming, from all sources, will have equivalent impact.

Shaming by a strategic partner is more effective for two reasons, corresponding to the direct or indirect relational costs incurred. First, when states shame their partners, they impose greater direct relational costs. The previous chapter explained leaders' reluctance to criticize their geopolitical allies for human rights abuses. When they do, they are often motivated by domestic pressure (for example, from an outraged public demanding condemnation of an abuse abroad) or genuine normative beliefs regarding human rights. In some cases, these incentives are strong enough to warrant a tough stance and risk undermining an otherwise beneficial partnership. The target government is more likely to comply to avoid further damaging a valued relationship. For example, after long-standing indifference, the United States finally yielded to global and domestic anti-apartheid pressures and issued sanctions on South Africa, despite its close economic and strategic partnership with the apartheid government.[21] It was precisely this preexisting relationship that enabled the sanctions to have such impact, first on the South African economy, and then on the strategic calculus of its leaders.

Second, shaming by friends and allies inflicts greater reputational damage because it is more credible. Having few strategic incentives to criticize a friend, such a shamer sends a costly signal that the shamer believes the target actually violated human rights. As a result, third parties are more likely to update their beliefs about the target country's record of compliance, resulting in diffuse social costs.

For example, in 2006 Iran was shamed for threatening to stone a woman to death (see my discussion of this case in chapter 6). Pressure on Iran escalated once Brazilian president Luiz Inácio Lula da Silva, a known ally and supporter of Ahmadinejad, offered asylum to the victim at the center of the case. Because of their existing strategic partnership, Brazil's interference threatened greater direct relational costs on the Islamic Republic. In addition, Lula was more credible compared to European officials because he stood to lose something valuable by angering Iranian officials and sabotaging

21. Klotz 1999.

Brazil-Iran relations. As a consequence, his interference embarrassed Iran and had a major impact on the case.

Shaming by an adversary is less likely to work through the pathways I just described. Because the target does not value its relationship with the shamer and receives no benefit from cooperation, it has few incentives to comply with the shamer's demands. Further, shaming by an adversary is less credible and thus less likely to inflict significant reputational damage. As I demonstrated in the last chapter, governments use human rights instrumentally to stigmatize their enemies. Leaders in the target country can exploit this fact by highlighting the source of criticism rather than its content, dismissing accusations as an exercise in political hostility rather than evidence of abuse. Indeed, this is how Chinese officials attempt to discredit Western criticism of China's treatment of Uyghurs in Xinjiang, characterizing such criticism as efforts "to smear China, undermine China's stability and contain China's development."[22] Western shaming is unlikely to endanger China's cooperative endeavors with other countries, especially those that are antagonistic to the West.

The key implication—that the effectiveness of shaming is conditional on the relationship between shamer and target—is not controversial. Many IR theorists acknowledge that social influence fails if the target lacks a positive relationship or shared identity with the shamer.[23] More rarely do these thinkers theorize what happens when shaming occurs within a context of relational *antagonism*, besides inducing a null effect. A key contention in my argument is that, even when shaming fails to promote compliance through international mechanisms, it can nonetheless influence states' human rights behavior by unleashing political forces *within* the target state, changing the domestic political game in ways that undermine human rights compliance and reward violations. It is to this dynamic that I now turn.

Domestic Reactions: Pressures to Defy

INTERNATIONAL SHAMING AND DOMESTIC DEFIANCE

Human rights pressure is not contained in the international sphere; it also has the potential to alter domestic politics in the target country. The predominant wisdom is that international shaming instigates domestic change in ways that ultimately favor *compliance* with global norms (see chapter 1 for details and important exceptions). But as scholars are increasingly

22. *Global Times* 2021.
23. Flockhart 2006; Johnston 2001; Schimmelfennig 2000.

documenting, external human rights pressure can also *backfire*, provoking strong, negative societal "counterreactions" that mobilize against human rights reforms.[24] Although rarely defined as such, these counterreactions are almost always described as conservative and right-wing in nature, rooted in "existing power structures or norms," and politically or ideologically vested in certain practices or policies that violate international (liberal) human rights norms.[25] For instance, authoritarian leaders may view certain rights claims as a threat to their power and attempt to mobilize societal opposition to human rights principles in order to mitigate the threat.[26] Or external advocacy for women's rights and sexuality rights may provoke conservative "anti-preneurs" into mobilizing against reforms in favor of the status quo.[27]

As such, most analyses of counterreactions are conceptually rooted in what I have described here as "behavioral interests." That is, opponents of human rights are presumed to hold preexisting political or ideological interests that conflict with the content of human rights norms. International shaming mobilizes these interests, but it does not, in this view, produce them. However, because these "pro-violation" movements are essentially driven by substantive preferences for regressive policies, it is not at all clear whether external pressure *causes* such movements or simply co-occurs along with a broader right-wing trend in the target state.[28]

I propose another possibility for how and why international shaming alters domestic politics in the target state. To do so, I build off and extend existing research on norm backlash while drawing from adjacent literatures on status and hierarchy in world affairs. In brief, international shaming often registers as a status threat to domestic audiences in the target country. When pervasive, the experience of status threat invokes a popular defensive reaction that degrades outside criticism and transforms norm violation into an expression of national identity and resistance. This defensive reaction alters the domestic political environment by introducing strategic incentives that constrain policymakers from complying with the demands of international shaming while rewarding those who resist. Together, these mechanisms advance the

---

24. Bloomfield and Scott 2016; Bob 2012; Chaudoin 2016; Dreier 2018; Nuñez-Mietz and Garcia Iommi 2017; Rafi and Chowdhury 2000; Symons and Altman 2015; Vinjamuri 2017. For a summary of this literature, see Strezhnev, Kelley, and Simmons 2021, 3–5.

25. Strezhnev, Kelley, and Simmons 2021, 5. See also Snyder 2020a, 2020b; Tsutsui, Whitlinger, and Lim 2012.

26. Risse, Ropp, and Sikkink 1999.

27. Ayoub 2014; Nuñez-Mietz and Garcia Iommi 2017; Symons and Altman 2015.

28. Strezhnev, Kelley, and Simmons 2021.

likelihood that states will not only ignore outside pressure but *double down* on norm violations as a response. The logic rests on three key insights.

Shaming invokes status threat in domestic audiences.

First, international shaming often registers with domestic audiences as a *status threat*—that is, as a hostile attempt to degrade the target country in a social hierarchy. It has been well established that national affiliation and citizenship constitute important social identities for many individuals.[29] People have deep emotional ties to their nation, and nationalism retains a great psychological power over how individuals see themselves in relation to others.[30] Status threat emerges when individuals believe that their group (country) is being devalued in relation to others—for instance, by being stigmatized or labeled inferior.[31] A large literature in IR demonstrates that individuals are sensitive to perceived threats to their country's status, ranging from military defeat to diplomatic snubs.[32]

Like other acts of status denial, human rights shaming registers as a threat insofar as citizens view it as an attempt to degrade their country on the world stage. As I underscored in previous chapters, shaming is a *stigmatizing* act that renounces not just a particular behavior but the violating actor or group as a whole. Importantly, national identity is routinely activated in human rights discourse, where the object of evaluation is typically the country (for example, Amnesty International's country reports, Freedom House country rankings, and the country-targeted resolutions of the UN High Commissioner for Refugees [UNHCR]). Some citizens come to associate international shaming with an attack on their country, especially if they have reasons to believe that such criticism is rooted in political animosity.

It is important to note that status threat is a subjective experience and may have only limited correspondence to objective conditions. Nevertheless, it is not totally unreasonable to suspect that human rights shaming is driven by hostile intentions. I have argued that international actors commonly weaponize shaming in order to degrade the target's position and advance their own. From the perspective of those who identify with the target, weaponized shaming arouses feelings of *harm* (the injury resulting from status degradation) and *wrong* (the sense that such harm is illegitimate, unfair,

---

29. Flockhart 2006; Mercer 1995.

30. Flockhart 2006; Mercer 1995; Ward 2017.

31. Branscombe et al. 1999; Ellemers, Spears, and Doosje 2002; Major and O'Brien 2005.

32. Dafoe, Renshon, and Huth 2014; Fattah and Fierke 2009; Lindemann 2011; Paul, Larson, and Wohlforth 2014; Towns 2012; Wohlforth 2009; Wolf 2011.

and imbued with ill intent). As such, shaming does not invoke remorse but instead indignation, rage, and resentment.[33]

Status threat stimulates defensive reactions.

Threat is a reactive force. Research in social psychology reveals that, when individuals perceive external criticism as a threat to their group's status, they not only fail to internalize that criticism but react defensively against it.[34] A defensive reaction drives perceptual, attitudinal, and behavioral changes that degrade outside criticism and place higher value on norm resistance as an expression of in-group identity. To illustrate, recall when supporters of Hillary Clinton styled NASTY WOMAN T-shirts during the 2016 presidential election, while Trump supporters donned apparel inscribed with BASKET OF DEPLORABLES. Before the campaign, these phrases carried very little symbolic meaning. But once hurled as epithets, they were quickly reappropriated by the very people they were designed to stigmatize and refashioned as totems of group identity. By changing the valence assigned to a particular practice, out-group criticism converts norm violation into a vehicle for expressing in-group identity, anger, and resistance. In this sense, external pressure *politicizes* a norm, transforming it into a symbolic boundary separating in-group from out-group.[35]

A similar dynamic occurs around international shaming. Foreign condemnation "internationalizes" the relevant issue in public discourse, suturing certain norms and practices (human rights) to intergroup conflicts (national status and honor).[36] Work on status and hierarchies in IR shows that status dissatisfaction provokes opposition to the norms and institutions undergirding a status hierarchy.[37] One way to effectively cope with the status-degrading effects of stigma is by rejecting the legitimacy of the stigmatizers and the norms they promote. To clarify, it is not the norms per se that incite opposition, but their use as technologies of stigma and status denial; international human rights enforcement implies a relation of domination and submission. An emerging body of experimental work further supports the notion that international shaming provokes oppositional reactions in

---

33. For more details on these psychological processes, see Snyder 2020a, 2020b.

34. Hornsey and Imani 2004. Interestingly, Matthew Hornsey and Armin Imani explicitly mention international human rights shaming when discussing potential implications. In such cases, shaming can backfire because "we are psychologically predisposed to deny the validity of the comments, even where they have a legitimate basis" (ibid., 366).

35. For a review on social and symbolic boundaries, see Lamont and Molnár 2002.

36. Gruffydd-Jones 2018.

37. Adler-Nissen 2014; Dafoe, Renshon, and Huth 2014; Evers 2017; Ward 2017; Zarakol 2010.

domestic publics, even in domains that ostensibly benefit citizens' well-being, such as human rights (see chapter 5).

Defensive reactions alter the domestic political landscape by introducing new incentives.

Finally, widespread feelings of status threat alter the political landscape in which elites compete for policy and influence.[38] Like any shift in public opinion or discourse, widespread feelings of status threat constitute a *legitimating resource* that transforms what is politically viable.[39] And like any resource, a defensive reaction to foreign shaming will not *determine* how policymakers choose to act, but it will systematically favor some policies, some messages, and some stances over others.

For one, prominent beliefs linking shaming to status threat *constrain leaders* from complying with international norms by increasing the political costs associated with "giving in" to foreign demands. When audiences associate human rights pressure with domination, politicians cannot acquiesce to such pressure without being perceived as kowtowing to the enemy. Even if leaders are inclined to comply with international norms on account of their foreign policy goals or genuine beliefs, they must reckon with domestic forces that associate compliance with weakness and a loss of political legitimacy.[40] Put differently, a compelling discourse on status threat amounts to an effective constraint on those who would advocate for complying with international demands.

This dynamic is likely to have occurred in Uganda once the United States threatened economic sanctions over the country's "Anti-Homosexuality Act" in 2014. President Yoweri Museveni—who by all accounts preferred a more moderate solution to the crisis—was backed into a corner. A *Foreign Policy* story quoted the Ugandan journalist Andrew Mwenda as saying, "The mere fact that Obama threatened Museveni publicly is the very reason

38. Ward 2017.

39. Patrick Thaddeus Jackson (2006, 23) describes legitimation as "the process of drawing and (re)establishing boundaries, ruling some courses of action acceptable and others unacceptable." For more on legitimation, see Jackson 2006; Krebs 2015; Krebs and Jackson 2007; Schimmelfennig 2001; Ward 2017; Williams 2003.

40. James Fearon (1994) writes of a similar mechanism in the context of international crises with his conception of "audience costs." Contrary to the common application of audience costs to explicit threats in military bargaining, Fearon's original conception involved much broader affective concerns over national honor and reputation. Whether in the context of military bargaining or other kinds of disputes, "backing down" is "costly for a leader because it gives domestic political opponents an opportunity to deplore the international loss of credibility, face, or honor" (ibid., 581). See also Dafoe, Renshon, and Huth 2014.

he chose to go ahead and sign the bill." And Museveni did so in a particularly defiant fashion, "with the full witness of the international media to demonstrate Uganda's independence in the face of Western pressure and provocation."[41]

Second, a defensive reaction among domestic publics *rewards opponents* of international norms. One insight from sociology is that norm-violating actors command legitimacy from those constituencies that do not feel well served by the group that said norms represent.[42] By flagrantly violating the norms of the out-group—thereby provoking their opprobrium and contempt—deviant actors demonstrate the authenticity of their identity with, and commitment to, the in-group. This dynamic then generates incentives to violate out-group norms as a strategy to accumulate prestige and symbolic capital from within one's social circle.[43]

In the international context, norm opposition performs resistance to foreign domination disguised as human rights criticism. Insofar as such criticism is understood as an attack on the nation, norm opponents can claim that they are defending the country's interests by standing their ground, thus accumulating political capital.[44] Such rewards benefit those who already hold behavioral interests in norm violation (such as repressive leaders or "norm antipreneurs") by providing a discursive focal point around which to mobilize their efforts. They also create inducements for politicians to demonstrate their opposition to norms in ways that would have been less attractive without foreign condemnation. For example, nationalists may seize on the opportunity to resist a particular norm—even if they were previously silent on the issue—to gain a political advantage.

Finally, a defensive reaction *punishes local advocates*. Many believe that international pressure legitimates and empowers local advocacy groups. However, external shaming can also *de*-legitimize local activists. When international pressure is deemed illegitimate, this illegitimacy is projected onto both the norm and the actors who promote said norm. Guilt by association damages the credibility of local NGOs, victims of human rights abuses, and others who are viewed as surrogates for antagonistic foreign powers.[45]

---

41. Allen 2014.

42. Hahl, Kim, and Zuckerman Sivan 2018, 3.

43. The sociological literature on deviant subcultures provides the clearest depictions of the "positive side" of negative identity. See Becker 2008; Cohen 1955, 1970; Goffman 2009; Lemert 1972.

44. Dreier 2018.

45. Nuñez-Mietz and Garcia Iommi 2017.

In Nigeria, for example, local advocates called on Western women's rights groups to cease actions on behalf of Amina Lawal, a Nigerian woman sentenced to be stoned to death in 2002. Many of the petitions and letters initiated by Western groups contained inaccurate information about the case and presented negative stereotypes of Muslims and Nigerians. These interventions damaged the credibility of local advocates—who were accused of colluding with foreign governments to embarrass Nigeria—and incited retaliatory violence by local vigilantes. Some officials reportedly became more committed to carrying out Lawal's death sentence after receiving various protest letters with Western postage.[46] As a result, the local advocacy group BAOBAB for Women's Human Rights published an open letter to global advocacy networks entitled "Please Stop the International Amina Lawal Protest Letter Campaigns."[47]

Together, these dynamics generate strategic incentives for leaders to resist international shaming to bolster domestic legitimacy. Indeed, when defensive reactions are particularly potent, it can be rational for policymakers to double down on violations even if they have no intrinsic preference against the norm *per se*. In this regard, the mechanism I describe differs from what some term "counterreactions," "blocking factors," or other forms of contestation wherein opposition to international shaming springs from behavioral interests in norm violation. Here, external shaming establishes the association of a particular norm with a relation of domination, thus animating opposition to that very norm, even when the target group was previously neutral or ambivalent. In effect, we see a reversal of the causal arrow centered in the norms literature, whereby the motivation to deviate results in an actor being shamed. Here, shaming produces the motivation to deviate.

CONDITIONS OF DOMESTIC REACTIONS

When should we expect to see a defiant reaction to international shaming? One plausible factor pertains to targeted elites and their behavioral interests within the domestic political context. Indeed, to the extent that it is advantageous, some leaders may want to manufacture a defensive reaction to legitimize and enable their behavior or rally up popular support. In other words, leaders who prefer to violate norms (on account of behavioral interests) have an incentive to mobilize collective feelings of status threat in their

---

46. Sengupta 2003.
47. BAOBAB for Women's Human Rights 2003.

domestic population. Further, elites have considerable agency in directing public opinion, including citizens' reactions to foreign criticism. For example, they can manipulate media discourse around international human rights dynamics, drawing on nationalist or anti-imperialist narratives to instill perceptions of status threat and cue a defensive response.[48] Some may even intentionally violate norms to provoke foreign condemnation and stir up a defensive reaction from relevant audiences. For example, some observers speculated that Vladimir Putin initiated the "Anti-Gay Propaganda" law precisely because he anticipated Western condemnation, which bolstered his popularity at home.[49]

This discussion raises an important question: To what extent does foreign human rights shaming play a *causal* role in this process, especially if leaders strive to manufacture a defensive reaction for their own political gain? Considering the degree to which policymakers manipulate domestic narratives on human rights and international relations, what difference does international shaming actually make? Here, it is important to acknowledge that while leaders may attempt to engineer public discourse on shaming, such attempts are not always successful. Put differently, elite interests may account for the *motivation* to provoke public defensiveness but not the *ability* to do so. To successfully manufacture a defensive reaction from key audiences, leaders must craft a compelling narrative of human rights as a status threat. The point is not that elites can manufacture this reaction *de novo* but rather that they can use real instances of international shaming to direct public opinion in ways that are politically favorable. Foreign criticism influences this process mainly by introducing a set of rhetorical resources that systematically favor one side or another in conflicts over international norms. Insofar as states condemn their strategic partners and rivals in systematically different ways, they introduce different legitimating resources that either constrain or enable the actions of leaders.

States shame their geopolitical rivals in precisely the kinds of ways that fuel a defensive reaction in target audiences. When states condemn their adversaries, observers can safely assume that they are motivated by hostile intentions, which not only discredit accusations of human rights abuse but also cultivate a sense of provocation and attack.[50] While governments

---

48. Dreier 2018.
49. Whitmore 2013.
50. Hall 2017; Dafoe and Weiss 2018.

take care not to offend a strategic partner, they condemn their adversaries using highly inflammatory and stigmatizing rhetoric—precisely the type that antagonizes target audiences and advances the likelihood of defensive reactions.[51] And as described in the last chapter, states take any opportunity to defame an enemy, even if the charges are substantively arbitrary, hypocritical, discriminatory, excessive, inaccurate, or otherwise untrustworthy.[52] Leaders in the target country can easily point to such bias and misinformation to damage the legitimacy of foreign critics and reinforce the view that shaming is driven by hostile motivations.[53]

For example, China often highlights American hypocrisy to discredit accusations of abuse in Xinjiang. When it came to genocide and crimes against humanity, Chinese foreign ministry Zhao Lijian remarked, "the 'hat' is a perfect fit for the United States." Around that time, China's English-language outlet published more than a dozen stories about the 1921 Tulsa massacre in the United States, while another state-run outlet publicized historical and contemporary violations committed by the United States and other Western countries. Pointing to Western hypocrisy is effective as a discrediting tactic because it implies that the accusations are motivated by politics, not principles. Zhao went on to call the accusations "the biggest lie of the century."[54]

Readers may wonder: If shaming backfires in this way, why do it at all? Some scholars recognize the potential for backlash and yet argue that human rights shamers "do not desire or intend pushback from perpetrators." But it is important to emphasize that the dynamics I am describing go beyond strategic blunders or shortsightedness. Recall from the previous chapter that political actors enforce norms not only, or even primarily, to compel compliance. For states wishing to stigmatize their geopolitical rivals, a defensive backlash is not only allowable but welcome insofar as it provides additional opportunities to tarnish the target's legitimacy. Similarly, for those responding to metanorm pressures, the primary reward is tied to the act of shaming itself, not necessarily to the outcome. In this sense, what may look like strategic mistakes are in fact the product of a structure of underlying incentives that fuels both harsh enforcement and steely resistance.

---

51. Hall 2017.

52. The criminologist Lawrence Sherman (1993, 460–61) argues that defiance of law enforcement is especially likely when sanctions are seen as unfair, arbitrary, or excessive.

53. See, for example, Joseph 2014.

54. Mantesso 2021.

A General Model of Target Response

These insights aggregate into a general model of responses to international shaming. As a reminder, I am holding *ex ante* behavioral interests—preferences for the norm-violating behavior *per se*—constant. All else equal, governments respond to international shaming by anticipating the potential reactions from different audiences and then figuring these reactions into their strategic calculus. The upshot is that leaders react to external pressure based on the constellation of relational forces, resulting in four ideal-typical outcomes (table 3.2).

COMPLIANCE

The upper-right quadrant of table 3.2 describes a target state's response to significant pressure to comply from friends relative to pressure from rivals. In this case, the incentives to comply vastly outweigh any benefits a leader can reasonably expect from resisting. This case is indicative of the canonical "norm life cycle" and "spiral" models of international norms and is most conducive to compliance.

Cases meeting this description usually resemble one of two scenarios: in one, an overwhelming global consensus among all observers—including friends and allies—shames the target for an egregious violation, such as happened in South Africa in 1985 when allies such as the United States and the United Kingdom were finally compelled to sanction the apartheid regime; in the other, the target is severely dependent—whether through colonial, imperial, or trade relations—on the state or states exerting normative pressure. In both scenarios, the international relational costs imposed by shaming are sufficient to secure compliance.

DEFIANCE

The lower-left quadrant of table 3.2 describes cases in which states are shamed intensely by adversaries—generating domestic outrage—but their actions are condoned by friends. Here, leaders experience significant incentives to resist compliance pressures in order to achieve political gains at home, and few counterbalancing incentives to comply are present.

These situations usually involve highly contested or polarized norms. For example, Putin's signing of Russia's "anti-homosexuality" bill in the lead-up to the 2014 Winter Olympics in Sochi generated intense outrage from

TABLE 3.2. General Model of State Responses to International Shaming

		Shaming from Geopolitical Rivals	
		HIGH	LOW
Shaming from Geopolitical Friends	HIGH	Response: *Deflection* Causal logic: Countervailing incentives for compliance and defiance	Response: *Compliance* Causal logic: Relational costs incentivize compliance; fewer incentives to defy
	LOW	Response: *Defiance* Causal logic: Collective reactions to status threat in domestic audiences incentivize defiance; fewer incentives to comply	Response: *Status quo maintenance*

mostly Western, liberal countries. On the other hand, Russia's allies, especially those in the Global South, not only failed to criticize Russia but largely rejected the legitimacy of sexual orientation and gender identity (SOGI) norms altogether.[55] In this context, Western shaming provoked a defensive reaction from both domestic *and* international audiences, who converged in their opposition to what they saw as an arrogant and high-handed attempt at cultural imperialism.[56]

Such scenarios in which the rewards for resisting international pressure vastly outweigh the costs create an environment that is conducive to defiance. By violating foreign (Western, liberal) norms, the defiant state bolsters its prestige in the eyes of those who resent being "pushed around" by domineering powers. In the absence of any countervailing force, these incentives drive leaders to take more and more extreme measures to showcase for defensive audiences their righteous resistance. The logical result is defiance and norm backlash, including the initiation of laws and policies that are antithetical to the norm in question. This is probably what occurred in Russia, which took a more polarized position on homosexuality following transnational pressure.[57]

As the Russia example suggests, defiance—and more generally the relational dynamics I have described—may assume a particular relevance under

55. Nuñez-Mietz and Garcia Iommi 2017; Symons and Altman 2015.
56. Rao 2014.
57. Symons and Altman 2015.

certain systemic conditions. Changes in the international system involving Western decline, bipolarity, or hegemonic transition inaugurate shifts in relational configurations—for example, by creating clusters of states that are densely connected internally but are lacking in strong dyadic ties among themselves. In that case, the dyadic dynamics I focus on here may aggregate into system-level trends, such as the polarization of norms. I return to the importance of system-level factors in the concluding chapter.

DEFLECTION

Finally, the upper-left quadrant of table 3.2 shows the effect of shaming by both friends and rivals: cross-cutting incentives for both compliance *and* defiance are generated simultaneously as leaders contend with different audiences that diverge in their interpretation of normative pressure. For instance, shaming by adversaries may provoke a powerful defensive reaction from domestic audiences, incentivizing leaders to resist. On the other hand, a state's foreign allies may be compelled to intervene by behavioral interests or metanorm pressures of their own. In this scenario, if target states resist too ostentatiously and consequently suffer relational costs from international allies, they may sabotage their foreign policy goals. At the same time, full compliance would generate disapproval from domestic audiences who interpret concessions as weakness. A political dilemma ensues.

When both compliance and defiance pressures are high, the optimal strategy for a state's leaders is *deflection*: deploying arguments that affirm the validity of the norm in question while minimizing perceptions that they violated said norm. Deflection provides a way to challenge international criticism without explicitly rejecting the legitimacy of the norm itself, thus ameliorating both compliance and defiance pressures.[58]

Deflection is optimal in this scenario because, as I explained in the previous chapter, norm enforcement is largely determined by political relationships.[59] States require of their geopolitical allies a lower standard for human rights performance, owing to their relational investment. However,

---

58. Zoltán Búzás (2018) makes a similar argument, positing that "norm evasion"—complying technically with the letter of the law while violating the principle of the norm—is an attractive strategy for governments facing a balance of pro-compliance and pro-violation coalitions. One difference in my argument is that, while Búzás highlights anti-compliance pressures rooted in preexisting behavioral interests, I emphasize anti-compliance pressures that emerge *as a consequence of shaming* and the animosity it engenders.

59. Donno 2010; Goodliffe et al. 2012; Terman and Voeten 2018.

leaders may also incur metanorm costs when turning a blind eye toward abuse; for instance, they may be lambasted by domestic critics for supporting an international pariah. From the perspective of shamers, deflection by an ally provides rhetorical cover, lowering the metanormative costs associated with tolerating deviance. Insofar as these friendly states' commitment to human rights norms is lower than their relational investment in the violator, a small change in the incentive structure is enough to tip the strategic calculus toward forbearance.[60] The same cannot be said for rivals, who impose more stringent demands for what they consider compliance.

Conclusion

To sum up, countries face multiple incentives when responding to international human rights pressure. In addition to the value that leaders extract from norm-violating behavior itself, shaming can undermine a target state's foreign relations and sabotage international benefits. Shaming can also alter the domestic political environment, which may favor either compliance or defiance. The latter two dynamics, I argue, are partly influenced by the *ex ante* geopolitical relationship between the shamer and the target. Pressure from geopolitical partners creates greater international incentives to comply while mitigating the potential for adverse reactions in the domestic sphere. Criticism from a geopolitical rival, in contrast, imposes negligible geopolitical costs and is more likely to fuel a defensive reaction in constituencies sympathetic to the target state, thus promoting defiance. When both compliance and defiance pressures are high, leaders often opt to deflect, affirming the validity of human rights norms while rejecting accusations that they violated those norms.

These claims are closely intertwined with the ones presented in the previous chapter. Shaming by an adversary is more likely to backfire partly because it signals hostile motives. Indeed, as I showed in chapter 2, states often shame their rivals in order to inflict political damage, using precisely the kind of stigmatizing and inflammatory rhetoric that ignites feelings of insult, provocation, and defiance. Shaming by geopolitical partners registers as more credible—and more effective—on account of the preexisting relationships with the target state. Unfortunately, this kind of shaming is also more difficult to mobilize for precisely the same reason: leaders are reluctant to criticize friends and allies because they value these relationships.

---

60. Hurd 2005, 519.

Only a surge of political will—typically induced by overwhelming metanorm pressures—will overcome these barriers to enforcement. The upshot is that shaming is most effective in situations where it is least likely to occur.

It is also worth noting how the theory diverges from conventional wisdom. Much of our current understanding of compliance centers on behavioral preferences: the interests that leaders bring to the violating behavior itself or the value they put on it. For instance, many accounts of "counterreactions" to human rights pressure focus on repressive governments or right-wing forces that are politically or ideologically vested in human rights violations; that is, they hold strong behavioral preferences against human rights compliance. But behavioral preferences alone cannot fully account for the range of responses to international shaming. Preexisting preferences may explain why some leaders initially resist compliance pressures but not why they adopt more divergent positions as a result of being shamed.[61] My theory shows that it can be rational for target actors to resist and defy human rights shaming even if they have weak preferences regarding the content of these norms.

Second, the theory complicates the widespread belief that international shaming inflicts legitimacy costs on targeted governments. If foreign criticism sparks domestic outrage, leaders are *rewarded* for noncompliance. In this sense, shaming is less a deterrent than an enabler of norm violations. Here, too, the logic diverges from more familiar accounts of "counterreactions" or "blocking factors," which are widely thought to lose credibility in the face of sustained international criticism.[62] Insofar as outside pressure fuels the mechanism I have described in this chapter, we should expect to see a higher commitment to norm violation as shaming increases in intensity. In brief, I argue that norm resistance arises *endogenously* from the process; it occurs because of, not in spite of, international shaming.

The next three chapters are dedicated to testing the argument. Because the theory generates empirical implications on multiple levels of analysis, I divide the empirical portions of the book into three parts: one chapter focuses on interstate interactions between shaming and target states, one on intrastate dynamics within target states, and the last on specific cases that tie these mechanisms together.

---

61. For a similar criticism, see Symons and Altman 2015, 74.
62. Risse and Ropp 1999, 262.

4

Interstate Shaming in the Universal Periodic Review

In February 2021, an American intelligence report was released showing that Saudi crown prince Mohammed bin Salman approved the assassination of the journalist Jamal Khashoggi in 2018.[1] But the newly elected Biden administration ultimately decided not to sanction Saudi Arabia's crown prince, citing foreign cooperation—particularly on counterterrorism and in confronting Iran—as the primary reason. "There isn't an issue in the Middle East where we don't need [the Saudis] to play a role," one veteran official explained. "If you sanction the crown prince directly you basically create a relationship of hostility."[2]

Anecdotes like this illustrate one of this book's central arguments: human rights enforcement is an inherently political exercise, mediated by the preexisting relationship between shamer and target. In chapter 2, I described how strategic relations shape states' decisions about whether and how to shame perceived human rights violations. Like the Biden administration in its approach to Saudi Arabia, leaders hesitate to shame their friends and allies in order to avoid undermining a valuable relationship. Meanwhile, they harshly condemn adversaries in an effort to inflict stigma and political damage. In chapter 3, I explained how these same ties affect subsequent responses by target states. There I argued that shaming can impose relational

1. This chapter draws off research in Terman and Voeten 2018 and Terman and Byun 2021.
2. Sanger 2021b.

costs in the international sphere, threatening the target state's foreign policy goals. Strategic ties serve as leverage, incentivizing leaders to comply with outside pressure so as to protect important relationships. Shaming from rivals, on the other hand, is easier to ignore. Because there is no valued relationship to protect, target states have fewer incentives to acquiesce to the shamer's demands.

This chapter tests these claims about the role of strategic relationships in international human rights enforcement. I focus on the *interstate* dimensions of the theory pertaining to interactions between states. (The next chapter turns to expectations concerning domestic politics.) If my argument is correct, we should observe the influence of strategic relations on the behavior of both shaming and target states. Testing these expectations, however, raises substantial empirical challenges. Existing studies tend to operationalize shaming as a homogenous count—how much a particular country is shamed in general—with two possible outcomes: improvement or *status quo ante*. Not only do such designs obscure the relational dynamics at the heart of the shaming process, but they also flatten important dimensions of variation on both the independent and dependent variables. We need to find a way to identify criticism from different actors and isolate the role of strategic relations in both the onset and response to international shaming.

To cope with that challenge, this chapter uses data from the most elaborate multilateral human rights process in the international system: the United Nations Universal Periodic Review (UPR), conducted by the UN Human Rights Council. In the UPR process, states "peer-review" one another's human rights records. As a laboratory to examine interstate shaming, this forum is ideal for several reasons. For one, it is the only international human rights mechanism that, in reviewing all 193 UN members, achieves 100 percent voluntary participation. Further, because the reviewers are the states themselves, researchers are able to trace the influence of political relationships in the enforcement of human rights. Importantly, the UPR represents a highly systematic, formalized, and repetitive environment that provides a granularity of information (who says what to whom) that is unmatched by other data sources.

Using statistical analysis, I examined over fifty-seven thousand recommendations from the first two cycles of UPR, examining the influence of three kinds of political relationships: geopolitical affinity, formal military alliance, and arms trade. The evidence shows that states do in fact spare their strategic partners in the review process by avoiding sensitive topics and giving milder commentary on average. But when friendly states offer criticism, their recommendations are more likely to be supported by the state under review compared to substantively identical recommendations coming from other countries. Adversaries, on the other hand, tend to shame one another in a more demanding and inflammatory fashion—precisely the kind of shaming that tends to fall on deaf ears or backfire. These results are remarkably robust, even after controlling for a number of factors that could influence human rights enforcement.

The rest of the chapter proceeds as follows. I first provide background on the UPR. The following section applies the book's general argument to interactions in the UPR, detailing several expectations. After describing the data and research design in the next section, I present the main results in the following two sections. The final section summarizes this chapter's findings and limitations.[3]

The Universal Periodic Review: Background

WHAT IS THE UPR?

The Universal Periodic Review (UPR) is a process conducted by the UN Human Rights Council (HRC) to periodically review the human rights practices of all UN member states. It was established by General Assembly resolution 60/251 in 2006, which also created the Human Rights Council. The HRC arose from the institutional ashes of the UN Human Rights Commission, which was heavily criticized for being too politicized.[4] As an attempt to create a fairer process, the HRC was mandated to

> undertake a universal periodic review, based on objective and reliable information, of the fulfillment by each State of its human rights obligations and commitments in a manner which ensures universality of coverage and equal treatment with respect to all States.

---

3. Although the UPR is unique in some ways, several other institutions also rely on peer review for implementation and enforcement, for example, the Working Group on Bribery and the Economic and Development Review Committee of the Organization for Economic Cooperation and Development (OECD); the Implementation Review Mechanism of the UN Convention against Corruption; and the Trade Policy Review Mechanism of the World Trade Organization (WTO). See Carraro, Conzelmann, and Jongen 2019; Koliev 2020. Mechanisms involving public votes on country-specific resolutions—the procedure, for instance, with the UN Human Rights Council and General Assembly—may exhibit similar patterns.

4. United Nations General Assembly 2005a, 182.

The UPR's peer-review system, Secretary-General Kofi Annan argued, would "help avoid, to the extent possible, the politicization and selectivity that are hallmarks of the Commission's existing system."[5] Beginning in 2008, the process is the first international human rights mechanism to achieve 100 percent voluntary participation, having now at least twice addressed all 193 UN countries.[6]

The UPR occurs in cycles: each UN member state is reviewed once per cycle. The first cycle ran from 2008 to 2011 and the second from 2012 to 2016. Reviews are facilitated by the UPR Working Group, which consists of the forty-seven member states of the Human Rights Council. However, any UN member—or permanent observer (the Holy See and Palestine)—can participate as a reviewer. The UPR Working Group meets three times per year in Geneva and reviews fourteen to sixteen states per session.[7]

Reviews take place through an interactive dialogue between the State under Review (SuR) and all other UN members (and permanent observers). First, the SuR presents a self-assessment of its human rights practices. All other states then have the opportunity to provide feedback in the form of specific recommendations. Each UN country can issue one or more recommendations per review, or none at all. The SuR must then publicly decide whether to support or reject each recommendation it receives and then voluntarily commit to those it supports. Once complete, an outcome report of the review is compiled, and the SuR has four and a half years to implement the recommendations it supported before undergoing another review in the next cycle.

THE UPR AS A LABORATORY OF INTERNATIONAL SHAMING

What can the UPR tell us about international human rights shaming? In chapter 1, I defined "shaming" as the public expression of disapproval of specific states for perceived violations of appropriate conduct. Many UPR recommendations would not be considered instances of shaming, as they fail to convey disapproval or identify violations. Importantly, however, they do offer an extremely useful proxy for the political dynamics underlying

5. United Nations General Assembly 2005b, para. 8.

6. Although not every state voted to pass resolution 60/251 (notably, the United States voted against it), participation in the UPR is voluntary, both as a reviewer and as a state under review.

7. The order of reviews during the first UPR cycle was determined through drawing of lots, and the same order was maintained during subsequent cycles.

interstate human rights enforcement and reveal a great deal about how international shaming works inside and outside the UN.

In principle, UPR reviews are supposed to be objective, with country delegations offering nonconfrontational recommendations to the state under review based on the UN Charter, the Universal Declaration of Human Rights, and the specific human rights obligations to which the target state has voluntarily committed.[8] In reality, however, delegations have broad leeway in what they choose to address and how. As a result, recommendations vary widely in both content and tone; they span the spectrum of potential human rights concerns, even when directed at the same country. Some admonish the state under review in scathing terms, representing shaming *par excellence* by identifying and condemning specific human rights violations. Others offer relatively gentle (if banal) suggestions or even praise the target state for improved conduct.

For example, consider Cuba's review in 2013.[9] North Korea recommended that Cuba "promote understanding, tolerance and friendship among the peoples of the world" and "continue to defend the cooperative approach, non-politicization and respectful dialogue in the field of human rights." The United States, in contrast, lambasted Cuba's repression of political dissidents and journalists and demanded that it "eliminate or cease enforcing laws impeding freedom of expression." Cuba, for its part, has used the UPR to accuse the United States of genocide, war crimes, and the repression of African Americans and indigenous peoples.[10]

Likewise, some delegations call for specific remedial actions (such as adopting a treaty or abolishing an abusive policy), while others use "softer" language to make vague and inexact suggestions. Regardless of valence, however, all UPR recommendations promote specific norms, whether implicitly or explicitly. For example, some recommendations call on the target state to ratify a particular international instrument, such as the International Convention on the Protection of the Rights of All Migrant Workers and Members of Their Families. In such instances, the reviewing state is identifying standards of appropriate conduct (the obligations detailed in the

---

8. General Assembly resolution 60/251 (United Nations General Assembly 2006), paras 1–2. Reviews are to be based on three documents: (1) a twenty-page national report prepared by the SuR; (2) a ten-page compilation of UN information prepared by the Office for the High Commissioner for Human Rights (OHCHR); and (3) a ten-page summary of information from stakeholders, also prepared by the OHCHR.

9. UN General Assembly 2013a.

10. UN General Assembly 2011.

convention) and implying that the target state has failed to fully adhere to those standards. Although perhaps not shaming *per se*, these recommendations nevertheless provide useful information on the reviewer's normative stance vis-à-vis the target state.

Importantly, both participants and observers view the UPR first and foremost as an *enforcement* mechanism that operates through interstate political pressure. Using surveys and semistructured interviews, Valentina Carraro finds that most delegations believe that the UPR generates both peer (state to state) and public pressure on states, and that this is its primary function. In this regard, the UPR differs from other human rights mechanisms such as monitoring by treaty bodies, which are thought to promote human rights through persuasion, learning, or information sharing. "Undoubtedly the UPR," even filtered through a highly technical and professionalized framework, "does 'name' and 'shame' transgressors."[11] More critically for our purposes, UPR recommendations mirror the enforcement logic of shaming: their bilateral nature provides a way for one state to punish or pressure another state into complying with certain normative standards. For these reasons, several studies have analyzed the UPR and similar forums in the theoretical context of international shaming and norm enforcement.[12]

From an empirical perspective, the UPR presents a laboratory to examine the politics of international human rights shaming that is ideal for at least two reasons. First, by virtue of its design, the process mirrors more informal dynamics outside the UN, thereby facilitating "external validity." In the everyday practice of world politics, governments enjoy significant flexibility in their position vis-à-vis other countries' practices, especially when it comes to something as complex and multifaceted as human rights. For any given issue in any given target state, the reactions of other countries will vary remarkably, regardless of the realities on the ground. The primary argument in this book is that both observing and target states alter their stance according to the expected political ramifications, and particularly with regard to their strategic relationships. These incentives also operate in the UPR, where delegations formulate their recommendations with a keen awareness of their geopolitical implications. Thus, the UPR's natural variation in review content allows us to examine the political dynamics of norm enforcement more generally.

Indeed, UPR recommendations are often representative of interactions outside the UN. For example, during one UPR cycle Canada issued

---

11. Carraro 2019, 1089.
12. Abebe 2009; Carraro 2017, 2019; Carraro, Conzelmann, and Jongen 2019.

recommendations to Iran concerning physical integrity and freedom of expression; then it focused on the plight of women and children when reviewing Saudi Arabia. As I discuss later, that difference reflects broader trends in the human rights postures of Canada and other Western countries, which appear relatively unafraid to pressure Saudi Arabia on women's rights issues while stringently avoiding more overt and sensitive political demands. In general, UPR recommendations are carefully constructed signals of states' broader human rights agendas, informed by the same dynamics that present in other diplomatic settings.

At the same time, the UPR distills these dynamics through a highly systematic, formalized, and repetitive environment that makes them amenable to empirical investigation and enhances "internal validity." By examining how patterns of geopolitical affinity condition the kinds of recommendations that states choose to offer in the UPR—scathing or soft, critical or condoning—we can precisely observe the theory's hypotheses at work.

Beyond its utility as a natural laboratory, the UPR may be consequential in itself. To date, studies on the UPR have been limited, and thus the significance of the process is still largely unknown. There are reasons to believe, however, that the process is more than just diplomatic performance or rhetorical maneuvering.[13] For one, governments and NGOs appear to invest a substantial amount of time and effort in the process—an indication of its perceived importance.[14] As I discuss in more detail later, states view the act of accepting recommendations as a kind of public commitment device that motivates them to implement those recommendations. And although media coverage of the UPR and public attention to the process remains limited,[15] many NGOs and activists rely on it to strengthen their domestic advocacy efforts—such as when the Electronic Frontier Foundation pointed to recommendations that Indonesia received to repeal its problematic criminal code.[16] As one Argentinian NGO representative put it, "UPR recommendations are used as a rationale to push the State to move forward concerning certain issues."[17] Nonetheless, regardless of the causal impact of the UPR itself, the

---

13. Menéndez 2022.

14. NGOs regularly submit shadow reports to the UPR—for example, Human Rights Watch has reported on the United States (Human Rights Watch 2019) and Earthjustice on Australia (Earthjustice 2020).

15. Joseph 2015. The UPR does receive some media attention, mostly concerning large countries, in ways that both support and criticize its authority; see, for example, Kuo 2018; Russell 2015.

16. Baghdasaryan 2022.

17. Menéndez 2022.

process offers an empirically useful proxy or window through which we can examine the political dynamics shaping international norm enforcement, both in and out of Geneva.

The Relational Politics of the UPR

This book takes a relational approach to human rights enforcement, emphasizing the political ties between source and target. In the previous chapters, I introduced the ideas of relational goods and relational costs, whereby leaders try to avoid offending other countries on which they depend for things they care about.[18] Relational goods can be economic, political, or ideational in nature, including humanitarian aid, foreign policy support, and military alliance. These goods are *relational* in that they are necessarily obtained through a strategic relationship that requires the participation of both partners. Because leaders value these relationships, they work to maintain them by anticipating potential reactions from their partners and behaving in ways that generate approval.

How does this general argument apply to interstate interactions in the UPR? If my argument is correct, we should observe the influence of strategic relations in the interaction between reviewer and target on the behavior of both parties, through two distinct but interrelated mechanisms.

First, governments will vary their evaluations in the UPR depending on their relationship with the target. In chapter 2, I described how states shame their friends and adversaries with different levels of severity: shaming by a friend tends to be more lenient and permissive, while shaming by an adversary is usually more demanding and adheres to stricter standards for what constitutes compliance. In the UPR, delegations enjoy broad leeway, in both content and tone, in the kinds of recommendations they offer. When evaluating a strategic partner, delegations often mute their criticisms so as to avoid retaliation, offering more lenient, safer, and more easily digestible recommendations. When evaluating an adversary, by contrast, delegations tend to take a tougher stance, issuing harsher and more demanding recommendations in order to stigmatize the target and demonstrate their own commitment to human rights.

Second, as chapter 3 explains, strategic ties should moderate the *reception* of criticism. Measuring the effect of interstate shaming is challenging, because we cannot always observe the target's reaction in a consistent

---

18. Goodliffe and Hawkins 2009b, 978.

fashion. To cope with that challenge, I exploit the fact that states under review are required to declare which recommendations they "support" or "accept."[19] Although supporting a recommendation does not necessarily signal a state's intent to implement, it nonetheless remains significant. In institutional terms, supporting a recommendation forces the state under review to follow up on that item during its next review. In theoretical terms, supporting a recommendation involves a kind of public commitment that may entrap a government in its own rhetoric.[20] This leaves the state under review vulnerable not only to transnational and domestic advocacy groups but to the recommending states themselves. For her rich qualitative study of the UPR, Carraro interviewed delegates who confirmed that states view recommendation support as a kind of commitment device or promise to the reviewer; the political relationship motivates them to implement the recommendation.[21] Indeed, observers of the UPR note that states do in fact implement a significant number of the recommendations they support.[22] For these reasons, recommendation support is a meaningful, if imperfect, sign of the intent to comply.

When deciding whether to accept a recommendation, states must factor in the political context, because recommendations send very different signals depending on their source. In a politicized environment, governments interpret criticism by their enemies as a cynical attempt to sully their country's reputation. The criticized government can exploit this by highlighting the source of a recommendation rather than its content in order to imply that it was motivated by political hostility rather than normative commitments. Moreover, publicly dismissing a geopolitical adversary's human rights concern is less likely to endanger other cooperative endeavors, especially with states that share the criticized government's hostile position vis-à-vis the

19. I use "support" and "accept" interchangeably, as does most of the documentation surrounding the UPR. HRC resolution 5/1 (para. 32) instructs rapporteurs: "Recommendations that enjoy the support of the State concerned will be identified as such. Other recommendations . . . will be noted." In reality, the nature of these responses has evolved significantly over the life of the UPR process as states have created categories such as "reject," "accept in part," and "already implemented." As of UPR Working Group session 17 in 2014, the group's reports have been standardized to itemize recommendations as either "supported" (or "accepted") or "noted." Sometimes states change their response after the review; for instance, both Rwanda and Denmark later accepted recommendations that they initially "noted" (UPR Info 2014).

20. Risse, Ropp, and Sikkink 1999; Simmons 2009.

21. Carraro 2019, 1084.

22. One study calculated that 48 percent of supported recommendations were either fully or partially implemented by midterm (two and a half years after the initial review) versus just 19 percent of the unsupported recommendations (UPR Info 2014, 5).

shamer. Not only does the target state have few incentives to acquiesce to demands from an adversary, but doing so may incur costs if it is seen as "kowtowing" to the enemy (a dynamic I examine in more detail in the next chapter).

On the other hand, recommendations send a very different signal when coming from a state that shares strong political, economic, or security ties with the target. As I explained in the previous chapters, some policymakers genuinely do care about human rights. This concern may originate in the behavioral preferences of state officials or in domestic metanorm pressures. Provided these forces are strong enough, delegations will issue a tough review and risk alienating an otherwise beneficial partnership. Publicly shaming a strategic partner sends a credible signal reflecting the critic's preferences on a particular issue. In this context, the target is more likely to accommodate the request in order to maintain a valuable partnership.

In sum, the theory generates two testable hypotheses. First, all else equal, states are more lenient with strategic partners and harsher with rivals. Second, states are more likely to support recommendations coming from strategic partners compared to how they receive substantively identical commentary issued by rivals.

Data and Research Design

THE DATA SET

I use data compiled by UPR Info, a nonprofit organization monitoring the process.[23] The sample includes all recommendations made during the first two cycles (twenty-six sessions) of the UPR working group ($n = 57{,}867$). During this time, 193 countries were reviewed twice, once per cycle. For each recommendation, data were collected on the state offering the recommendation (the *reviewer*), the SuR receiving the recommendation (the *target*), and the SuR's response to the recommendation (the *response*). UPR Info researchers also hand-labeled each recommendation according to the kind of action demanded on the part of the SuR (*severity*) and the specific human rights *issue(s)* involved, from a set of fifty-four categories (such as "women's rights," "detention," and "international instruments") that are not mutually exclusive (see appendix A for details). Table 4.1 presents three example observations.

---

23. See UPR Info, https://www.upr-info.org.

TABLE 4.1. Examples of Universal Periodic Review Recommendations

From (Reviewer)	To (Target)	Session	Text	Issue(s)	Severity	Response
Argentina	Antigua and Barbuda	12	Continue with the efforts to prevent, punish, and eradicate all forms of violence against women.	Women's rights	1	Accepted
Australia	Antigua and Barbuda	12	Accede to the Second Optional Protocol to the International Covenant on Civil and Political Rights, aimed at abolishing the death penalty, and take all necessary steps to remove the death penalty from Antigua and Barbuda law.	Death penalty, international instruments	3	Noted
Australia	Antigua and Barbuda	12	Improve conditions in Antigua and Barbuda's prisons and detention facilities.	Detention	2	Accepted

DEPENDENT VARIABLES

The hypotheses concern two main dependent variables: the severity of the recommendation and the response to the recommendation. The response simply records whether or not the SuR supported a recommendation. The severity measures the level of the leniency or harshness of the recommendation's content based on the actions demanded of the SuR. Some delegations call for highly specific actions (such as adopting a treaty or abolishing an abusive policy), while others offer vague and inexact suggestions couched in "softer" language.

In the UPR, the specificity of a recommendation is a highly informative proxy for its severity. More specific recommendations reflect more severe

demands because they are more difficult to comply with. Such recommendations raise the bar for what the target state must do to claim that it implemented the recommendation. Inversely, less specific recommendations are
more lenient, and the standards for compliance are more permissive. It is much
easier for a government to claim that it "considered" adopting a treaty or abolishing a law than it is to claim that it "ratified" the treaty or "abolished" the law.
Keenly aware of this, both reviewing and target states consider the language
of recommendations carefully and intentionally. Across cases, the first verb in
a recommendation is highly indicative of its specificity and thus its severity.

UPR Info researchers coded each recommendation according to a five-
point categorical variable based on the first verb and the overall action contained in the recommendation. From these action codes, I constructed a
three-point ordinal measure of recommendation severity (see appendix A
for details). Higher values on the severity scale denote more demanding recommendations. Recommendations coded as 1 on this scale would not be
considered "shaming" in the conventional sense: they either praise the SuR
or request minimal change (for example, to "share best practices," or "request
technical assistance"). Unsurprisingly, recommendations of this type are very
likely (95 percent) to be supported by the SuR. Recommendations coded as 2
are the most common and contain a general behavioral element (for example,
"encourage," or "engage with"). Of these, 85 percent are supported. Recommendations coded as 3 are the most severe and demand that the SuR change
its behavior in tangible ways ("eliminate," "ratify, "enforce"). Only 55 percent
of such recommendations are supported. In some of the subsequent analyses, I limit the sample to recommendations with severity levels of 3 in order
to ensure that the hypotheses hold with only the most critical interactions.

EXPLANATORY VARIABLES

The hypotheses predict that certain strategic ties will influence the outcomes
of severity or response. To evaluate these claims, I examine three types of
strategic relationships in which foreign policy support, formal defense
agreements, and military arms, respectively, are exchanged. Clearly there
are additional dimensions of strategic relations beyond these three. By focusing on these ties, however, I offer a broad sample of relational goods that
are likely to influence interstate criticism in the UPR. Any effects that we
observe corresponding to some or all of these strategic dimensions will
lend credence to the overall claim that shaming is fundamentally mediated
by political relationships.

First, I capture foreign policy support by examining the degree of *geopolitical affinity* (hypothesis 1). States that have embraced the neoliberal order advanced by the United States and other Western states may easily brush off criticism from those who rebel against that order (and vice versa). In contrast, harsh criticisms from governments with similar foreign policy dispositions cannot be dismissed as easily. Geopolitical affinity is measured by taking the absolute distance between country ideal-points, estimated using votes in the UN General Assembly and multiplying this by minus one.[24] Larger values represent smaller distances and thus higher levels of ideological convergence on global issues.

Second, I look at the effects of formal *military alliances* on state interactions in the UPR. Formal military alliances hinge on the belief that states will come to each other's defense. Public discord may undermine that belief and sabotage a mutually beneficial partnership. Thus, states are more likely to be constrained when addressing their military allies. If alliance partners do criticize each other, the target may have a stronger incentive to support the recommendation in order to squash concerns about a conflictual relationship. To test effects of a formal military alliance (hypothesis 2), I use the Correlates of War (COW) formal alliance (version 4.1) data indicating whether or not a formal alliance exists between reviewer and target.[25]

Finally, I test the influence of *arms and weapons trade*. Countries that import arms may fear criticizing their supplier too harshly, lest they sabotage this valued relationship. At the same time, arms exporters and aid donors face similar incentives with respect to their recipients. The United States exports arms to Saudi Arabia not just for financial gain but also because it values a strategic partnership. More generally, arms exports are at least partially driven by shared interests between donor and recipient.[26] Thus, even powerful states benefit from the maintenance of such relationships and avoid provoking negative judgments from their clients.[27] Moreover, powerful states may wish to mitigate the perception that they aid and abet a human rights violator.

Consider, for example, when the Obama administration approved $1.3 billion in military aid to Egypt following Abdel Fattah el-Sisi's crackdown on dissenters. The move attracted widespread scrutiny; the journalist Glenn Greenwald, for instance, commented that the administration "lavished the

---

24. Bailey, Strezhnev, and Voeten 2015. Data are available through 2015.
25. Gibler 2008. Data are available through 2012.
26. Blanton 2005.
27. Esarey and DeMeritt 2017.

TABLE 4.2. Hypotheses about the Impact of Strategic Ties on UPR Responses

Explanatory Variable	Relevant Actor	Hypotheses
GEOPOLITICAL AFFINITY	Reviewer	*Hypothesis 1A:* All else equal, states are more lenient toward states that share their geopolitical ideology.
	Target	*Hypothesis 2A:* All else equal, states are more likely to support recommendations coming from states that share their geopolitical ideology.
FORMAL MILITARY ALLIANCE	Reviewer	*Hypothesis 1B:* All else equal, states are more lenient toward states with which they share a formal military alliance.
	Target	*Hypothesis 2B:* All else equal, states are more likely to support recommendations coming from states with which they share a formal military alliance.
ARMS TRADE	Reviewer	*Hypothesis 1C:* All else equal, states involved in an arms trade are more lenient toward each other.
	Target	*Hypothesis 2C:* All else equal, arms importers (exporters) are more likely to support recommendations coming from their exporters (importers).

regime with aid, money, and weapons" while ignoring its repression.[28] In fact, Secretary of State John Kerry did mention Egypt's human rights issues while announcing the renewed military relationship, but only obliquely and in a series of platitudes as he sat next to his Egyptian counterpart in a joint press conference. As the *New York Times* put it, Kerry was signaling that American officials "would not let their concerns with human rights stand in the way of increased security cooperation with Egypt."[29]

In sum, both weapons suppliers and weapons clients are incentivized to protect these strategic relationships when offering or receiving human rights recommendations. To test the effects of arms and weapons trade (hypothesis 3), I record two binary variables indicating whether the reviewer supplied arms to the target and vice versa, using data from the Stockholm International Peace Research Institute's Arms Transfers Database.[30] In the models shown here, all relational variables are lagged one year.

28. Greenwald 2015.
29. Gordon and Kirkpatrick 2015.
30. Stockholm International Peace Research Institute 2019. The data cover the entire time period.

I also consider a number of potential confounding variables that could influence interstate human rights shaming, including an indicator for whether the reviewing country was undergoing a review during the same session as the target (*reviewer UPR*), an indicator for whether the reviewer and target belonged to the same geographic region (*shared region*),[31] and measures of *physical integrity rights protections* for both reviewer and target.[32] All models include fixed effects for reviewer, target, and year to account for unobserved factors associated with stable state characteristics and time, respectively. In both analyses, I report results from OLS models for ease of interpretation, but I also include a number of robustness tests, including those related to potential selection bias. Those robustness tests, as well as details on controls and model specifications, can be found in appendix A.

Analysis of Reviewer Behavior

Conditional on participating in a review, how do states modulate their recommendations depending on their relationship with the target? The results from the statistical model, summarized in table 4.3, confirm that states are less severe on their strategic partners and harsher on their adversaries. Hypothesis 1A finds especially strong support. A one-point (one standard deviation) increase in geopolitical affinity reduces the mean level of severity by about 0.13 (on a three-point scale). Formal military allies (hypothesis 2A) also offer more lenient recommendations, although the magnitude of this effect is not as strong as geopolitical affinity.

I also find that states engaged in arms trade (hypothesis 3A) make less stringent recommendations for one another. That is, countries that import arms are more lenient toward their suppliers, perhaps to avoid undermining an important aid relationship, and arms exporters are also more lenient toward those to whom they provide weapons, possibly in an attempt to evade responsibility for providing material support to human rights abusers. Because the United States provides arms to Egypt, for example, American representatives may participate cautiously in Egypt's review in order to avoid charges of complicity in abuse.

In general, states are less likely to recommend in the UPR that their strategic partners take strong remedial *actions*.[33] But how do interstate relation-

---

31. From the Correlates of War (COW) project.

32. Fariss 2014. Data are available up to 2013.

33. The effects of control variables run generally as expected. There is some evidence that countries belonging to the same region are more lenient toward one another, all else equal.

TABLE 4.3. Determinants of UPR Recommendation Severity

	Mean Level of Severity			
	Model 1	Model 2	Model 3	Model 4
GEOPOLITICAL AFFINITY	−0.101***	−0.104***		
	(0.005)			
ALLIANCE	−0.030**		−0.055***	
	(0.015)			
ARMS (REVIEWER TO TARGET)	−0.007			−0.031*
	(0.017)			
ARMS (TARGET TO REVIEWER)	−0.098***			−0.137***
	(0.024)			
UPR (REVIEWER)	−0.010	−0.009	−0.009	−0.011
	(0.012)	(0.012)	(0.012)	(0.012)
SAME REGION	0.010	0.003	−0.038***	−0.052***
	(0.009)	(0.008)	(0.009)	(0.008)
PHYSICAL INTEGRITY RIGHTS (REVIEWER)	0.025	0.026	0.028	0.025
	(0.021)	(0.021)	(0.021)	(0.021)
PHYSICAL INTEGRITY RIGHTS (TARGET)	−0.090***	−0.089***	−0.090***	−0.089***
	(0.026)	(0.026)	(0.026)	(0.026)
N	39,896	39,896	39,896	39,896

***p <.01; **p <.05; *p <.10

Notes: Results from linear probability models. Fixed effects for target, reviewer, year, and issue are omitted. Robust standard errors in parentheses.

ships influence the kinds of *issues* addressed in recommendations? That is, do delegations avoid particular subject matter when reviewing a partner? To examine this question, figure 4.1 reports the marginal effect of geopolitical affinity on the number of recommendations offered by a given reviewer in each issue category, controlling for other factors.

The plot shows that, when reviewing geopolitical partners, states tend to avoid highly sensitive human rights issues—such as those that threaten the target's ruling regime—in favor of what Sarah Bush terms "regime-compatible" topics. Writing about international democracy promotion, Bush defines "regime-compatible" programs as those that "target-country leaders view as unlikely to threaten their imminent survival by causing regime collapse or

---

However, as indicated by model 1, this effect is likely collinear with geopolitical affinity. In addition, states are more likely to issue severe recommendations to countries with poor human rights records on average. There is no evidence that countries undergoing a UPR review in the same session are more lenient in their recommendations.

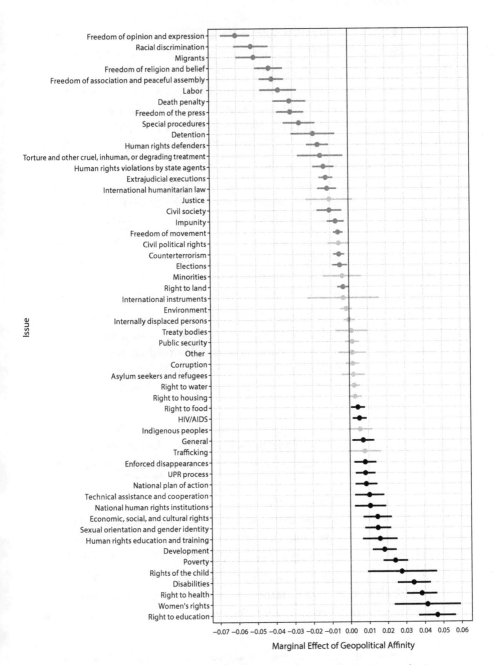

FIGURE 4.1. The Effect of Geopolitical Affinity on Recommendation Counts, by Issue
The plot reports the marginal effect of geopolitical affinity on the number of recommendations offered by a given reviewer for each issue category, controlling for other factors. Error bars indicate 95 percent confidence intervals. Shading indicates the sign and significance of the effect of geopolitical affinity on the number of recommendations. See appendix 3 for further details on model specifications.

overthrow."[34] Indeed, Bush's typology of regime-compatible and incompatible democracy-assistance programs overlaps a great deal with the empirical findings reported in figure 4.1.[35]

For example, higher levels of geopolitical affinity are associated with safer topics, such as socioeconomic rights (for example, the right to education, or the right to health) and the protection of vulnerable populations (women's rights, the rights of the child, trafficking). Because abuses in these domains typically take place in the private sphere, state actors are absolved as perpetrators of human rights abuse and allowed to project a role for themselves as protectors and providers. Not only do such rights fail to undermine regime survival, but they may even reinforce its power by legitimating state expansion and capacity.[36] By gravitating toward politically safer issues, delegations can claim that they are promoting human rights by participating in the UPR—thus satisfying metanorm pressures—while at the same time protecting their geopolitical relationships from damaging confrontation.

In contrast, lower levels of geopolitical affinity (in other words, greater hostility) are associated with more politically sensitive issues, such as those concerning civil-political liberties (for example, freedom of opinion and expression, or elections) and physical integrity violations (such as torture or human rights violations by state agents). Recommendations on these issues tend to be more threatening to target countries because they attribute abuse to state actors (torture, impunity), promote open political competition and dissent (freedom of opinion and expression, elections), or impose demanding constraints on domestic rule (migration, including citizenship and refugee issues).

Substantively, conditional on participating in a review, a one-point (one standard deviation) increase in geopolitical affinity is associated with 0.047 *more* recommendations about the right to education but 0.061 *fewer* recommendations about freedom of opinion and expression. Although these effects appear small in magnitude, note that they indicate changes relative to a very modest baseline. For example, the average number of recommendations addressing freedom of opinion and expression across all reviewers is

34. Bush 2015, 60.

35. I elaborate on the conceptual distinction between "sensitive" and "safe" human rights issues in Terman and Byun 2022.

36. Of course, some international discourse surrounding women's rights directly challenges state actors and threatens their rule. But in the UPR, most of the recommendations addressing women's rights concern abuses conducted in the private sphere, such as domestic violence, and thus remain "apolitical" and nonthreatening to the ruling regime. Bush (2015, 72–73) observes something similar with the role of women's groups in foreign-funded democracy promotion.

only about 0.083 per review. A change of 0.061 is therefore quite substantial; it nearly nullifies (in one direction) or doubles (in the other direction) the average amount of criticism in this area.

A good illustration of these dynamics is found in Canada's review of Iran and Saudi Arabia. Canada issued five recommendations to Iran during its 2014 review, focusing on sensitive issues related to physical integrity, freedom of speech and expression, the death penalty, and racial and religious discrimination. These recommendations were also quite damning; some demanded punishment for Iranian state actors or the rollback of their authority. For example, Canada urged that Iran "investigate and prosecute all those responsible for the mistreatment or abuse of detained persons in Iran." It also recommended that Iran "amend its press law to define the exceptions to article 24 of its Constitution in specific terms and that do not infringe upon freedom of expression."[37]

By contrast, Canada's recommendations to Saudi Arabia during the same cycle highlighted the plight of vulnerable groups such as women, children, and religious minorities while refraining from directly incriminating the Saudi government. Compared to those issued to Iran, Canada's recommendations to Saudi Arabia were noticeably indeterminate, as when it urged "necessary measures to ensure the effective enjoyment and protection of the right to freedom of religious belief, with a view to promoting the equality of all peoples and respect for all faiths."[38]

It is difficult to ascribe such contrasts to differences in Iran's and Saudi Arabia's human rights records. Indeed, prominent human rights surveys tend to evaluate the former more favorably than the latter on various dimensions of political and civil rights.[39] Canada's discriminating approach is better explained by its relationship of geopolitical affinity with and dependence on Saudi Arabia and its concomitant adversarial relationship with Iran. Saudi Arabia not only cooperates with Canada on key issues such as counterterrorism and refugees but is also its second-largest foreign supplier of oil.[40] By contrast, as a member of NATO and a close ally of the United States, Canada has long been hostile to the Iranian regime, going so far as to sever formal diplomatic relations in 2012.

---

37. United Nations General Assembly 2014, 23, 24.

38. United Nations General Assembly 2013b, 17.

39. For example, Freedom House's (2014) *Freedom in the World* reports rated Iran a 6 on both political rights and civil liberties (on a 1-to-7 scale, with 7 being the least free). The same report rated Saudi Arabia a 7 on both political rights and civil liberties.

40. Kaplan, Milke, and Belzile 2020.

It is also worth noting how Syria's approach in the same UPR cycle reverses these patterns. Syria admonished the Saudi government to "refrain from preventing Syrian pilgrims from practicing their religious duties as it constitutes a flagrant violation of freedom of belief and religion." Meanwhile, it encouraged Iran to "continue efforts to highlight the negative repercussions of both terrorism and unilateral coercive measures [imposed by the United States] on national development plans and on the enjoyment of basic human rights by its citizens." Syria further prefaced its recommendation to Iran by cautioning other reviewers "against basing human rights reviews on confrontation, politicization, and double standards."[41] Again, geopolitical relations provide the most likely explanation: Syria's relationship with Saudi Arabia has long been strained, owing to bitter regional disputes, whereas it has often acted as Iran's "brother-in-arms" on an array of important issues.[42]

Overall, the evidence shows that states moderate their criticism of human rights conditions depending on their geopolitical relationship with the target. Representatives reserve their most stigmatizing commentary for their geopolitical rivals, with whom they address particularly sensitive and politically damaging human rights issues. Meanwhile, states are more lenient with their strategic partners, issuing softer criticism on safer and less threatening topics. In doing so, delegations can respond to metanorm pressures by displaying their identity as "good citizens" of the international human rights regime. At the same time, they can secure their geopolitical interests by refraining from offending their partners while inflicting as much damage as possible on adversaries.

These findings are robust across a number of specifications. One of the most serious threats to inference is the potential selection bias resulting from voluntary participation (see appendix A). In this data set, participation is identical for states under review (each country was reviewed twice) but highly uneven for states qua reviewers. While all UN states are invited to offer feedback in every review, they are not forced to do so. To account for the possibility of selection bias, I estimated two-step Heckman selection models. The results, reported in appendix A, indicate that states are more likely to participate in the reviews of their strategic partners but less severe in their commentary on average.

Still, governments *do* rebuke their strategic partners on occasion. For example, the data contain 1,448 instances in which a state issued a

---

41. United Nations General Assembly 2013, 24, 14, 5.
42. Hokayem 2012, 7.

recommendation at the highest level of severity to a military ally and 920 instances of such a recommendation to an arms client. What happens when states demand specific actions of their strategic partners?

Analysis of Target Behavior

The second analysis explores the behavior of the target state. To recall from earlier in this chapter, target states must publicly report whether or not they support each recommendation they receive during a review. What drives states to support or reject UPR recommendations?

Of all the recommendations made, 73 percent were eventually supported. However, there was wide variation according to the topic addressed. Figure 4.2 plots the marginal effects of each issue category on the likelihood of target support while controlling for other factors, including geopolitical affinity between reviewer and target. The plot shows that states appear more open to some human rights issues than others. Namely, recommendations involving human rights education and training and recommendations around disabilities are widely accepted by target states. In contrast, recommendations relating to the death penalty are more than thirty-six percentage points *less* likely than average to be accepted. Those addressing civil political freedoms and migration also appear to be highly intolerable to states. Notably, the same topics that we saw in figure 4.1 are *most* likely to be scrutinized by geopolitical rivals are the ones *least* amenable to target states (see figure 4.2).

Regardless of a recommendation's substantive content, my theory predicts that target states will base their response partly on the *source*. To test this hypothesis, I examined the effect of strategic relationships on the likelihood of support. Here, the statistical models control for the thematic issue involved in a recommendation as well as the severity of the source's demands. By controlling for issue and severity, the analysis aims to isolate the effects of dyadic relationships across substantively similar recommendations. I also control for whether the SuR sits on the Human Rights Council, as council members may be incentivized to accept more recommendations on average. Again I control for shared region and for physical integrity rights, and I include fixed effects for reviewer, target, and year. Full model descriptions can be found in appendix A. Table 4.4 reports estimates from linear probability models, although the results are robust to logit specifications (see appendix A).

As a reminder, severity measures the level of demandingness in a recommendation (higher numbers indicating more severe demands). In the results reported here, severity 2 and severity 3 refer to the effects of

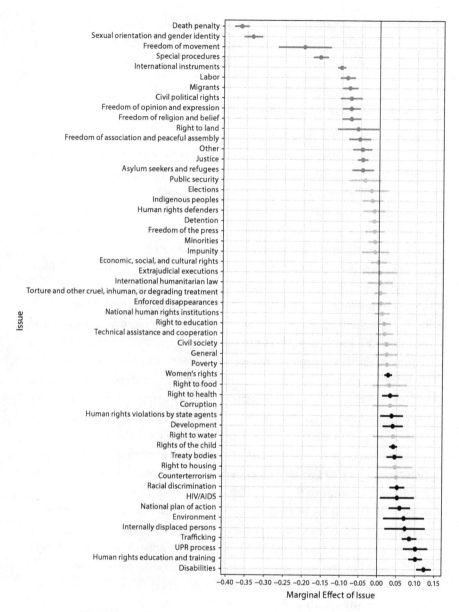

FIGURE 4.2. The Effects of Issue on Probability of Recommendation Support
The plot shows the marginal effect of each recommendation issue on the likelihood
of target support, controlling for other factors. Error bars indicate 95 percent confidence intervals. Shading indicates the sign and significance of the effect of recommendation issue on the likelihood of target support. The results are estimated using
the same model reported in table 4.4, model 2. See appendix 3 for further details on
model specifications.

TABLE 4.4. Target State's Response to UPR Recommendations

	Probability of Supporting Recommendation			
	Model 1	Model 2	Model 3	Model 4
SEVERITY 2	−0.048***	−0.049***	−0.059***	−0.058***
	(0.004)	(0.004)	(0.004)	(0.004)
SEVERITY 3	−0.217***	−0.217***	−0.230***	−0.229***
	(0.005)	(0.005)	(0.005)	(0.005)
GEOPOLITICAL AFFINITY	0.059***	0.061***		
	(0.003)	(0.003)		
ALLIANCE	−0.007		0.008	
	(0.008)		(0.008)	
ARMS TRADE (REVIEWER TO TARGET)	0.024**			0.035***
	(0.011)			(0.011)
ARMS TRADE (TARGET TO REVIEWER)	0.047***			0.066***
	(0.014)			(0.014)
HRC MEMBER (TARGET)	0.014*	0.013*	0.015*	0.016**
	(0.008)	(0.008)	(0.008)	(0.008)
SAME REGION	−0.010**	−0.012***	0.018***	0.020***
	(0.005)	(0.004)	(0.005)	(0.004)
PHYSICAL INTEGRITY RIGHTS (REVIEWER)	0.005	0.004	0.003	0.004
	(0.011)	(0.011)	(0.012)	(0.012)
PHYSICAL INTEGRITY RIGHTS (TARGET)	−0.095***	−0.095***	−0.097***	−0.097***
	(0.017)	(0.017)	(0.017)	(0.017)
N	39,896	39,896	39,896	39,896

***p <.01; **p <.05; *p <.1

Note: Results from linear probability models. Fixed effects for target, reviewer, year, and issue are omitted. Robust standard errors in parentheses.

recommendations coded as a level 2 or level 3 in severity, respectively, compared to those coded as 1 (the omitted category). Unsurprisingly, states are more likely to accept those recommendations that involve vague or congratulatory language (severity 1) over those involving more specific demands (severity 2 and severity 3). Lenient recommendations are easier to comply with and thus are accepted at a higher rate.

Remarkably, however, even after controlling for the substantive content of recommendations (that is, for issue and severity), I find that relational variables correlate strongly with target response. As predicted by hypothesis

1B, states are more likely to accept recommendations coming from geopolitical sympathizers. Countries under review are six percentage points more likely to support a recommendation as the reviewer state moves one standard deviation in its UN voting pattern, even after controlling for the substantive characteristics of the recommendation. States are also more likely to accept recommendations from their arms suppliers or from their clients (hypothesis 3B). On the other hand, the effects of alliance (hypothesis 2B) do not reach conventional levels of statistical significance.[43]

I tested the robustness of these findings in two ways (see appendix A). First, because some reviews focus more on praising improved practices than on shaming violations, I repeated the analysis on a subsample of the most critical recommendations (that is, those at security level 3). Second, I estimated logit models instead of OLS, as the outcome is a binary indicator of support. The results are consistent with the main analysis.

In sum, the findings present strong support for hypothesis 1B on geopolitical affinity and moderate support for hypothesis 3B concerning arms dependence. These relational ties appear to be important considerations for state delegations as they decide whether or not to support the recommendations they receive in the UPR. We are less certain about the significance of formal military alliance (hypothesis 2B), perhaps because limited data coverage suppresses the statistical power of these models.

Overall, however, these results confirm the importance of political relationships in states' receptivity to shaming. On the one hand, states may feel pressured to accept recommendations coming from their geopolitical friends, lest they sabotage important partnerships and the relational goods they provide. As one of Carraro's interviewees put it: "It is so difficult to reject a recommendation because after each recommendation in the parenthesis you have the name of the country that made the recommendation."[44] On the other hand, leaders may feel safe rejecting recommendations from adversaries, whom they can accuse of having hostile motives or being politically biased. Following China's third UPR in November 2018, for instance,

---

43. Once again, the coefficients on the controls run generally as expected. Members of the Human Rights Council are more likely to accept UPR recommendations, probably to endorse the process that they themselves lead. Because region is collinear with UN General Assembly voting patterns, the marginal effects of shared region switch directions when combined with geopolitical affinity in the same model. Not surprisingly, countries with poor human rights records are less likely to accept UPR recommendations on average. Interestingly, target states are no more likely to accept recommendations coming from countries that boast strong human rights protections themselves, challenging the supposed credibility of "defenders of the faith," such as Canada or Norway.

44. Carraro 2019, 1090.

Vice Foreign Minister Le Yucheng brushed off criticism of China's alleged detention of human rights defenders and use of internment camps, claiming: "We will not accept the politically driven accusations from a few countries that are fraught with biases, with total disregard for facts."[45]

To illustrate, consider Iran's review during the UPR's seventh session in 2010. Brazil recommended that Iran "extend the rights guaranteed in Iranian legislation to all religious groups, including the Baha'i community." During this period, Brazil was by all accounts friendly with Iran. As I detail in chapter 6, then-president Mahmoud Ahmadinejad was working to develop stronger ties with Latin America, opening six new embassies in the region from 2005 to 2009. In November 2009, just one year before Iran's review in the UPR, Ahmadinejad became the first Iranian president to visit Brazil since the Islamic Revolution. The Iranian delegation supported Brazil's recommendation on religious groups and the Baha'is, a widely persecuted minority in Iran.

During the same review, France issued a remarkably similar recommendation: "End acts of repression against persons belonging to ethnic or religious minorities, particularly the Baha'i, and to respect their rights." Like Brazil's recommendation, this recommendation addressed the status of the Baha'i and other religious minorities and called on Iran to protect their rights. Both recommendations were coded as severity level 2, which calls on the state under review to take general action toward some goal. But unlike with Brazil, Iran only "noted" the recommendation from France, essentially rejecting it.

Similar patterns can be observed in the Netherlands' 2012 review, during which four countries recommended that the Netherlands combat violence against women. Uzbekistan recommended that the Netherlands "adopt practical measures to ensure absolute prohibition of violence against women and cruel treatment of children." Cuba recommended that the country "adopt effective measures to combat violence against women and to fight poverty." The United States asked the Netherlands to "ensure that existing statutes prohibiting gender discrimination are properly implemented and enforced, and increase through effective implementation and enforcement efforts to address violence against women and children." Chile recommended to the Netherlands that it "continue strengthening the functions of the competent institutions and use of adequate mechanisms to more efficiently combat domestic violence, which mainly affects women and children."

45. Kuo 2018.

Each recommendation used similar wording, differing only slightly, to implore the Netherlands to take additional steps to eradicate violence against women. But the Netherlands delegation supported only two of these recommendations—from the United States and Chile—while rejecting those from Cuba and Uzbekistan. Combined with the statistical evidence reported here, the conclusion is clear: two recommendations that address identical human rights violations and make similar demands can elicit very different reactions depending on the source.

Conclusion

This chapter has presented evidence relating to the interstate dimensions of my theory. As a dialectic process, shaming is not determined by target-country characteristics alone. States condemn norm violations selectively based on their strategic relationship with the violator. Likewise, a state's sensitivity to normative pressure depends on its relationship with the source of that pressure. Of course, the results are limited in a number of ways. I analyzed only three dimensions of strategic relationships, setting aside others such as trade. And the UPR is not totally representative of international shaming writ large, even if it distills shaming's essential features. These caveats notwithstanding, the findings confirm the importance of relational ties in international human rights enforcement.

And yet this investigation can address only portions of my overall argument. The theory also claims that criticism from adversaries may not only fail to secure compliance but encourage targeted governments to double down on abuses. This can happen when international shaming unleashes domestic political forces *within* the target state, igniting a defensive reaction that works to delegitimize outside criticism, disempower local advocates, and generate incentives for politicians to defy foreign demands. Although the UPR offers an unusually fine-grained picture of interstate shaming, these potentialities lie beyond what these data can tell us. To better explore shaming's variegated effects, we must dive deeper into the domestic sphere of the shamed state.

5

International Shaming and Domestic Politics

The previous chapter examined the *interstate* dimensions of my theory. I presented evidence supporting the view of shaming as an inherently relational and strategic exercise. States hesitate to criticize their friends and allies in order to safeguard their foreign policy interests; if and when they do criticize their allies, however, the added geopolitical leverage advances the likelihood of compliance. Meanwhile, governments reserve the harshest commentary for their rivals, with an eye toward stigmatization.

The fact that interstate shaming is determined more by political imperatives than by normative commitments has led many observers to question the power of human rights institutions to influence governments via international mechanisms.[1] However, as I discussed in previous chapters, human rights shaming is not confined to the international sphere. One popular argument is that international norms instigate change primarily through *domestic* channels, especially by mobilizing social movements to pressure norm-violating governments "from below" (see chapter 1).

My theory complicates this conventional wisdom. In chapter 3, I argued that shaming often not only fails to mobilize local support for human rights but backfires by inciting a defensive reaction from domestic audiences. Given widespread efforts to weaponize human rights to stigmatize geopolitical rivals, citizens in the target state register external human rights pressure

1. For example, Simmons 2009, chap. 4.

as a threat to their country's status and react in defensive ways that degrade the validity of outside criticism and transform norm violation into an expression of national identity and resistance. When such reactions are pervasive, leaders face incentives that penalize compliance with foreign norms and reward outright resistance violations, even if they have no strong preference for norm-violating behavior.

This chapter examines these *intrastate* aspects of my argument, focusing on how international shaming alters domestic politics—particularly public opinion—in the target state. I use survey experiments to examine individual reactions to foreign human rights criticism. Contrary to some received wisdom, I find scant evidence that international shaming encourages domestic mobilization for human rights. Instead, the findings suggest that international shaming has the counterproductive effect on public attitudes of heightening nationalist sentiments and hostility toward advocacy efforts. Importantly, these defensive reactions are not reducible to preexisting beliefs regarding specific human rights issues or the content of relevant norms. Indeed, foreign shaming can incite defensive reactions even among those individuals who are otherwise sympathetic to human rights causes.

These findings trouble a pervasive assumption held by scholars and activists alike: that outside pressure mobilizes domestic movements for human rights. If the results from the experiment are any indication, international criticism may provide information to members of the public about human rights violations and—under a limited set of conditions—generate modest concern about those violations. At the same time, however, foreign shaming threatens citizens' national attachments, reinforcing positive views about their country and diminishing support for activism or political mobilization in defense of human rights. Insofar as public opinion influences national policymaking, widespread reactions of this kind could inhibit the ability of leaders to comply with outside demands, while enabling active resistance to international norms and their advocates.

The following discussion proceeds in four parts. I begin by establishing the importance of public opinion for theories about international shaming. The next section describes international shaming's potentially counterproductive effects on public opinion in the target country as well as the expectations derived from these effects. I then turn to the survey experiments and present their results and significance. I conclude by discussing the implications of these findings for elite decision-making and for domestic responses to international human rights pressure.

Why Public Opinion?

The goal of this chapter is to examine how international shaming alters the target country's domestic political environment. I take an experimental approach to this problem, testing the effects of international human rights criticism on domestic public opinion. Although public opinion is not the only avenue through which international shaming affects domestic politics, exploring citizens' reactions to foreign criticism is informative for both substantive and methodological reasons.

For one, domestic audiences play an important constraining and enabling role in national policymaking, even in nondemocratic settings.[2] They are particularly prominent in canonical accounts of international human rights dynamics. As described in chapter 1, many commentators believe that international shaming works by mobilizing domestic opposition and social movements in target countries. While this can occur through a variety of pathways, public attitudes are relevant to all of them. For example, some posit that international actors provide *credible information* to domestic audiences, validating accusations of their country's norm violations.[3] Outside criticism is also thought to extend *legitimacy* to local NGOs and advocates, broadening their coalitions and strengthening their mobilization efforts.[4] International shaming can also delegitimize norm-violating governments in the eyes of ordinary citizens.[5] In brief, public opinion is important theoretically: international shaming is thought to alter the target country's domestic political environment by shifting public perceptions and attitudes in ways that favor human rights compliance.

And yet, despite widely held assumptions regarding shaming's positive impact on public attitudes, we lack conclusive evidence supporting this view. Some studies suggest that shaming is effective in moving public opinion in a positive direction.[6] Others, however, document unintended or adverse consequences. Jamie Gruffydd-Jones finds that foreign human rights

2. Dafoe et al. 2022; Weeks 2008.

3. Dai 2005; Donno 2013.

4. Simmons 2009, 140–48.

5. As Finnemore and Sikkink (1998, 903) put it: "[States] care about international legitimation because it has become an essential contributor to perceptions of domestic legitimacy held by a state's own citizens."

6. Ausderan 2014; Davis, Murdie, and Steinmetz 2012; Tingley and Tomz 2022. Kyla Jo McEntire, Michele Leiby, and Matthew Krain (2015) explore the ways in which human rights organizations mobilize support among third parties (generating metanorms), but they do not address how the *targets* of such appeals respond to their efforts.

criticism can spark a defensive, nationalistic reaction among Chinese citizens; he shows that that this reaction, in turn, bolsters regime support.[7] Similarly, Brian Greenhill and Dan Reiter show that shaming by international NGOs backfires among American observers and that government defenses can overpower any external criticism.[8] Similar effects have been shown for other kinds of international norm enforcement, like boycotts[9] and legal rulings.[10] Together, these findings suggest that international human rights pressure may backfire by shifting public opinion in a counterproductive way. Unfortunately, given the centrality of public opinion in major theories of international norms, the empirical literature to date has been unable to adjudicate between these two competing predictions.

A focus on public opinion also provides several methodological advantages by enabling the use of experimental methods. Survey experiments can estimate causal effects in ways that are often inaccessible through observational designs. Concerns surrounding endogeneity and reverse causality trouble nearly all cross-national studies on human rights, especially when, as I have suggested, external pressure stimulates additional violations. Experiments afford the researcher some degree of control and with it the opportunity to test various dispositional and contextual factors that moderate the effect of foreign criticism on citizens' attitudes. The result is a more precise and empirically valid picture of shaming's effects on the individual level, and that picture, in turn, informs our understanding of domestic reactions to international pressure more generally and ultimately illuminates why such efforts promote compliance in some cases and defiance in others.

Hypotheses

In chapter 3, I described how international shaming can register as a status threat to domestic audiences in the target country, especially when it emanates from a geopolitical adversary. Status threat emerges when individuals see their social group (nation) being degraded on a salient dimension of comparison.[11] People derive much of their self-esteem from group identity, and if they feel that their group is not doing well compared to others—that in fact it is being stigmatized, criticized, denounced, discriminated against, or dominated—they

---

7. Gruffydd-Jones 2018.
8. Greenhill and Reiter 2022.
9. Grossman, Manekin, and Margalit 2018.
10. Brutger and Strezhnev 2018; Chapman and Chaudoin 2020; Madsen et al. 2022; Voeten 2020.
11. Branscombe et al. 1999; Ellemers, Spears, and Doosje 2002; Major and O'Brien 2005.

will feel personally attacked. Existing research in IR shows that national identity is a salient social identity for many people and that individuals are sensitive to perceived threats to their country's status.[12] Like other acts of status denial, human rights shaming registers as a threat insofar as citizens view it as a hostile attempt to degrade their country on the world stage.

Importantly, the experience of status threat provokes a defensive reaction that alters people's attitudes, their attachments, and ultimately their behavior. In this section, I elaborate these changes and derive testable expectations. To do so, I draw from a large literature in sociology and social psychology pertaining to shaming, social influence, and intergroup relations, as well as existing applications of such insights to IR research.

Before proceeding, it is worth underscoring the difficulties involved in applying theories of intergroup relations to world politics. It is not obvious how we should differentiate in-group from out-group in the global environment, and multiple identity dimensions—regional, racial, religious, ethnic, and so on—are likely to be relevant. However, as discussed in chapter 3, the importance of national affiliation cannot be underestimated, especially in the context of international human rights shaming. Not only is nationality a core social identity for many people, but it is also routinely primed in human rights discourse, where the country is typically the object of reference.

THREE DIMENSIONS OF ATTITUDINAL CHANGE

Which attitudes and beliefs are sensitive to international shaming? In the first place, we can reasonably expect shaming to affect individual attitudes about the *substance* of human rights criticism, that is, the specific human rights violations or reforms raised by critics. Shaming could also affect what scholars call "related beliefs"—those that relate not to the substance of the criticism but to other salient subjects.[13] Two sets of beliefs are relevant: attitudes about one's country as a whole and attitudes toward human rights activists and advocacy. The latter is particularly important given the widespread assertion that international shaming legitimates and empowers local activists. I first theorize how shaming could impact attitudes concerning one's country, followed by issue-related beliefs and, finally, support for human rights activism.

---

12. Dafoe, Renshon, and Huth 2014; Fattah and Fierke 2009; Lindemann 2011; Paul, Larson, and Wohlforth 2014; Towns 2012; Wohlforth 2009; Wolf 2011.
13. Little 2019.

In-group Favoritism

First, the experience of status threat is thought to generate an overall psychological movement toward the in-group. One way this happens is by intensifying the *salience* of group identity, that is, its perceived relevance in a situation. Ashley Jardina, for instance, finds that White Americans exposed to group status threats are more likely to view the world through the lens of their racial identity and to prioritize the collective interests of their group.[14] In addition to group salience, status threat drives greater in-group favoritism, which leads people to rally behind their group or its leadership.[15] In-group favoritism occurs when members emphasize distinct and positive characteristics of their group while downplaying intragroup diversity or shortcomings.[16] Scholars hypothesize that affirming the positive aspects of one's group bolsters self-esteem, offsetting the anxiety imposed by status threat.[17]

In the context of international human rights shaming, we can expect foreign criticism to enhance the salience of observers' national identity, along with efforts to affirm positive aspects of their country. For example, we may see higher nationalist sentiments or assertions that human rights are generally well protected.

Issue-Related Beliefs

Second, the experience of status threat shapes beliefs and attitudes vis-à-vis the substantive object of normative criticism: the salient norm, policy, practice, or event at play. Research has shown that social identity dynamics condition how people form and update salient beliefs by directing their appraisal of new information.[18] In controlled experiments, group-directed criticisms are seen as less accurate when conveyed by an out-group member compared to identical criticism stemming from an in-group member.[19] Because out-group critics are presumed to be driven by hostile intentions, their claims are seen as less reliable and thus are weighted as less important, even if they

---

14. Jardina 2019, 38–39.

15. Branscombe et al. 1999, 46–47; Major and O'Brien 2005, 405–6.

16. Brewer 1999; Tajfel and Turner 1986.

17. Branscombe et al. 1999; Lüders et al. 2016; Sherman et al. 2007; Spencer-Rodgers et al. 2016.

18. Nugent 2020, 5.

19. This is known as the *intergroup sensitivity effect*. See Ariyanto, Hornsey, and Gallois 2009; Esposo, Hornsey, and Spoor 2013; Hornsey 2005; Hornsey and Imani 2004; Hornsey, Oppes, and Svensson 2002; Hornsey, Trembath, and Gunthorpe 2004; Jeffries et al. 2012.

have objective merit.[20] Interestingly, the authors of one such study, Matthew Hornsey and Armin Imani, explicitly mention international human rights shaming when discussing potential implications. In such cases, they argue, shaming can backfire because "we are psychologically predisposed to deny the validity of the comments, even where they have a legitimate basis."[21]

The experience of status threat does not merely negate the influence of outside criticism but also produces attitudes by inciting motivated reasoning.[22] In their efforts to defend the target group, members tend to counterargue, constructing reasons and rationales designed to neutralize criticism and ameliorate the psychic costs associated with devalued status. For example, they may argue that norm violations are not a big deal or that they were justified in violating the norm. Importantly, this kind of reasoning can drive polarization: a shift in attitudes about the norm or behavior in question toward more extreme positions and away from those advocated by the critic.[23] As Howard Becker observes, "A person who quiets his own doubts by adopting the rationale moves into a more principled and consistent kind of deviance than was possible for him before adopting it."[24]

In the context of international human rights shaming, we should expect to see foreign shaming shaping individual attitudes vis-à-vis the specific rights or norms at issue. Specifically, we should expect to see signs of identity concerns and motivated reasoning as individuals assess the message of foreign critics.

Support for Human Rights Activists and Advocacy

Finally, status threat fuels hostility toward dissent, activism, and other interventions aimed at normative change. It is not uncommon for individuals to maintain private beliefs critical of their group while simultaneously opposing efforts to air such criticism in the public sphere. This second-order inclination arises from enhanced in-group attachment. Status threat discursively connects normative debates—which may or may not have been salient to social identity *ex ante*—to the survival and integrity of the group itself. In this context,

20. Hornsey, Oppes, and Svensson 2002. These findings do not seem to vary with the quality of the message or the experience of the critic (Esposo, Hornsey, and Spoor 2013; Hornsey and Imani 2004).

21. Hornsey and Imani 2004, 366.

22. Social influence is effective to the extent that observers identify with the source of the message. When conveyed by out-group members, criticism results in either no attitude change or a move in the opposite direction of the advocated position (Cialdini and Goldstein 2004, 612).

23. Isenberg 1986; Myers and Lamm 1976; Nugent 2020; Sunstein 2002.

24. Becker 2008, 39.

dissenters must follow certain "identity rules" governing when and how criticism is appropriate.[25] For instance, criticism must not be aired in front of an out-group audience (the "airing our dirty laundry" effect). Likewise, criticism should be silenced if the group is engaged in an explicit intergroup conflict (the "united we stand" effect).[26] When these rules are violated, even sincere in-group critics can be seen as betraying the group by contributing to its status degradation, thus diminishing the legitimacy of their cause.

In the context of international human rights shaming, we should expect that foreign shaming will engender hostility toward critics and inhibit people's willingness to support or engage in human rights advocacy. Individuals may admit that human rights violations need to stop, and that abusive policies must be reformed, while at the same time rejecting efforts to pressure their government to do so.

CONDITIONAL EFFECTS

Shaming does not evoke status threat in all situations or among all observers. While the process by which status threat arises is complex, two factors are worth emphasizing. First, as highlighted throughout this text, the *source* of shaming affects its reception. On an interpersonal level, psychologists have observed that the experience of social threat relies on situational cues that confirm or refute the hypothesis that one's group is being attacked.[27] One of the most powerful cues is the identity of the shamer and the shamer's relationship to the target.[28] In the absence of other information, criticism from a member of a hostile out-group is assumed to be driven by hostile intentions, an attempt to degrade the status of the target group.[29] Likewise, as I explained in previous chapters, criticism emanating from a geopolitical rival is more likely to invoke status threat because observers attribute such criticism to political animosity and an intention to harm the target. Shaming by a geopolitical ally or friend, on the other hand, is less likely to conjure the perception of ill will.

Second, it is important to remember that status threat is a subjective perception, not an objective condition. Thus, beliefs about shaming—whether it reflects legitimate criticism or a hostile attack—can vary across observers, even if they are subject to the same environment. Although a number of

25. Hornsey 2005, 302.
26. Ariyanto, Hornsey, and Gallois 2009; Chekroun and Nugier 2011.
27. Branscombe et al. 1999; Major and O'Brien 2005, 399; Steele, Spencer, and Aronson 2002.
28. Steele, Spencer, and Aronson 2002.
29. Hornsey and Imani 2004, 367.

individual traits are important, social psychologists emphasize the degree to which individuals *identify* with the targeted group.[30] High identifiers depend on group membership for a significant share of their self-concept and are therefore more sensitive to status threat when faced with group criticism.[31] Applying this insight to world politics, Steven Ward proposes that nationalists are more sensitive to derogations of their country's status and more likely to cope by championing hawkish and revisionist policies.[32] If so, international human rights shaming might provoke status threat in individuals with higher national identity attachments, as well as in those who identify with the targeted regime, such as through partisan ties.

Finally, it is worth emphasizing that the mechanisms I have described are primarily *relational* in nature, not substantive. That is, hostility toward international shaming is not reducible to individuals' preexisting beliefs regarding human rights or related issues; rather, it is a function of social context. In other words, even if observers are personally sympathetic to the *content* of the message, they may nonetheless reject it in certain social *contexts*.

Experimental Evidence

I conducted two survey experiments to inspect the effect of human rights shaming on public opinion in the country being shamed. It is important to note up front that the following studies are based on samples of Americans and are therefore limited in their ability to generalize to other countries. Deeply rooted discourse on American exceptionalism may render US citizens particularly intransigent in their response to outside criticism.[33] Nevertheless, the United States represents both a theoretically and empirically important case in the debate surrounding human rights shaming. Empirically, the United States is the most shamed country by Amnesty International and draws comparable attention from similar NGOs.[34] It is also routinely scrutinized by other countries; indeed, the United States has received the most recommendations of any state in the Universal Periodic Review. Theoretically, investigating a wealthy democracy such as the United States provides needed balance to a literature that is largely focused on developing and autocratic settings. Moreover, other countries commonly criticized for human rights violations, such as Iran or

30. Major and O'Brien 2005, 400.
31. Ellemers, Spears, and Doosje 2002, 176–78.
32. Ward 2017; see also Herrmann 2017.
33. Ignatieff 2009.
34. This statistic comes from my own analysis of Amnesty urgent actions from 1985 to 2015.

China, exhibit similar political cultures of nationalism and exceptionalism. Thus, the features distinguishing the United States may be not so distinct after all and could plausibly apply to other cases.

Both experiments exposed a sample of Americans to a fictional article reporting an instance of international human rights shaming surrounding violations in the criminal justice system. I selected the issue of criminal justice for three reasons. First, criminal justice is a highly salient topic in the human rights space, commanding considerable attention from advocacy groups such as Amnesty International and Human Rights Watch as well as from state actors. Second, criminal justice affords the study some degree of external validity insofar as it applies to other countries, unlike the War on Terror or other arenas that are distinctive to the United States. Finally, criminal justice reform presents a "hard case" of defiance: it is a relatively popular issue among American citizens, especially compared to other issues on which the United States is commonly shamed (for example, immigration and the death penalty). Nevertheless, evidence from pilot studies suggests that the main findings hold across different human rights issue areas, including those pertaining to immigration, criminal justice, the War on Terror, and human trafficking.

The first experiment manipulates the *target* of shaming. All participants read about an instance of human rights shaming regarding violations in the criminal justice system. For some participants, this criticism was directed abroad, while for others it targeted the United States specifically. This design allows us to better isolate the effect of international shaming—that is, the experience of seeing one's country criticized—apart from any priming effects related to specific issues. So if we do observe a defensive reaction, we know that participants were defensive not toward human rights or criminal justice reform in general (the control) but toward external criticism itself (the treatment).

The second experiment manipulates the *source* of shaming. In the first experiment, the shamer was said to be a fictitious NGO in order to minimize any effects arising from individual attitudes toward a given group or country. However, a key component of my argument is that international shaming can geopoliticize a particular human rights issue, transforming it from a domestic policy debate into a concern over international status and rivalry. The identity of the critic matters to this dynamic. Thus, in the second experiment, all participants were exposed to human rights criticism of the American criminal justice system. However, some participants were told that such criticisms emanated from a particular country—Canada, France, China, or Iran—in order to examine how the source of shaming shaped its reception.

Study 1

EXPERIMENTAL DESIGN

The first survey experiment was fielded from September 14, 2018, to October 17, 2018, to the AmeriSpeak panel of the National Opinion Research Center (NORC), a probability-based panel designed to be representative of the US household ($n = 775$).[35] The survey first collected pretreatment variables on demographic information, partisanship, racial resentment, and national identity attachments.[36] It then randomly assigned participants to one of two groups. To ensure proper comparability, both groups were asked to read a news article about an international advocacy group ("Human Rights Action Committee," or "HRAC") that was shaming human rights violations. Although using a fictitious NGO strains credulity, it also facilitates internal validity; participants may bring their own idiosyncratic views toward any known actor (such as Amnesty International).

In the control treatment, HRAC shamed multiple unnamed countries for violations of human rights in the area of criminal justice. The treatment group, in contrast, read that HRAC was targeting the United States specifically, as shown here.

STUDY 1 [CONTROL / TREATMENT]

Rights Group Condemns Abuses Worldwide
March 1, 2017

Human Rights Action Committee (HRAC), an international advocacy organization based in Geneva, Switzerland, accused [multiple governments / the United States] today of repeated violations of human rights throughout their criminal justice system.

A HRAC spokesperson said: "[In many countries, the / The United States'] criminal justice system is plagued with injustices, including discrimination, excessively harsh sentencing, and inhumane prison conditions."

The group said it would publish a report about the violations and launch an international campaign urging states and other members of the international community to denounce these abuses.

35. The study was funded and facilitated by Time Sharing for Social Sciences (TESS). Full data and study materials can be found at OSFHome, "Human Rights Shaming, Compliance, and Nationalist Backlash," osf.io/q8ra3.

36. Three measures of national identity attachments were taken from Huddy and Khatib 2007. The measures were then summed to one index and rescaled from 0 to 1. The three are highly internally consistent (Cronbach's alpha = 0.852).

TABLE 5.1. Study 1: Survey Outcomes

Dimension	Measure	Instrument
ATTITUDES TOWARD IN-GROUP (NATIONAL) FAVORITISM	National superiority	The world would be a better place if other countries were more like the United States.
	Human rights perceptions	In general, human rights are well respected in the United States. (reversed)
ATTITUDES TOWARD HUMAN RIGHTS REFORM	Support of criminal justice reform	The US government needs to take concrete steps to reform the criminal justice system to ensure that detainees' human rights are protected.
	Tolerance of human rights violations	Sometimes it is necessary to violate people's human rights in order to maintain order in society. (reversed)
SUPPORT FOR INTERNATIONAL HUMAN RIGHTS ADVOCACY (ATTITUDINAL)	Support of international campaign	I support an international campaign focusing on human rights violations in the United States.
	Support of UN resolution	I support a UN resolution condemning human rights violations in the United States.
SUPPORT FOR INTERNATIONAL HUMAN RIGHTS ADVOCACY (BEHAVIORAL)	HRAC donation	Are you willing to donate $1 to the Human Rights Action Committee to support its campaign to push for criminal justice reforms in the United States? If you select "yes," a link to the donation page will appear at the end of this survey.
	Criminal justice reform petition	Are you willing to sign a petition to urge the US government to implement criminal justice reforms in the United States? If you select "yes," a link to the petition page will appear at the end of this survey.

Note: Instruments have been edited slightly to conform to book style.

Following the prompt, subjects answered questions on three sets of attitudinal measures corresponding to the three dimensions described here (see table 5.1). First, I measured in-group (national) favoritism using two questions, one about national superiority and the other about perceptions of human rights conditions in the United States. I then asked respondents about their attitudes toward the specific issue at hand (criminal justice reform) as well as toward the general norm (adherence to international human rights standards). Finally, respondents answered four questions about human rights activism. The first two questions were designed to measure their attitudinal support for international advocacy targeting the United States. The second two were quasi-behavioral measures of participants' personal willingness to (1) donate to HRAC and (2) sign a petition to support efforts to reform the criminal justice system in the United States.[37]

These measures were rescaled to standardize direction and aid interpretation. In the results reported here, an increase in any given measure indicates a *compliance* effect, or individuals' tendency to report perceptions and attitudes that align with human rights advocates and favor pro-compliance mobilization. Lower numbers indicate a *defiance* effect: shaming shifts public opinion in the opposite direction from the position advanced by advocates.

RESULTS

General Effects of International Shaming

How do Americans respond generally to human rights shaming of their country? Figure 5.1 reports the effect of the treatment on each outcome variable. Overall, I find no evidence to support the view that human rights criticism mobilizes pro-compliance efforts among American citizens on average. On the other hand, criticism of the United States backfires on several dimensions and makes citizens *less* willing to mobilize for human rights norms.

First, the results indicate overall movement toward in-group favoritism, consistent with social identity expectations on intergroup criticism. Compared to the control (HRAC shaming multiple unnamed countries), shaming of the United States in particular increased feelings of national superiority ($p = 0.055$). We also observe backlash on participants' support for international advocacy. Exposure to foreign shaming decreased support for an international campaign focused on human rights abuses in the United States by 8.5 percentage points; decreased support for a UN resolution against the United States by 5.6 percentage points; and decreased willingness to donate to the fictitious "Human Rights Action Committee" by 5 percentage points.

---

37. Principal components analysis suggests different factors for people's oblique support for international advocacy and their own personal advocacy, suggesting that we should view these as two separate constructs.

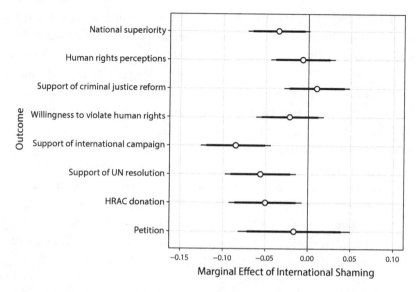

FIGURE 5.1. The Effects of Foreign Shaming of the United States
Results from an OLS regression in which each outcome (scaled to unit length) is regressed on a binary treatment indicator that has the value of 1 for respondents who were assigned to treatment 1 (foreign shaming of the United States) and 0 for respondents in the control (foreign shaming of unnamed countries). Models do not include any controls. Thick bars represent 90 percent confidence intervals; thin bars represent 95 percent confidence intervals.

The last effect was particularly striking: 12.7 percent of respondents in the control group said that they would donate to HRAC, but just 7.6 percent said that they were willing to donate to HRAC in the treatment group—a 40 percent decrease.

On the other hand, I found neither defiance nor compliance effects on outcomes directly addressing policy issues. On average, shaming the United States exerted null effects on participants' perceptions of domestic human rights conditions, support of criminal justice reform, or tolerance for human rights violations. I also found little change in subjects' willingness to sign a petition demanding criminal justice reform.

Partisan Differences

One might suspect these responses to be conditioned by partisan identity. In the current US political climate, partisanship not only reflects ideological preferences but constitutes an important *social identity*.[38] A large literature

38. Huddy and Bankert 2017; Iyengar, Sood, and Lelkes 2012.

on source cues shows how partisanship mediates the influence of outside messages on mass attitudes.[39] Further, those human rights issues commonly leveraged against the United States—such as those related to criminal justice, immigration, and national security—are also some of the most partisan.[40] Because Democrats tend to be sympathetic to human rights discourse in general, and to criminal justice reform in particular, shaming could strengthen these prior attitudes, generating a compliance effect. Republicans, on the other hand, might perceive human rights criticism as an attack on their group and its associated worldview.[41] As a reminder, Donald Trump was in the White House at the time this survey took place.

I find that shaming exerted counterproductive effects among both Republicans and Democrats, albeit in different ways (figure 5.2). Democrats exposed to human rights shaming of the United States exhibited no significant change with regard to their perceptions of human rights conditions or support for criminal justice reform. They did, however, withhold their support for international advocacy targeting the United States (both the campaign and the UN resolution). This suggests that international shaming fails to produce pro-compliance attitudes among Democrats, while potentially alienating them vis-à-vis international interventions.

In general, Republican participants exhibited a more consistent defensive reaction than their Democratic counterparts. Compared to those in the control group, Republicans who were exposed to foreign criticism of the United States displayed more in-group favoritism, including higher nationalist sentiments and a more positive perception of domestic human rights conditions. They also expressed more hostility toward advocacy efforts: they rejected an international campaign focused on the United States and were also less willing than Republicans in the control group to donate to HRAC.

Nevertheless, Republicans were *more* likely to agree that the US government should reform the criminal justice system after exposure to foreign criticism. This unexpected finding presents something of a puzzle. One possible interpretation is that criminal justice reform is increasingly a bipartisan issue in the United States and that it is becoming more popular among Republicans in particular. Perhaps Republicans no longer view criticism arising from criminal justice issues as an attack on their partisan worldview

39. Bush and Jamal 2015; Druckman, Peterson, and Slothuus 2013; Nicholson 2012.

40. Human Rights Watch lists "criminal justice, immigration, and national security" as their priority areas in the United States. See Human Rights Watch, "United States," https://www.hrw.org/united-states (accessed August 15, 2018).

41. Nyhan and Reifler 2010.

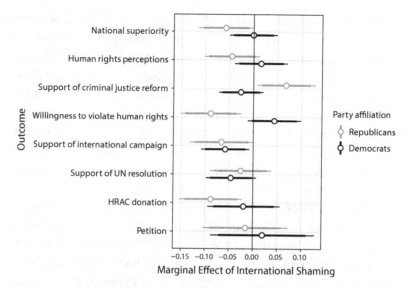

FIGURE 5.2. The Effects of Foreign Shaming of the United States, by Party Identity

Results from an OLS regression in which each outcome (scaled to unit length) is regressed on a binary treatment indicator that has the value of 1 for respondents who were assigned to treatment 1 (foreign shaming of the United States) and 0 for respondents in the control (foreign shaming of unnamed countries). Models do not include any controls. Thick bars represent 90 percent confidence intervals; thin bars represent 95 percent confidence intervals.

and are more open to supporting efforts by the Trump administration to integrate this issue into its policy agenda.

Nevertheless, the fact that Republicans appear to support criminal justice reform renders the other results even more striking. In addition to higher nationalism and diminished support for advocacy, Republicans in the treatment group exhibited greater tolerance of human rights violations for the sake of social order. Thus, even as they acknowledged the specific problem of abuses in the criminal justice system, these participants also felt that some human rights violations were justifiable. This logic appeared to allow Republicans to compensate for recognizing faults with their country. For supporters of the incumbent government, the heightened sense of threat intensified the desire to affirm other positive aspects of the United States, resulting in higher nationalist sentiments and an insistence that the country respects human rights in general.

In short, we cannot attribute Republican backlash to these participants' distaste for the *content* of the criticism; in fact, they appeared to be quite amenable to demands for criminal justice reform. Rather, insofar as Republicans exhibited hostility to shaming, this hostility seemed to be driven by the relational *context* of enforcement, not by preexisting beliefs regarding the validity of the message. As one Republican respondent put it succinctly, "Although I somewhat agree with their [HRAC's] findings, it's up to us [the United States] to fix the problem, and they should stay out of our business."[42]

National Identity Attachments

Another potential moderating factor is presented by national identity attachments. As I discussed earlier, the literature on status threat places special emphasis on the degree to which individuals *identify* with the targeted group—that is, how psychologically significant membership in that group is to them and the extent of their commitment to the group's well-being. High identifiers are more likely to experience criticism as a status threat and are more likely to cope with that threat by reacting defensively. Thus, we might expect greater backlash overall from individuals with strong national identity attachments.

The survey results confirm these intuitions, showing that backlash was markedly stronger among participants with stronger attachments to American identity. Figure 5.3 shows the interaction between people's national identity attachments and foreign shaming. I consider participants "highly nationalist" if they are above the median on the pretreatment *national identity attachment* measure. Among members of this group, exposure to foreign shaming of the United States decreased support for campaign activities—a result that aligns with the full sample. Unlike the full sample, however, highly nationalist participants were also less likely to sign a petition supporting criminal justice reform. Not only did shaming not work among strong nationalists, but it also inhibited their willingness to act in support of human rights improvements.

Open-Ended Responses

In addition to reporting discrete measures, I also asked subjects to write about how the news article about HRAC made them feel "about human rights conditions in the United States." Although brief, their responses provide additional insights into the patterns guiding their thinking. I analyzed these open-ended responses in two steps.[43] First, responses were coded for

---

42. This response had been edited lightly for grammar and punctuation.

43. Two graduate student coders, blind to main hypotheses and treatment conditions, read and coded the responses based on the following dimensions, with an interrater agreement statistic (Cohen's kappa) ranging from 0.73 to 1.00, depending on the specific dimension

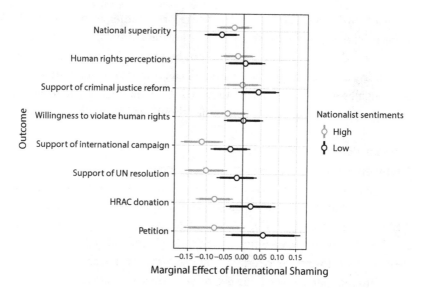

FIGURE 5.3. The Effects of Foreign Shaming of the United States, by National Identity Attachments

Results from an OLS regression in which each outcome (scaled to unit length) is regressed on a binary treatment indicator that has the value of 1 for respondents who were assigned to treatment 1 (foreign shaming of the United States) and 0 for respondents in the control (foreign shaming of unnamed countries). Models do not include any controls. Thick bars represent 90 percent confidence intervals; thin bars represent 95 percent confidence intervals.

their overall *alignment* with the views expressed in the article: responses were marked as "agree" when they generally accepted that human rights violations are a problem in the US criminal justice system and require redress; they were marked as "disagree" if they overtly rejected this claim; and they were marked as "ambivalent" when they neither fully agreed nor disagreed.[44] Thus, alignment provides an overall snapshot of the degree to which respondents leaned toward a compliant or defiant position vis-à-vis rights abuses in the United States.

Figure 5.4 reports the marginal effect of the treatment on the responses' general alignment with the article.[45] We observe that respondents exposed

---

of interest. The appendix B provides more detail on these codes, their prevalence, and their interrater reliability.

44. Note that while the control condition did not explicitly mention the United States, the open-ended question asked respondents to speak on the US justice system.

45. The plot reports the marginal effect of the treatment on the likelihood of open-ended responses coded as "agree," "disagree," or "ambivalent"—the three most common codes in the data set. Less common codes, such as "no opinion" and "unsure," are excluded from the plot.

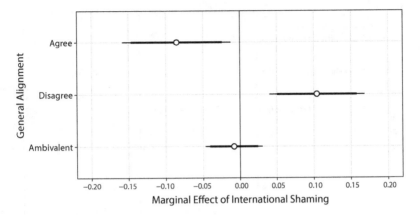

FIGURE 5.4. The Effects of Foreign Shaming of the United States on Open-Ended Responses: General Alignment with the Article
Results from an OLS regression in which general alignment of open-ended responses is regressed on a binary treatment indicator that has the value of 1 for respondents who were assigned to treatment 1 (foreign shaming of the United States) and 0 for respondents in the control (foreign shaming of unnamed countries). Models do not include any controls. Thick bars represent 90 percent confidence intervals; thin bars represent 95 percent confidence intervals.

to foreign shaming of the United States were less likely to overtly *agree* with the views expressed in the article and more likely to overtly *disagree*. This finding provides compelling evidence of a generalized defensiveness on behalf of respondents in the face of human rights criticism of the United States.

Second, responses were coded based on their *substantive content*. Using an iterative process accounting for both theoretical knowledge of the topic as well as inductive observations of the data, I generated a series of codes corresponding to six broad themes: (1) human rights, (2) the justice system, (3) race, (4) HRAC and other human rights advocates, (5) political partisanship, and (6) comparing the United States with other countries. Figure 5.5 reports the marginal effect of the treatment on the likelihood of respondents raising a particular topic. We see that participants who were exposed to the treatment were more likely to discuss HRAC (the advocacy group mentioned in the article) and human rights critics, as well as the US criminal justice system. On the other hand, they were *less* likely to explicitly address the issue of race.

Just knowing that a topic was mentioned tells us little about *how* it was discussed. For each topic mention, I coded whether the valence favored a generally compliant or defiant position. For example, some responses

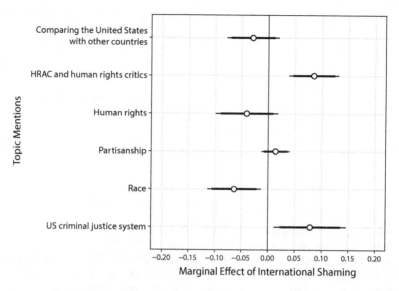

FIGURE 5.5. The Effects of Foreign Shaming of the United States on Open-Ended Responses: Mentions of Particular Topics

Results from an OLS regression in which mentions of particular topics are regressed on a binary treatment indicator that has the value of 1 for respondents who were assigned to treatment 1 (foreign shaming of the United States) and 0 for respondents in the control (foreign shaming of unnamed countries). Models do not include any controls. Thick bars represent 90 percent confidence intervals; thin bars represent 95 percent confidence intervals.

brought up the US justice system in order to criticize the abuses endemic in that system (favoring compliance), while others defended the system against outside attacks (favoring defiance). Similar patterns in valence can be observed with other topics; a response favored defiance when it *defended* the state of human rights in the United States, *criticized* HRAC, *affirmed* the superiority of the United States compared to other countries, and so on. Figure B1 in appendix B reports the marginal effect of foreign shaming on the valence of particular topics.

Together, findings from the open-ended analysis both confirm and refine the trends already reported in several respects.[46] First—and most noticeably—participants were far more likely to express hostility toward the Human Rights Action Committee after reviewing their criticism of the

---

46. Unless otherwise noted, the findings I discuss here are statistically significant at the $p < 0.05$ level.

United States. While participants drew on a variety of tactics to undermine HRAC and its report, one of the most common strategies—especially among Republicans and strong nationalists—was to call into question the *motives* and *political biases* of the group.

> I would want to know more about this organization, who founded it, who its members are, and who funded it. I also feel that state sovereignty is extremely important and the US should not be directed by foreign actors. I believe there are organizations that believe that the US should be diminished for their own reason and will use all means, including skillful propaganda and illegitimate tribunals, to accomplish this end. (male, age fifty-seven, Republican, high nationalism)

> The international community and UN are totally socialist/communist. I totally disregard anything they say or think. (female, age sixty-nine, Republican, high nationalism)

> Organizations with suspicious source of funding are meddling with US politics and societal life. (male, age forty-two, independent, low nationalism)

> I believe any group from Europe, especially the EU, is especially hypocritical and holds the US to higher moral and financial expectations than they do for themselves. They also have an entirely different form of government which does not subscribe to the same expectations Americans hold for themselves. Any research from such a group is conducted staunchly biased. (male, age thirty-two, Republican, high nationalism)

> HRAC has no business in our judicial process. They need to keep their opinion in Geneva. (male, age fifty-eight, Republican, high nationalism)

Indeed, Republicans in the treatment group were significantly more likely to excoriate HRAC and associated actors (the United Nations, groups from Europe) by seventeen percentage points—the strongest substantive effect in the analysis.

Second, participants in the treatment group were more likely to attempt to defend the US criminal justice system. Here, a common strategy was to compare the US record to those of other countries.

> It made me feel like the USA is unfairly judged by other countries that have just as much, if not more inhumanity and injustice in their systems.

"Pot calling kettle black syndrome." (male, age sixty-three, Republican, high nationalism)

I feel once you are convicted, you give up your rights. Plus . . . I'd rather be arrested in the United States than North Korea. (male, age forty-two, Republican, low nationalism)

While I agree that there are issues with the justice system in the United States, I would think that another country's focus would be, or should be, more drawn to the human rights conditions in other places where people are suffering far worse and in greater amounts than here in the United States. I do think the international attention would help shine a brighter light on issues we should be managing better at home, but I find it hard to believe that Geneva actually cares that much about our issues. (female, age forty-four, Democrat, high nationalism)

In comparing the United States to other countries, respondents engaged in group differentiation, highlighting the positive dimensions of their group (the United States) in contrast to the negative attributes of others. They also insinuated that the HRAC's criticism was hypocritical, using the logic that if activists *really* cared about human rights violations, they would focus their attention elsewhere instead of on the United States. Some cast additional doubt on the HRAC by implying that the organization was motivated by a desire to vilify the United States.

Finally, it is worth noting what was *absent* in these reactions. Specifically, the findings do not indicate greater defensiveness among respondents on the issues of race or human rights ideals—two key elements of the article they read. This may indicate that they were preoccupied less with the specific normative content of the report's findings than with its targeting of the United States specifically. In other words, respondents focused not on the message but on the messenger. Nor did participants in the treatment group express enhanced partisanship—for instance, by ridiculing the opposing party. Instead, defensive participants focused their hostility on the HRAC, Geneva, and Europeans. In doing so, they engaged with the prompt through the lens of a distinctly *American* identity, displaying prominent signs of in-group attachment and favoritism.

I would say if the American government is abusing any humans in prison, jails, or other detaining facilities, I would want to see this for myself. I believe in the American people to respect all human rights.

I am proud to be an American. (female, age twenty-nine, Democrat, high nationalism)

[I'm] very disappointed. [The] United States is and will always be one nation, home of the free and land of the brave. (male, age forty, Republican, high nationalism)

I really don't care what folks in Geneva, Switzerland, think about what goes on in my country. (female, age fifty-two, Republican, high nationalism)

In all, the findings suggest that respondents viewed international human rights shaming as both salient and threatening enough to their American identity to evoke defensive reactions.

Study 2

EXPERIMENTAL DESIGN

The second survey experiment was fielded on July 22, 2021, via Lucid Theorem, a convenience panel widely used by social scientists ($n = 2,820$).[47] As with the previous experiment, the survey first collected pretreatment variables on demographic information, partisanship, racial resentment, and national identity attachments.[48] It then randomly assigned participants to one of five conditions—four treatment groups and a control. Participants in the control group were asked to read the following prompt before proceeding to the outcome questions:

STUDY 2: CONTROL

Some people accuse the United States' criminal justice system of human rights violations, including discrimination, excessively harsh sentencing, and inhumane prison conditions. We're interested in what you think.

I asked participants in the four treatment groups to read some version of the following article, varying the source of foreign criticism. Although the

47. Compared to Mechanical Turk, Lucid's sample more closely matches national benchmarks in terms of both demographics and political identification, ideology, and interest (Coppock and McClellan 2019).

48. Three measures on national identity attachments were taken from Huddy and Khatib 2007. The measures were then summed to one index and rescaled from 0 to 1. The three are highly internally consistent (Cronbach's alpha = 0.852).

article is fictitious, it is worth noting that each of these countries has in fact condemned the United States in ways that are comparable to the prompt.[49]

STUDY 2 [TREATMENTS 1, 2, 3, 4]

[Canada / France / Iran / China] Condemns Abuses in United States
July 1, 2021

A spokesperson for the **[Canadian / French / Iranian / Chinese]** government accused the United States today of repeated violations of human rights throughout the criminal justice system.

The statement read: "The United States' criminal justice system is plagued with injustices, including discrimination, excessively harsh sentencing, and inhumane prison conditions."

[Canada's / France's / Iran's / China's] representative went on to urge other countries and members of the international community to denounce these abuses.

Subjects in the four treatment groups were then asked, "Why do you think [Canada / France / Iran / China] made this statement?" They were provided with the following options and asked to select all that applied: "[Canada / France / Iran / China] (1) is knowledgeable about human rights violations; (2) is biased against the United States; (3) cares about protecting human rights; (4) wants to raise its own profile; and (5) has a political agenda." All respondents answered the same set of questions as in study 1 (see table 5.1).[50]

RESULTS

Overall, this experiment resulted in more null results compared to study 1. This is not too surprising given the nature of the control. In the previous experiment, respondents in the control group were told of abuses occurring elsewhere, but in this study *all* participants were primed with information disparaging the United States, which could have induced defensiveness. This feature may explain the smaller differences between the control and treatment groups in study 2.

---

49. For example, Feng 2020; Hernández and Mueller 2020; Salem 2020.

50. One exception was the question labeled "HRAC donation." Because the prompt did not mention the HRAC, the wording of the question was changed to: "Are you willing to donate $1 to support a human rights campaign to push for criminal justice reforms in the United States? If you select 'yes,' a link to the donation page will appear at the end of this survey."

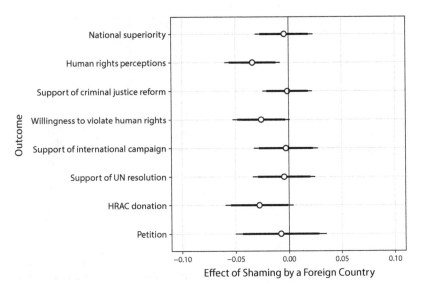

FIGURE 5.6. The Effects of Shaming by a Foreign Country
Results from an OLS regression in which each outcome (scaled to unit length) is regressed on a binary treatment indicator that has the value of 1 for respondents who were assigned to treatments 1–4 (shaming by foreign country) and 0 for respondents in the control. Models do not include any controls. Thick bars represent 90 percent confidence intervals; thin bars represent 95 percent confidence intervals.

Nevertheless, I find partial support for two main findings. First, compared to the control (which did not specify a shaming agent), shaming by a foreign country provoked marginally greater defensiveness. Figure 5.6 reports the marginal effect of shaming by a foreign country, pooling the four treatment groups ($n=2{,}247$) and comparing these responses to those of the control ($n=573$).[51] Overall, I find no evidence that shaming by a foreign country promoted views favorable to compliance. There is some evidence, however, that foreign criticism backfired on several dimensions. Respondents exposed to shaming by a foreign country were more likely to agree that human rights were well respected in the United States. They were also more willing to violate human rights for the sake of social order and less likely to donate to human rights advocacy efforts.

As with the previous study, I disaggregated these results by party identification and by nationalist attachments (figures reported in appendix B). As with the previous study, the main results do not appear to be driven by a sole

51. See appendix B for results disaggregated by treatment group.

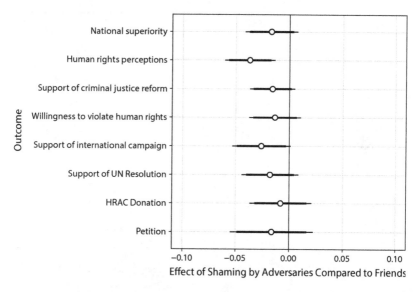

FIGURE 5.7. The Effects of Shaming by Adversaries versus Friends
Results from an OLS regression in which each outcome (scaled to unit length) is regressed on a binary treatment indicator that has the value of 1 for respondents who were assigned to treatments 1–4 (shaming by foreign country) and 0 for respondents in the control. Models do not include any controls. Thick bars represent 90 percent confidence intervals; thin bars represent 95 percent confidence intervals.

partisan identity; both Republicans and Democrats displayed signs of defensiveness. I did, however, find consistent trends in national identity attachments: highly nationalistic individuals appeared to be particularly sensitive to shaming by a foreign country. In addition to the three main results described already, strong nationalists were also less likely to sign a petition supporting criminal justice reform following exposure to foreign criticism.[52]

The second suggestive finding is that shaming by US adversaries is more likely to backfire than shaming by friends and allies on average. I pooled participants in the China and Iran groups and compared their responses to those in the Canada and France groups. Figure 5.7 reports the marginal effect of shaming by an adversary compared to a friend. Point estimates for all outcomes were in the direction of defiance effects, with two showing

52. Among less nationalistic individuals, the treatment induced null results for all measures. To clarify, this does not necessarily mean that the effect of foreign shaming is significantly different for strong nationalists compared to weak nationalists. The interaction of the treatment with national identity attachments is significant for the following outcomes: willingness to violate human rights for social order, stated support for criminal justice reform, and willingness to sign a petition calling for criminal reforms.

statistical significance: human rights perceptions (respondents evaluated US human rights conditions more positively) and support for an international campaign (respondents decreased their support of an international campaign advocating for criminal justice reform in the United States).

Again, these results were not exclusive to Republicans. Indeed, Democrats were less likely to support human rights advocacy through donation or petition when exposed to shaming by adversaries compared to friends. And unlike the previous finding, shaming by adversaries induced defensiveness in both strong and weak nationalists (see appendix B for figures).

Why does shaming by adversaries induce greater defensiveness than shaming by friends? Part of the story might have to do with perceptions of motive—*why* were these countries interfering in US affairs? Figure 5.8 summarizes how participants evaluated the motives of various countries shaming the United States. As expected, respondents ascribed different motives to different actors. More than Canada or France, China and Iran were seen as criticizing the United States because they had a political agenda, were biased against the United States, and wanted to raise their own profile. Canada and France, in contrast, were thought to care about human rights and, to a lesser degree, to be knowledgeable about the issue. Of course, these differences in perceived motive are rooted in multiple factors. Not only are Iran and China actors widely regarded as adversaries and threats to the United States, but they also lack credibility on human rights promotion on account of their own poor records. Both associations—geopolitical rivalry and hypocrisy—are likely to have played a role in shaping respondents' perceptions.

Overall, the results from this study are not as conclusive as results from the first study, owing to the number of statistically insignificant results. In addition, effect sizes were relatively small in magnitude, possibly because the experimental treatments, by manipulating only a few words, were relatively subtle. In real life, people usually witness their country being shamed in much more flamboyant ways, as well as editorialized through the reactions of their own political leaders. For example, as Jamie Gruffydd-Jones finds, Chinese state media strategically publicize certain types of international human rights pressure, presumably because leaders anticipate a defensive, nationalistic reaction among their population that, in turn, will bolster regime support.[53] Not surprisingly, shaming from major geopolitical rivals (in China's case, the United States) is more likely to be "passed on" to the general public.

53. Gruffydd-Jones 2018.

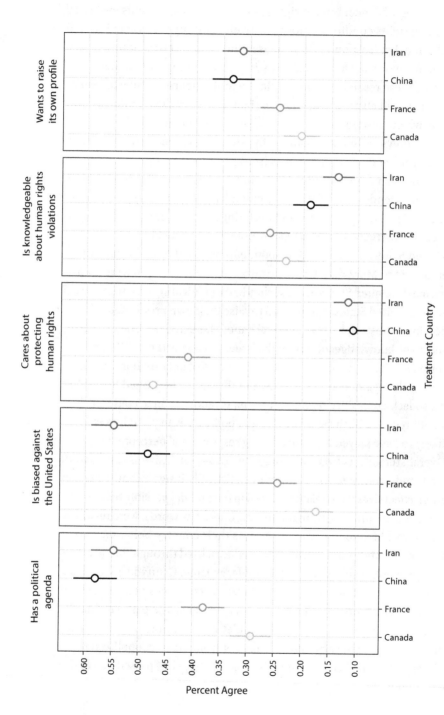

FIGURE 5.8. Perceptions of Motive for Countries Shaming the United States
The *y*-axis represents the percentage of the sample in a given treatment condition who identified a certain motive for the country shaming the United States. Bars represent 95 percent confidence intervals.

Conclusion

International shaming is commonly thought to fuel domestic mobilization for human rights. Nevertheless, we lack a full account of how this tactic affects one key audience—the population of the target state. Although shaming has the potential to mobilize domestic populations against the rights-violating state, it may also engender a defensive reaction that heightens nationalist sentiments and degrades outside criticism. This chapter has tackled this question with experimental methods.

There are three main takeaways. First, I find little evidence that international shaming produces attitudes that are conducive to human rights mobilization. An important exception was Republicans in the United States who expressed verbal support for criminal justice reform, even as they lent less material support for activists working toward this goal. On all other measures, however, the findings fail to support the widespread assumption that international shaming shifts public opinion toward the side of human rights advocates.

Second, there is some evidence that international shaming backfires by inciting a defensive reaction among domestic audiences. International shaming—particularly by an adversarial country—appears to fuel national favoritism, driving Americans, for instance, to see the United States and its human rights record in a more positive light overall. Another consistent trend is the public becoming less willing to support activism to improve human rights in the United States, including by international institutions and civil society groups, in the face of foreign shaming. I observed a change not only in discourse but also in material support: participants were less willing to donate to a (fictitious) human rights organization once they learned that it was criticizing the United States, and also following criticism by a foreign country, even with no mention of the organization. Thus, even if shaming does change people's private views, it may nonetheless undermine political mobilization or activism aimed at reform.

Finally, this defensiveness appears to be *relational*—not substantive—in nature. In the first study, identical criticism directed at other countries garnered broad support, even as it evoked hostility when applied to the American context. In the second study, participants changed their attitudes based solely on the identity of the messenger. This suggests that an antagonistic response to international shaming is not simply an artifact of preexisting ideological positions of opposition to human rights or criminal justice reform. Rather, defensiveness derives from the relational context. Foreign shaming—particularly when done by an adversarial country—activates national identity attachments, which in turn shape human rights attitudes.

These findings are important because public opinion plays a key role in mediating the influence of international human rights shaming on government decisions in the target state. In chapter 3, I explained how a widespread defensive reaction alters the domestic political landscape in three ways: (1) by constraining leaders from complying with international norms; (2) by rewarding those who double down on alleged violations and resist foreign pressure; and (3) by punishing and delegitimizing local human rights advocates. The experimental results presented here, while focused on the individual level and not the domestic political level, lend plausibility to these mechanisms. A heightened sense of threat and nationalism drives citizens to withdraw support for leaders who are seen as "giving in" to the enemy, while increasing support for those who are seen as standing up to a bully.[54] In the context of human rights enforcement, this translates into constraining compliance and rewarding resistance to international shaming. Importantly, foreign shaming appears to make the domestic public less willing to support activism to improve human rights, thereby directly hurting the work of local advocates and hindering their efforts at mass political mobilization.

Of course, this study was limited to a single case, the United States, whose several unique features—including hegemonic status and American exceptionalism—may limit the ability to generalize to other contexts. That said, it is not difficult to find similar trends in other countries. China is a prominent example. Gruffydd-Jones's work shows that Chinese citizens have a defensive, nationalist reaction when exposed to human rights shaming from the United States (an adversarial country) but not to shaming from the African Union (a neutral source). Interestingly, the backlash effect is neutralized when shaming is directed explicitly at the Chinese government rather than the country as a whole, congruent with social identity and status threat mechanisms.[55]

Like American respondents, Chinese leaders often attempt to discredit international criticism by questioning the motives and political biases of critics. In one characteristic comment, a spokesperson for the Chinese mission to Geneva, Liu Yuyin, responded to a UN report alleging rights abuses in Xinjiang by calling it "a politicized document that disregards facts, and reveals explicitly the attempt of some Western countries and anti-China

54. Fearon 1994; Dafoe and Weiss 2017.
55. Gruffydd-Jones 2018.

forces to use human rights as a political tool."[56] Such narratives—that the West is using human rights to smear China—are rampant within Chinese public discourse and likely serve to rile up citizens' defensive reactions, which in turn drive additional support for government policies. Similar trends occur in Israel, where foreign condemnation over policies in the occupied Palestinian territories appears to increase support for hard-line policies and decrease support for international norms in general.[57] All of these instances support the general idea that international normative pressure arouses defiant reactions among citizens in the target country, especially when they have reason to suspect hostile motives, and that those reactions translate into increased support for the policies in question.

The evidence presented here is subject to other limitations. To begin with, I was able to measure only short-term reactions. It could be that sustained exposure to international pressure shifts public response over time, perhaps by inducing long-term cultural shifts.[58] Additionally, this study examined ordinary citizens using a nationally representative sample. One could argue that the real audience for international shaming is not public opinion in the target country writ large but local activists, oppressed minorities, and other marginalized groups with a vested interest in human rights compliance.[59] The nature of the sample, however, precluded any measurement of the effect of international shaming on the opinion of these groups with adequate precision.

Finally, it is important to underscore that public opinion is just one factor in a complex process linking international shaming to domestic political outcomes. Inferences about individual attitudes are not enough; we need to know how these attitudes aggregate and alter the broader political landscape to affect the behavior of policymakers. The next chapter draws these linkages through real-life case studies.

56. Kuo and Rauhala 2022.
57. Grossman, Manekin, and Margalit 2018; Bassan-Nygate 2022.
58. Merry 2006; Simmons 2009.
59. I thank Beth Simmons for raising this point.

6

Applications

The previous two chapters employed quantitative and experimental evidence to test key components of my relational theory of international shaming. This chapter shows how these components fit together by applying the framework to real-world cases. To clarify, the purpose of this chapter is not to empirically test the theory. Rather, my primary goals are to (1) explore how the book's theoretical arguments unfold on the ground, (2) elucidate causal mechanisms linking the patterns described in the previous chapters to concrete outcomes, and (3) compare the theory's explanatory power to alternative explanations.

I center cases that diverge from the typical story commonplace in the literature on international shaming, in which foreign normative pressure effectively elicits target compliance. While I do not deny that shaming can work in some cases, my theory predicts that such cases are unusual, for two reasons. First, norm enforcement is most effective when it occurs between geopolitical partners, but states face strong disincentives to shame their friends and allies and thus do so less frequently and seldom forcefully. Second, leaders typically reserve human rights shaming, especially in its harshest form, for their enemies and adversaries. But here they are less effective at inducing compliance and more likely to provoke resistance.

The pair of cases I discuss in this chapter exemplify these two logics. The cases are similar in many respects. Both feature a target state in the Middle East that is widely regarded as a pariah regime—Saudi Arabia in one case and Iran in the other. Both feature clear and compelling evidence of human rights abuse. Both involve the same observing countries—the United States and its Western allies—that must decide whether and how to condemn these abuses. The studies diverge, however, on both the independent variable (the geopolitical relations between potential shamer and target) and the dependent variables (the behavior of the potential shamer and the target vis-à-vis human rights pressure). In the first case, the target, Saudi Arabia, is an important strategic partner to the United States and other Western countries, while the second case features an adversary of the West in Iran. Despite comparable abuses, Saudi Arabia avoided significant punishment, while Iran faced harsh condemnation. In addition, by featuring within-case variation both on the shaming side and in the target's response, the latter case provides additional leverage to evaluate applications of the theory.

I first examine the US position on human rights in Saudi Arabia, focusing on the death of the *Washington Post* journalist Jamal Khashoggi. The case highlights the politics of shaming between geostrategic partners; in this case, America's reluctance to alienate an important ally led policymakers to avoid strong denunciations or sanctioning. This case represents "the dog that didn't bark"—that is, it features an absence of significant shaming efforts. However, using counterfactual reasoning, I argue that the Khashoggi situation was a missed opportunity: human rights pressure, had it been applied, could have had a meaningful effect.

The second case turns to Iran, focusing on the 2010–2011 "Save Sakineh" campaign, a massive and global shaming operation in response to an Iranian woman being sentenced to death by stoning for adultery. The case complements the Saudi example, as the same potential shamers, the United States and its allies, differed markedly in their response to comparable abuses: they went easy on Saudi Arabia while forcefully condemning Iran. I show that international shaming by Iran's adversaries unleashed political forces inside Iran that inhibited policymakers' ability to comply with international pressure, not because of material interests or ideological commitments but rather because of an imperative to defy foreign—especially Western—demands. At the same time, significant metanorm pressures compelled Iran's geopolitical partners (notably Brazil) to also shame the Iranian regime. Faced with competing pressures to comply and defy, Iran ultimately responded to international shaming with a strategy of deflection, thus satisfying geopolitical allies while avoiding the image of succumbing to perceived Western domination disguised as human rights pressure.

The case narratives employ qualitative evidence from a range of sources, including news articles, public relations material, NGO reports, official statements, original interviews, and existing research. The goal is to comprehend both the choice to shame human rights violations and the consequences of that choice, reconstructing the strategic interaction between (potential) shamers, target countries, and relevant audiences. After providing a brief background of the alleged violation, I first examine the decision-making of potential shaming countries, documenting the key factors: enforcement costs, behavioral preferences, metanorms, and stigma imposition. I then turn to decision-makers in the target country to account for the various inducements influencing their reaction, including preferences reflected in the norm-violating behavior, international costs, and domestic reactions. I close by addressing the subsequent outcomes and aftermaths of the two cases.

Jamal Khashoggi and US-Saudi Relations

BACKGROUND

The Kingdom of Saudi Arabia is an absolutist monarchy headed by King Salman bin Abdulaziz Al Saudi; his son, Crown Prince Mohammed bin Salman (MBS), is considered the *de facto* ruler. When it comes to human rights, Saudi Arabia ranks among "the worst of the worst": the nation severely restricts civil, political, and physical integrity rights. In 2020, Freedom House gave Saudi Arabia an overall score of 7 out of 100 (1 out of 40 for political rights and 6 out of 60 for civil liberties), the seventh-lowest score among independent nations (tied with Somalia).[1] In addition to broad repression of civil, political, and physical integrity rights, the regime routinely violates the human rights of women, children, religious minorities, and expatriate laborers.[2]

In 2018, the prominent Saudi journalist and dissident Jamal Khashoggi was assassinated at the Saudi consulate in Istanbul, Turkey. Khashoggi once had close ties with the monarchy, but he eventually grew critical of the regime. In 2017, he fled to the United States, where he began writing for the *Washington Post*. As a columnist, Khashoggi sharply criticized the Saudi regime for its repression of free speech and dissent, brutal war in Yemen, arrest of women's rights activists, and general deficit of democracy and political freedoms.[3] Before his death, Khashoggi was also involved in several projects to promote human rights, democracy, and free expression

1. Repucci 2020.
2. Amnesty International 2021; Human Rights Watch 2021; US Department of State 2021.
3. Khashoggi 2018.

in Saudi Arabia. In retaliation for his dissent, Khashoggi was continually harassed online by Saudi-backed troll farms, and his cell phone was infected by spyware reportedly linked to the Saudi government.[4] Shortly before his assassination, US intelligence officials reportedly discovered plans by Saudi officials to capture Khashoggi.[5]

On October 2, 2018, Khashoggi visited the Saudi Arabian consulate in Istanbul in order to obtain documents for his upcoming marriage. CCTV recorded him entering the consulate but did not record him exiting. Saudi officials initially said that Khashoggi was alive when he left the embassy; they later changed the story to say he was strangled inside the consulate during a "fistfight."[6] Following an investigation, American intelligence officials concluded that Khashoggi was assassinated by order of Crown Prince Mohammed bin Salman.[7] Several months later, the UN special rapporteur on extrajudicial, summary, or arbitrary executions, Agnes Callamard, released a report summarizing a six-month investigation; it concluded, "Mr. Khashoggi's killing constituted an extrajudicial killing for which the State of the Kingdom of Saudi Arabia is responsible."[8] As of this writing, the crown prince continues to deny having ordered the attack or having any prior knowledge of it.

US-SAUDI ALLIANCE

The United States and Saudi Arabia maintain a close, long-standing strategic partnership. The relationship was forged in 1943, when President Franklin D. Roosevelt inaugurated an "oil for security" arrangement wherein the Saudis provided access to their massive oil reserves (the second largest in the world as of 2016) in exchange for America's security assistance and protection against foreign threats. Despite the manifest differences between the two nations in government, religion, and geography, Saudi Arabia and the United States have sustained a partnership for nearly eighty years, cooperating on a wide range of security, economic, and diplomatic issues.

The US–Saudi Arabia relationship is one of mutual—if asymmetric—dependence. The United States relies on the Saudis for several foreign policy objectives, chiefly around oil production and counterterrorism. Saudi Arabia

4. Benner et al. 2018.
5. Morris, Mekhennet, and Fahim 2018.
6. Hubbard 2018.
7. Harris, Miller, and Dawsey 2018; Schmitt and Fandos 2018.
8. United Nations General Assembly 2019.

is the third-largest supplier of America's imported oil, providing around half a million barrels per day.[9] The United States also maintains numerous military bases on Saudi territory and depends on Saudi cooperation to secure its strategic interests in the Middle East. The two countries work closely to counterbalance Iran, a mutual adversary. In return, the United States provides Saudi Arabia with critical military, technical, and financial support. Saudi Arabia is the second-largest buyer of American arms (active foreign military sales total $100 billion[10]), and it relies on US assistance for intelligence services (including on "internal security" matters[11]), as well as for logistical and military reinforcement in its conflict with Yemen.[12] Although this strategic partnership has certainly been strained at various times over the years, it remains one of the most durable bilateral relationships in the international system.

SHAMING COSTS AND BENEFITS

As argued in chapter 2, states shame other states on human rights abuses for three potential reasons. First, leaders may want to deter unwanted behavior and reinforce compliance with a preferred norm—what I term "behavioral preferences." Second, shamers are rewarded by third-party audiences, such as domestic publics, for punishing human rights abusers—what I term "meta-norm pressures." Third, states may want to undermine the target government's legitimacy and status by tarnishing their reputation—what I term "stigma imposition." The last motive is largely irrelevant in this discussion, because the United States would receive negligible geopolitical benefits from the stigmatization of Saudi Arabia.[13] To what extent, however, do the other motives apply to the United States vis-à-vis the Khashoggi affair?

Conceivably, behavioral preferences might have motivated American leaders to sanction Saudi Arabia—that is, they may have had a genuine interest in achieving global compliance with international human rights

---

9. US Department of State 2020.

10. Ibid. American arms account for 73 percent of Saudi military imports, according to the Stockholm International Peace Research Institute (2020). Arms sales appear to have increased significantly during Saudi Arabia's war in Yemen (Riedel 2021).

11. Greenwald and Hussain 2014.

12. Al-Mujahed and DeYoung 2015.

13. As explained in chapter 2, states (such as the United States) may want to stigmatize other countries (such as Saudi Arabia) as a *tactic* to achieve compliance with human rights. But this is distinct from the *goal* of stigma imposition, which is motivated by the desire to inflict political damage on a rival. Using stigmatization as a tactic would fall under "behavioral preferences."

and diplomatic law, and they may also have been genuinely displeased by the Saudis' wanton disregard for these institutions. Although behavioral preferences are difficult to observe in isolation, the evidence suggests that such preferences have varied significantly across presidential administrations. The Trump administration's apparent indifference to human rights and international law in general extended to US-Saudi relations. The Biden administration was more ambiguous in this regard. President Biden himself may have held genuine normative beliefs favoring compliance with international human rights institutions, while also wanting to see better compliance from Saudi Arabia. Other individuals in the Biden administration may have pushed to prioritize human rights in foreign policy in general and within US-Saudi relations in particular.[14]

Regardless of policymakers' personal dismay over the actions of the Saudi government, they were clearly pressed by third parties to punish Saudi Arabia for Khashoggi's murder, which unleashed ferocious outrage both at home and abroad. Metanorm pressures were imposed from multiple angles. One major source was civil society, including human rights groups and media outlets. Notably, the *Washington Post*, as Khashoggi's employer, made significant efforts to lobby President Trump and others to hold the Saudis accountable. One editorial read:

> Businesses that withdrew this week from an investment conference in Riyadh should continue to shun contact with the crown prince; Washington lobbyists should refuse to accept more of his cash. Congress should block all arms sales and deliveries. US relations and cooperation with Saudi Arabia must continue but only after they have been put on a new footing.[15]

Khashoggi's fiancée, Hatice Cengiz, also beseeched the US government to take action, writing: "I implore President Trump and first lady Melania Trump to help shed light on Jamal's disappearance."[16]

Some of America's foreign allies also wanted to see the Saudis punished, most notably Turkey. According to the *New York Times*, President Recep Tayyip Erdoğan—a personal friend of Khashoggi—used intelligence leaks to cultivate global media attention to the case, intending to pressure Western

---

14. Sanger 2021a.
15. *Washington Post* Editorial Board 2018.
16. Cengiz 2018.

countries to sanction the Saudi crown prince, whom he saw as a geopolitical threat.[17]

Perhaps most importantly, metanorm pressures came from within the
US government, as Khashoggi's murder incited unusual bipartisan uproar in
Congress. In a letter written to President Trump, twenty-two US senators
called for an investigation into the murder and the possibility of imposing sanctions. Republican senators, including Marco Rubio, Lindsay Graham, Bob Corker, and Rand Paul, broke with the Trump administration to
demand stronger punitive actions.[18] "If they're [Saudi Arabia] this brazen, it
shows contempt," said Lindsay Graham. "Contempt for everything we stand
for, contempt for the relationship."[19] (Note the emphasis on the integrity
of the strategic relationship, over and beyond abstract international norms.)

Two months after Khashoggi's death, the US Senate unanimously passed
a resolution holding MBS personally responsible. It also voted 56–41 (with
seven GOP yeses) to pass legislation ceasing US military assistance for Saudi
Arabia's intervention in Yemen, marking the Senate's first-ever invocation
of the War Powers Act.[20] While largely symbolic, the two resolutions were
widely viewed as a rebuke of both Saudi Arabia for Khashoggi's killing and
President Trump for refusing to condemn Saudi rulers. Of course, US lawmakers themselves may have been performing outrage for their constituents,
under the influence of metanorm pressures. Regardless of their personal
motivation, however, public outcry—particularly by Republican leaders—
compounded the pressure on foreign policymakers to sanction the kingdom.

Despite these pressures to punish the Saudis, American foreign policymakers nevertheless faced significant enforcement costs. In my theory, enforcement costs arise from provoking a negative reaction and upsetting a valuable
relationship. The more a country values its relationship with the violator, the
higher the enforcement costs. Indeed, this is precisely what we observed in
the Khashoggi affair: many foreign policymakers were skittish about angering the kingdom. Defense Secretary Jim Mattis and Secretary of State Mike
Pompeo held closed-door meetings with members of Congress to warn them
against any action that would undermine the US-Saudi partnership.[21] In the
first place, straining the US-Saudi alliance, they argued, would sabotage
billions of dollars in military sales, costing American jobs and wealth in

17. Gall 2018.
18. Pappas 2018.
19. Riotta 2018.
20. Davis and Schmitt 2018. Congressional action was narrowly blocked in the House.
21. Ibid.

the security sector. Although Trump exaggerated in claiming that planned weapons sales totaled $110 billion, the actual figure of $14.5 billion was still a significant amount at stake.[22] Alienating the Saudis could also raise oil prices, rattling the global economy. "If you want to see oil prices go to $150 a barrel," Trump told reporters, "all you have to do is break up our relationship with Saudi Arabia."[23] Then there was the Saudis' critical role in America's efforts to isolate Iran, as well as its strategic importance in the region.

The Saudis, for their part, reaffirmed these risks by threatening retaliation should the United States attempt to punish the kingdom for Khashoggi's killing. According to *Al Arabiya*—a Saudi-run news outlet—an official Saudi source warned that "any action against the Kingdom will be responded to with greater reaction."[24] Writing in the same issue, Turki Aldakhil, general manager of *Al Arabiya*, enumerated "catastrophic scenarios" should the United States impose sanctions on Saudi Arabia.[25] Punitive action, he warned, would increase oil prices, causing America to "stab its own economy to death," halt the exchange of critical intelligence protecting "millions of Westerns" from terrorism, and drive Riyadh closer to Russia and China, resulting in a Russian military base in Tabuk. Of course, it is impossible to discern the credibility of these threats. Nevertheless, the very real anxiety displayed by American foreign policymakers indicates at least some plausibility to these potential enforcement costs.

OUTCOME

The Trump and Biden administrations clearly took different approaches to the Khashoggi affair, and yet both were plagued by the same central dilemma. On the one hand, domestic and international outrage over Khashoggi's murder—to say nothing about the beliefs of individual policymakers—pressured American policymakers to punish Saudi Arabia, and specifically the crown prince. On the other hand, the risk of alienating an important strategic partner posed significant enforcement costs. In the end, those enforcement costs proved to be prohibitive: they prevented any significant punishment and most likely emboldened the Saudis.

In the immediate aftermath of Khashoggi's disappearance, Trump appeared open to curbing the Saudis, warning of "severe punishment" should

22. Landler 2018.
23. Ibid.
24. *Al Arabiya* Staff Writer 2018.
25. Aldakhil 2018.

high-level Saudi officials be shown to have been responsible. However, once the CIA's reports assigning culpability to MBS were leaked, Trump dropped any pretense of entertaining a potential response of punishment and publicly affirmed his intention to stand by the Saudis. In a public statement on November 20, 2018, Trump defended his decision not to sanction the kingdom, explicitly using transactional reasoning: America simply could not afford to sabotage a strategic relationship with Saudi Arabia. Contradicting CIA reports, Trump refused to acknowledge that MBS had knowledge of the assassination, writing, "Maybe he did and maybe he didn't!" "In any case," Trump continued, "our relationship is with the Kingdom of Saudi Arabia."[26] The statement, which was reportedly dictated by Trump himself, warned that alienating the Saudis would destroy American jobs in the arms industry, destabilize oil prices, and give an edge to America's adversaries.[27] He followed up by telling journalists:

> I'm not going to tell a country that's spending hundreds of billions of dollars and has helped me do one thing very importantly—keep oil prices down, so that they're not going to $100 and $150 a barrel. Right now, we have oil prices in great shape. I'm not going to destroy the world economy. And I'm not going to destroy the economy for our country by being foolish with Saudi Arabia. . . . It's about America first. The CIA has looked at it [Khashoggi's killing]. They've studied it a lot. They have nothing definitive. And the fact is maybe he [Crown Prince MBS] did, maybe he didn't.[28]

Instead of blaming the crown prince, the Trump administration imposed sanctions and visa restrictions on seventeen Saudi nationals who, it said, were involved in Khashoggi's murder. The policy was widely criticized as perfunctory and insufficient.[29]

Trump continued to stand by the Saudis throughout his presidency. In April 2019, Trump vetoed a bipartisan resolution forcing the United States to withdraw from Saudi Arabia's war in Yemen—the first time war powers legislation passed Congress with bipartisan support.[30] A few months later, he vetoed three bills that would have halted arms sales to the kingdom.[31]

---

26. White House Office of the Press Secretary 2018.
27. Landler 2018.
28. Ibid.
29. DeYoung and Fahim 2018.
30. Landler and Baker 2019.
31. Cohen and Klein 2019.

In 2020, the Trump administration bypassed the 1987 Missile Technology Control Regime—an international pact to control arms races—to sell weaponized drones to the Saudis.[32] Jared Kushner, Trump's son-in-law and senior adviser, continued to court MBS, meeting with him privately in Saudi Arabia.[33] Reflecting on the episode in an interview with Bob Woodward, Trump took credit for protecting MBS from any major fallout from the Khashoggi situation, boasting, "I saved his ass."[34]

Biden initially took a very different approach. As a presidential candidate, he promised to adjust US-Saudi relations and treat the Saudi regime as "the pariah that they are."[35] In a statement given to the Council on Foreign Relations, Biden vowed to withdraw the kingdom's "dangerous blank check," saying: "We will make clear that America will never again check its principles at the door just to buy oil or sell weapons."[36] (Biden eventually withdrew that official position.)

Once in the White House, Biden appeared intent on following through with these promises and, in the words of White House press secretary Jen Psaki, would "recalibrate" Washington's relationship with Riyadh. Unlike Trump, Biden declined to engage directly with MBS, instead speaking to his father the king. The Biden administration paused sales of "smart bombs" and announced an end to US military support for "offensive" operations in Yemen (although it was left unclear what "offensive" meant).[37] Perhaps most impactful, the Biden administration declassified an intelligence brief concluding that MBS ordered the assassination of Khashoggi.

Despite Biden's vow to hold the moral high ground, however, realpolitik eventually prevailed. According to reporting by David Sanger of the *New York Times*, a consensus emerged within the White House that punishing the crown prince would inflict a severe breach on the US-Saudi relationship, and that the costs of such a breach—particularly in Saudi cooperation in the Middle East—was simply too high. Sanctioning MBS, one veteran official explained, would "force [the Saudis] to show that there is a high price the United States has to pay for that."[38] Following the chaotic exit from Afghanistan, Biden's reliance on the Saudis only deepened. Speaking to

---

32. Wong 2020.
33. Kirkpatrick et al. 2018.
34. Sheth and Haltiwanger 2020.
35. Sanger 2021a.
36. Council on Foreign Relations 2019.
37. Gould and Mehta 2021.
38. Sanger 2021b.

The Hill, the security analyst Varsha Koduvar explained: "The administration has put itself in a bind where it cannot be as forceful on human rights without fearing some loss of cooperation with Saudi Arabia or a disruption to its regional strategy."[39]

Once the reality of this cost-benefit calculation became clear, the Biden administration began to retreat from its earlier promises and toned down the scathing rhetoric. In February 2021, Biden decided that he would forgo sanctions or any other major penalty against MBS, explaining:

> We held accountable all the people in that organization—but not the crown prince, because we have never, that I'm aware of . . . when we have an alliance with a country, gone to the acting head of state and punished that person and ostracized him.[40]

The Biden administration later approved a new $500 million military contract, which included weapons used by Saudi offenses in Yemen, contradicting the earlier policy to ban offensive weapons sales.[41] Even Trump remarked that Biden appeared to be "viewing [Saudi Arabia] maybe in a similar fashion" to the approach taken by his own administration.[42]

Reactions by other countries followed a similar pattern: those with a direct tie to Saudi Arabia either stayed silent or came out in direct support of the Saudi regime. Many Arab allies characterized the affair as a smear campaign orchestrated by the kingdom's enemies. Several of Saudi Arabia's Western partners—including Canada, the United Kingdom, France, and Germany—witnessed internal debates on their continued partnership with the Saudis, with opposition parties calling for the Saudi regime to be punished. Ultimately, however, few Western countries implemented significant changes in their dealings with Saudi Arabia. Leaders in France, the United Kingdom, and Spain rejected calls to end arms sales in order to protect jobs in the arms industry.[43] Several countries considered freezing military sales, only to reverse their position following Saudi threats of retaliation.[44]

39. Kelly 2021.

40. Guardian Staff and Agencies 2021.

41. Kirchgaessner and McKernan 2021.

42. Knickmeyer 2021.

43. Reynolds 2018.

44. For example, Spain backtracked on its plan to halt bomb sales after Riyadh threatened to cancel a $2 billion contract for warships, a deal linked to six thousand jobs in a country already struggling with unemployment (Shalaby 2018). Likewise, Canada considered freezing sales but eventually proceeded with new deals.

DISCUSSION

Overall, America's reaction to the assassination of Jamal Khashoggi fits well with a relational theory of international shaming. Ultimately, enforcement costs from damaging a valuable strategic partnership outweighed any potential benefit from human rights improvements. While the Khashoggi situation was perhaps unusual in the level of popular attention it received, the dilemma it posed was by no means unique. By failing to punish the Saudis for Khashoggi's assassination, American foreign policymakers continued a long tradition of ignoring Saudi Arabia's human rights abuses in exchange for strategic cooperation. This pattern aligns with my prediction that high enforcement costs will make states less likely to shame strategic partners.

The US-Saudi relationship reveals another aspect of my theory—that when states do shame their allies (for example, when coming under intense metanorm pressures), they tend to do so in less offending ways. Leaked cables reveal that American authorities have called on Saudi Arabia to end its prohibition on women driving, but they appear much less willing to address more sensitive issues such as free speech, torture, and the imprisonment of dissidents—a trend we also observed in the UPR in chapter 4.[45] For the Saudi regime, criticisms on issues like women's rights and social freedoms are easy to embrace, at least compared to overtly political demands like free speech. Indeed, shortly after assuming the throne, MBS eagerly lifted the ban on women driving and implemented other reforms, for which he was lauded by Western pundits as a modernizer and revolutionary.[46] Meanwhile, experts warned that such changes amounted to little more than a "smokescreen" and "women-washing" to palliate the abuses of a repressive regime.[47]

This kind of selective criticism reflects a deeper pattern when it comes to US-Saudi relations. Insofar as American policymakers push the Saudis on human rights, they tend to focus on easily digestible and relatively inoffensive reforms—reforms that easily align with the regime's agenda—while avoiding the kind of criticisms that could spark a rift in the relationship. Thus, what initially presents as the United States holding its allies accountable is actually an attempt to moderate metanorm pressures while simultaneously shielding important strategic partners from genuine confrontation.

45. Leigh 2011.
46. Friedman 2017; O'Donnell 2018.
47. Mahdawi 2018; Bayoumi 2018.

While my theory explains why America chose not to shame Saudi Arabia in the Khashoggi case, it also suggests that human rights pressure, had it been applied, could have had a positive effect. On the counterfactual, it is impossible to know what would have happened if the United States had imposed meaningful sanctions for Khashoggi's murder. However, some clues support the conjecture. First, MBS appeared to open to human rights concessions when Biden initially took office and was still maintaining a tough stance and promising to recalibrate US-Saudi relations. In what some analysts called a "peace offering," MBS released Loujain Al-Hathloul, a prominent women's rights activist who attracted global attention for defying Saudi Arabia's ban on women driving. She was arrested in May 2018 and released after 1,001 days in prison. Trump had shown little interest in Al-Hathloul's plight, but the Biden administration appeared to press for her release. Senior Saudi officials reportedly viewed Al-Hathloul's release as a relatively low-risk gesture of goodwill toward a seemingly hostile US administration. There were also signs that Saudi officials were willing to release additional political prisoners, such as Abdulrahman Al-Sadhan, who was sentenced to twenty years in prison for running a Twitter account critical of the kingdom. Speaking to *The Hill*, Al-Sadhan's sister reported that Biden's tough rhetoric offered glimmers of hope; around the time of Al-Hathloul's release, her brother called the family saying he expected to be freed from jail.[48]

Unfortunately, Al-Sadhan's situation changed rapidly once Biden announced that he would not be sanctioning MBS. "Clearly there wasn't enough accountability to the brutal murder of the journalist Jamal Khashoggi," Al-Sadhan's sister said. "That, by itself, has emboldened the Saudi officials to continue committing human rights abuses." More generally, America's eventual acquiescence may have ultimately emboldened MBS to ramp up human rights violations. After Biden reversed course on US-Saudi policy, any attempt at human rights pressure lost credibility, enabling MBS to continue targeting dissidents with impunity. "[The Saudis have] had more than eight months now to size up the administration," said the foreign policy analyst Bruce Riedel to *The Hill*, "and they've come to the conclusion that it's not serious on this issue."[49]

In all, America's reaction to the assassination of Jamal Khashoggi fits well with a relational theory of international shaming. Ultimately, enforcement costs from damaging a valuable strategic partnership outweighed any potential benefit from human rights improvements. However, the Khashoggi case

48. Kelly 2021.
49. Kelly 2021.

also reflects a missed opportunity: had American policymakers displayed the political will to prioritize human rights over strategic cooperation, Saudi leaders might have taken human rights criticism more seriously.

Iran

BACKGROUND

The Islamic Republic of Iran is a hybrid regime that includes elements of both electoral democracy and theocratic authoritarianism, with ultimate power held by "Supreme Leader" Ayatollah Ali Khamene'i. The regime is widely criticized for constraining civil liberties and abusing human rights. In 2020, Freedom House gave Iran an overall score of 17 out of 100 (7 out of 40 for political rights and 10 out of 60 for civil liberties).[50] The current regime was established following the Islamic Revolution of 1979, which not only succeeded in removing the dictatorial Pahlavi regime but also introduced far-reaching social, economic, and political changes to Iranian society. Following the revolution, Iran became a major adversary of the United States and many other Western countries.

Stoning was practically unheard of in Iran before 1979. The practice was first introduced shortly after the Islamic Revolution as part of a broad "anti-corruption" campaign that aimed to combat "cultural counterrevolution" by cleansing the postrevolutionary society of any infiltration of "Western" gender relations.[51] Stoning was then codified in law with the passing of the Islamic Penal Code in 1983. The Code prescribes stoning as the punishment for adultery and specifies the details of how it should be performed. Article 102 states that men shall be buried up to their waists and women up to their breasts for execution. Article 104 states that the stones used should "not be large enough to kill the person by one or two strikes; nor should they be so small that they could not be defined as stones (pebbles)." At the same time, the Code stipulates that adultery convictions require multiple confessions or eyewitnesses, a burden of proof that is practically impossible to achieve. Partly for this reason, adultery convictions—and by extension stoning sentences—are extremely rare.

Stoning has been highly controversial in Iran since its inception.[52] Immensely unpopular among domestic and foreign populations alike, the

---

50. Repucci 2020.
51. Paidar 1997, 345; Yeganeh 1993.
52. Abbasgholizadeh 2007.

penalty was rarely enforced and typically commuted to other punishments.[53] Stoning was put back on the agenda during the presidency of the reformist Mohammad Khatami (1997–2005). In December 2002, while in negotiations with the European Union, Iran imposed an official moratorium on stoning, while again keeping the law officially "on the books." Under hard-line president Mahmoud Ahmadinejad (2005–2013), stoning remained taboo, but the checks that had kept lower-level judges from imposing the punishment dissolved. By the time Sakineh's case captured international attention, at least nine women and two men were awaiting stoning sentences in Iran.

Sakineh Mohammadi Ashtiani[54] was born around 1968 in Osku, a rural area of East Azerbaijan Province in Iran.[55] She is a member of the Azeri ethnic minority and a mother to two children.[56] In 2005, Sakineh's husband, Ebrahim Ghaderzadeh, aged forty-four, was murdered via electrocution by his cousin Isa Taheri. Sakineh was charged and convicted as an accessory to murder under article 612 and sentenced to the maximum of ten years in prison.[57] Her conviction was later commuted to a lesser charge of "complicity in murder," and her sentence was reduced to five years, the maximum allotted for this charge.

In May 2006, apparently arising out of the investigations into her husband's murder, Sakineh was convicted of "illicit relations" and given ninety-nine lashes.[58] Despite this conviction, a different court recharged her with "adultery while married"—a more serious offense. Despite a lack of evidence, Sakineh was convicted based on a legal loophole known as *elm-e ghazi*, or the judge's "knowledge" or "intuition."[59] On September 10, 2006, in a split decision, the court sentenced her to death by stoning.[60]

---

53. Judges were encouraged to find alternative punishments for adultery, but some low-level courts—usually clustered in particular provinces like Tabriz—ordered it anyway. We do not know how many stonings took place between the ratification of the Islamic Penal Code in 1983 and 2002 because they were conducted secretly in private prison compounds and the media was prohibited from reporting on them. Ultimately, leaks from prisons and other covert sources indicated that at least two dozen stonings occurred. Ibid.; Sadr 2010.

54. Following campaign materials, I refer to Sakineh Mohammadi Ashtiani and her son by their first names to avoid confusion.

55. Amnesty International 2010.

56. Lévy 2010.

57. Amnesty International 2010.

58. Ibid.

59. Article 105 of the Islamic Penal code allows a judge to rule according to his own "intuition" if his ruling is based on documented evidence. Critics argue that these rulings are often biased and faulty, stemming from the judges' perception instead of hard evidence. Terman and Fijabi 2010.

60. Amnesty International 2010.

In 2007, Sakineh's son Sajjad secured the assistance of Mohammad Mostafaie, an Iranian defense attorney known for his advocacy in cases of adultery and juvenile executions.[61] Mostafaie agreed to take up Sakineh's case and served as her lawyer until he was forced to flee to Norway in August 2010 at the height of the global campaign surrounding his case. Sajjad also attracted the interest of Mina Ahadi, an Iranian expatriate and human rights activist living in Germany, who played a major role in publicizing Sakineh's case worldwide.

SHAMERS

In 2010, having exhausted domestic avenues for recourse, Ahadi and Mostafaie used their connections in the transnational human rights network to elicit global attention to Sakineh's case. By the end of their "Save Sakineh Campaign," officials in at least forty countries had publicly condemned her sentence, including Iran's adversaries in North America and Europe as well as allies such as Brazil. In this section, I compare the strategic incentives driving Iran's friends and enemies to intervene in Sakineh's case. For Western countries, the combination of behavioral preferences, metanorm pressures, and stigma incentives led to swift, unequivocal, and defamatory shaming efforts. In Brazil, metanorm pressure and possibly behavioral preferences induced President Luiz Inácio Lula da Silva to interfere and risk Brazil's budding partnership with Iran; however, the rhetorical tone of his intervention was markedly less stigmatizing and offensive than the rhetoric of Western countries.

The United States, North America, and Europe

Sakineh's stoning sentence was condemned throughout Europe and North America, including by officials in the United Kingdom, Canada, Italy, France, Spain, Sweden, Norway, Finland, Denmark, Iceland, the United States, and the European Parliament.[62] Western shaming efforts were rooted in a synergistic combination of behavioral preferences, metanorm pressures, and political hostility toward Iran.

First, behavioral motivations were strong by virtue of the visceral disgust conjured by stoning. It is not difficult to see why many people, including

---

61. Iran Solidarity 2010.

62. *Agence France-Presse* 2010; Akin 2010; International Committee against Stoning 2010; *RFI* 2010; *EFE News Service* 2010; *Europe 1* 2010; *CNN* Wire Staff 2010; European Parliament 2010.

foreign policymakers, preferred a strong norm prohibiting the practice. It is also likely that political leaders were genuinely horrified by Sakineh's plight. Here was a poor mother and member of a marginalized ethnic minority who had been sentenced to die, in one of the most horrific ways possible, for what most people in the West do not consider a crime. Some political figures even adopted the case as a personal cause. French first lady Carla Bruni-Sarkozy, for example, wrote a public letter to Sakineh promising, "France will not abandon you."[63]

Second, activists and media outlets were able to mobilize tremendous interest and outrage from Western publics, animating metanorm pressures on governments to intervene in Sakineh's case. Resembling Clifford Bob's account in *Marketing of Rebellion*, Mina Ahadi formulated a media-savvy outreach strategy complete with a compelling story of horrific abuse, captivating photos of the victim, and emotional pleas from Sakineh's children as they fought to save her.[64] The campaign also relied heavily on what Kyla Jo McEntire and her colleagues call "motivational frames," which "motivate individuals to act by creating feelings of agency and efficacy—suggesting that they can act, and that their actions can create the desired outcomes."[65] Sakineh's story captivated audiences precisely because her stoning sentence was imminent but not inevitable. Ahadi and others insisted that Western publics had the power to save Sakineh, if only they would generate enough outrage. The human rights community was nearly unanimous on this point, expressing little doubt that Western pressure would be helpful and effective in this case.

Such narratives fueled considerable public concern, turning the "Save Sakineh" campaign into a cause célèbre throughout Europe, Canada, and the United States. In the months between July 2010 and January 2011, Sakineh's name was printed in over 300 newspapers worldwide. Protests on her behalf took place in over 100 cities around the world. A petition for her release drew 137,000 signatures, including from celebrities like Michael Douglas, Annie Lennox, and Lindsay Lohan.[66] Media outlets not only covered the story but assumed an activist role, starting their own petitions and letter-writing campaigns.[67]

---

63. *RFI* 2010.
64. Bob 2005.
65. McEntire, Leiby, and Krain 2015, 411.
66. Spivak 2010.
67. Fletcher 2010a. Martin Fletcher from *The Times* (London) and Saeed Kamali Dehghan from *The Guardian* covered Sakineh's case extensively for months, and both took credit

As the campaign gained momentum, it demanded the attention of Western governments. Regardless of their personal beliefs, leaders had enormous incentives to intervene in Sakineh's case. Otherwise, it is difficult to apprehend why Sakineh in particular commanded such a spotlight, given that at least eleven other individuals were awaiting stoning sentences in Iran but had gone mostly unnoticed. The distinctive attention to Sakineh's case emerged, in large part, from metanorm pressures that her advocates generated by promoting her case on what Clifford Bob terms the "global morality market."[68]

Finally, the widely felt animosity toward Iran among both leaders and citizens reinforced the urge to stigmatize the Islamic Republic. Unlike Saudi Arabia, where stoning is similarly legal and rare, Iran was easy to condemn.[69] Not only were there negligible enforcement costs, but undermining the legitimacy of the Islamic Republic had been a central element in America's long-standing campaign to destabilize the regime. Indeed, Sakineh's case featured many of the general themes—religious extremism, oppression of women, brutality, and backwardness—that featured prominently in Western narratives demonizing the Islamic Republic.[70] And when the case ignited in 2010, the Islamic Republic was already receiving intense scrutiny for its contested 2009 presidential election and its controversial nuclear program. Against this backdrop, Sakineh's advocates leveraged popular and political antipathy toward Iran, turning Sakineh into a symbol of the regime's brutality. In the words of one commentator, Sakineh was a "microcosm of all that the rest of the world recognizes is so terribly and glaringly wrong with Iran."[71]

Behavioral rewards, metanorm pressures, and stigma incentives rarely work independently. In Sakineh's case, the intensity of Western shaming emerged from a mutually reinforcing synergy between the three. While mobilizing metanorms, activists animated behavioral preferences by disseminating information about Sakineh's plight. Widespread public outrage encouraged Western politicians to take a strong denunciatory stance, while the fact that the perpetrator was Iran—a long-standing adversary for many Western governments—nullified any enforcement costs that might arise from harsh condemnation. At the same time, many of Sakineh's advocates

---

for breaking the story and sparking the international campaign (ibid.). *The Times* was especially active, publishing 538 articles mentioning Sakineh's name, usually with Martin Fletcher's byline.

68. Bob 2005.
69. Hubbard 2020.
70. Moallem 2005.
71. *The Times* 2010.

were also hostile to the Islamic Republic. In fact, Ahadi confirmed that the campaign was an *intentional* attack on the Iranian government. She wrote, "This is a movement against the Islamic regime of Iran, which perpetrates murder and crime."[72]

As a result of these synergies, Western shaming was particularly harsh and inflammatory and often sensationalist. Shaming actors, including government officials and activists, used highly derogatory and antagonistic rhetoric, calling Iran "barbaric," "uncivilized," and medieval."[73] Some of these denunciations extended to Islam in general, especially those made by Ahadi, a known secular activist who once wrote an autobiography entitled: *I Have Apostatized: Why I Fight for Freedom and against Islam.*[74]

At times, Western shamers also propagated claims that were inaccurate or lacked credibility. For example, some of Sakineh's advocates vehemently denied that Sakineh was charged with being an accessory to murder, despite evidence to the contrary.[75] The media frenzy surrounding Sakineh's case fueled sensationalist and misleading reporting. In one instance, *The Times* of London printed a photo claiming to depict Sakineh "unveiled," but in fact it showed Susan Hejrat, an Iranian exile living in Sweden and an anti-regime activist. Sakineh's son Sajjad claimed that the incident caused his mother to be sentenced to ninety-nine lashes for disseminating a photo of herself without hijab, another claim that was widely circulated yet unverified. Similarly, informed by Ahadi, several outlets falsely reported in December 2010 that Sakineh had been freed, only to issue retractions when they realized their mistake.[76]

This kind of misinformation led to internal strife among Sakineh's advocates, particularly between Ahadi and Sakineh's lawyer Mohammad Mostafaie. "Being dishonest in human rights work always hurts human rights work," Roya Boroumand, an activist involved in the campaign, told me. She added:

> Human rights advocates don't have a lot of power. But they have the moral superiority. It is a psychological war. We don't have bombs. In this

72. Ahadi 2010.

73. Burt 2010.

74. Originally published in German as *Ich habe abgeschworen: Warum ich für die Freiheit und gegen den Islam kämpfe.*

75. Not only did Ahadi and other campaigners downplay the fact that Sakineh had been found guilty of being an accessory to murder, but they may have intentionally obscured court documentation suggesting as much. Personal interview (anonymous).

76. Dehghan and Black 2010.

psychological war we have to have the moral high ground in order to sometimes, rarely, make a difference. Once you start messing with the facts, you are losing and giving ammunition to the other side. Because then they know you are a liar too.[77]

As I discuss in the next section, these inaccuracies were quickly detected by Iranian officials, who used them to discredit the campaign.

Brazil

That Iran's Western adversaries were eager to chastise Iran is not surprising. But few people expected Brazil to join them. On July 31, 2010, President Lula offered Sakineh a home in exile in Brazil. The announcement was reported internationally as an unexpected twist, not only in Sakineh's fate but also in Brazil-Iran relations.

Unlike Western countries, which had nothing to lose by intervening in Sakineh's case, Brazil had a friendly relationship with Iran. At the time Ahmadinejad was making a concerted effort to extend Iran's influence in Latin America; six new embassies had been opened in the region from 2005 to 2009.[78] Iran was paying special attention to Brazil, the largest economy in the region. In November 2009, Ahmadinejad became the first Iranian president to visit Brasília since the Islamic Revolution. For Brazil's leadership, a relationship with Iran was part and parcel with an overall foreign policy ambition to achieve international independence and partnerships beyond the United States.[79] In this spirit, Brazilian president Lula publicly defended Iran's right to peaceful nuclear energy and voted against UN sanctions, infuriating the United States.[80] The flourishing Brazil-Iran relationship, along with Brazil's long-standing policy of non-interference, led to widespread surprise when Lula interfered in Sakineh's case. Indeed, only a few days before the announcement, Lula had repeated that Iran's domestic laws needed to be respected.[81]

Multiple forces probably contributed to Lula's about-face. One adviser alluded to something like behavioral incentives when explaining Lula's change of heart. "He listened to his conscience and was moved by her story," the adviser told the *New York Times*. It is certainly possible that Lula had a

77. Roya Boroumand, interview with the author, April 18, 2015.
78. Arnson, Esfandiari, and Stubits 2010.
79. Ibid.
80. Leyne 2010; *The Economist* 2010.
81. Barrionuevo 2010.

genuine desire to save Sakineh and that this preference was strong enough to risk confronting Iran.[82]

Importantly, the widespread outrage ignited by Sakineh's case among the Brazilian public generated significant metanorm pressures. A petition on her behalf circulated in Brazil and drew 114,000 signatures, including signatures from many Brazilian public figures such as former president Fernando Henrique Cardoso. Public protests used slogans like "And Now, Lula?," demanding action from the government on Sakineh's case. Some commentators speculated that Lula offered Sakineh asylum as a response to these domestic pressures.[83]

In chapter 2, I explained that while some governments may criticize strategic partners under conditions of strong behavioral or metanorm pressures, they tend to do so in less offensive, demanding, and sensationalist ways. Even as he strove to assuage domestic outrage and protect Sakineh's life, Lula ultimately wanted to maintain positive relations with Iran. Thus, unlike denunciations from Europe and North America, his offer was carefully worded and respectful, characterizing Sakineh more as an inconvenience for the Iranian government than as a victim of its cruelties.[84] "If my friendship and affection for the president of Iran [Mahmoud Ahmadinejad] matters," Lula said, "and if this woman is causing problems there, we will welcome her here in Brazil."[85]

TARGET

In chapter 3, I posited that leaders respond to international human rights pressure by weighing three kinds of inducements: behavioral interests (the value they extract from norm-violating behavior itself), relational costs (such as undermining valued geopolitical partnerships), and domestic reactions (such as a defensive reaction favoring defiance to international pressure).

First, leaders must consider their preferences and interests in the norm-violating behavior itself, *ex ante* any external criticism. In this case, the evidence suggests that behavioral preferences were not a major factor and, if anything, discouraged Iranian leadership from carrying out Sakineh's stoning sentence. Sakineh herself posed no material threat; she was a provincial, apolitical figure, irrelevant to security or stability concerns. Unlike

---

82. Ibid.
83. *The Economist* 2010; Camarena 2010.
84. *The Economist* 2010.
85. Barrionuevo 2010.

challenges to its acts of political repression, Iranian leadership had little material interest in executing Sakineh. A more likely possibility is that Iranian leadership shared an ideological commitment to stoning as prescribed by traditional Islamic jurisprudence. But even this is dubious. Stoning is an intensely taboo topic in the Iranian public sphere, in part because the practice is so widely despised. Although some officials may value the policy for ideological reasons—such as the local judges who initially sentenced Sakineh—such preferences are hardly widespread among top-level elites. This aversion partially explains why stoning is so seldom carried out in Iran, even for those who are sentenced. In similar cases outside the global spotlight, officials typically commute stoning sentences to other punishments.[86]

Once Sakineh's case captured international attention, two other sets of incentives became important. First, Western shaming provoked a defensive reaction from Iranian officials, particularly from hard-line factions of the political elite and their supporters, who viewed it as a hostile attempt to defame Islam and Iran in the eyes of the world. As I explained in chapters 3 and 5, foreign condemnation can "internationalize" a particular issue in the target state, linking it to national status and honor. When this happens, international human rights pressure becomes associated with foreign domination. Western shaming in Sakineh's case had all the features that encourage such a defensive reaction: activists like Ahadi explicitly conveyed hostile intentions toward the Islamic Republic, acknowledging that their goal was to destabilize the regime. Western governments and media used antagonistic and stigmatizing rhetoric, calling Iran (and Islam) uncivilized and barbaric. And human rights pressure evoked powerful historical narratives, particularly around the Islamic Revolution, wherein Western interference (especially in sexual matters) was closely tied to cultural imperialism, counterrevolution, and threats to national security.

Insofar as Western shaming transformed Sakineh from an apolitical figure into a fulcrum of international conflict, releasing Sakineh became a political liability. For hard-liners, succumbing to Western domination was intolerable, and the more Western actors interfered in the campaign the less willing these leaders were to capitulate. Ramin Mehmanparast, a spokesperson for the foreign ministry, articulated the political stakes this way: "The other side is only looking for pretexts against the Islamic establishment, and if . . . we give in to their demands . . . there will be nothing left of the revolution and

---

86. Sadr 2010.

the establishment."[87] Indeed, defying Western condemnation was not only acceptable but *rewarding* insofar as it bolstered the narrative of Iran as an Islamic protagonist standing up to imperialist enemies. In a stump speech to his base in Gorgan in October 2010, Ahmadinejad referred to Sakineh to malign the United States, which he said used "humane values as a tool to dominate other nations."[88] After linking the campaign to America's military campaign in the Middle East—a direct attack on Iran's status and security interests—Ahmadinejad heralded the "Iranian nation's great revolution" leading the global resistance.[89] By framing the situation this way, Ahmadinejad and other hard-liners effectively constrained the judiciary from making any move that could be seen as succumbing to Western pressure.

On the other hand, pressure from Iran's allies—especially Brazil—meant something very different than pressure from Western nations. Unlike the latter, Brazil was an important ally to Iran and one of the few to defend its nuclear program.[90] Brazil's disapproval imposed greater relational costs on Iran by threatening this valued geopolitical partnership. The enforcement costs that Brazil would incur also made Lula's criticism more credible than that of Western officials; his interference embarrassed Iran and undermined its self-styled reputation as an anti-imperialist leader of the Global South. On the domestic side, pressure from Brazil could not arouse the same kind of defensive reactions; it lacked the hostile intentions, inflammatory rhetoric, and historical connotations associated with pressure from the West.

Not surprisingly, Lula's intervention garnered a very different reaction from Iranian officials than criticisms from Western nations. In response to Brazil's offer of asylum, Mehmanparast called Lula "a very humane and emotional person" who had been misinformed on the case.[91] In contrast, the conservative newspaper *Kayhan*—widely considered the mouthpiece of Supreme Leader Ayatollah Khamene'i—responded to Carla Bruni's involvement by calling her a "French prostitute" and a "home wrecker."[92]

These competing pressures—from the West and Brazil—culminated in a dilemma for Iranian leadership. Criticism from Brazil imposed direct and indirect relational costs, incentivizing Iranian officials to release Sakineh. At the same time, Brazil's involvement only emboldened Western campaigners,

87. *Emirates 24/7* 2010.
88. *Islamic Republic of Iran News Network* 2010b.
89. Ibid.
90. Leyne 2010; *The Economist* 2010.
91. *Associated Press* 2010.
92. *Islamic Republic of Iran News Network* 2010a.

generating defensive reactions and the temptation to defy. Haleh Esfandiari summed up the conundrum this way:

> There are those in the regime who wish this whole affair would disappear because they see it as an embarrassment for Iran, and there are those who argue that the government should not cave in to international pressure and are looking for ways to carry out the sentence and hang her.[93]

Faced with this conundrum, Iranian officials pursued a strategy of *deflection*: deploying counterarguments that attempted to justify their actions and delegitimize foreign criticism, while carefully avoiding the issue of stoning directly so as not to alienate Brazil. This involved a two-pronged strategy.

First, Iran's spokespeople attempted to normalize Sakineh's case as a *murder* conviction, thereby defending their actions as a criminal matter and not one of human rights. "This dossier looks like many other dossiers that exist in other countries," Mehmanparast told *Press TV*, Iran's English-language television outlet.[94] "If in human societies we were expected to release those who commit serious crimes, we would also have to ask you to release your murderers."[95] Iranian officials also put Sakineh herself on state television four times, a startling decision given the taboo nature of the subject. In each appearance, Sakineh confessed to aiding the murder of her husband and denounced Western interferers, referring to Mostafaie and Ahadi by name. "Ms. Mina Ahadi, this is none of your business," she said in one video. "I committed a sin." One particularly horrific "documentary," produced by the English-language outlet *Press TV*, showed Sakineh reenacting the murder of her husband in gruesome detail, with her son Sajjad playing the role of his dead father. To clarify, Mehmanparast and other judicial spokespeople never explicitly denied that Sakineh had been sentenced to stoning for adultery. But they were careful not to mention stoning directly, saying only that "the verdict regarding the extramarital affairs has stopped and it's being reviewed."[96] Sakineh's "death sentence," Mehmanparast insisted, was related to the murder charges against her.[97]

Second, Iran went on the offensive by discrediting Sakineh's advocates as enemy political operatives. Here, officials leveraged the hostile intentions, sensationalism, and inaccuracies propagated by Western shamers as

93. Esfandiari 2010.
94. *Al Arabiya* 2010.
95. *Radio Zamaneh* 2010.
96. *Al Arabiya* 2010; *New York Times* 2010.
97. *Al Arabiya* 2010.

rhetorical resources to delegitimize the campaign. Special attention was paid to Ahadi, who was accused of manipulating Sakineh's case to attack, stigmatize, and turn public opinion against Iran. Officials emphasized Ahadi's past involvement with Komaleh, an armed Kurdish separatist group,[98] warning: "The West must be careful not to allow itself to be misled by people who seek to harm our reputation."[99] Iran's publicists also repeatedly gloated about the "dissemination of half-truths about the case by Western officials and media outlets," which they saw as proof of the "Western campaign to undermine the Islamic Republic system."[100] "The hostile Western media campaign regarding the case," Malek Ajdar Sharifi, head of the judiciary in East Azerbaijan, explained, "aims to invent poisonous propaganda against the Islamic Republic of Iran rather than sticking to their main duty of objectively disseminating information."[101] Finally, Iranian officials accused Western nations of hypocrisy, reinforcing the perception of hostile intentions while cultivating a sense of outrage. Speaking to a group of Muslim students during his New York City tour, President Ahmadinejad compared the "Western media storm" over Sakineh to the silence over Teresa Lewis, a forty-one-year-old grandmother from Virginia on death row.[102]

It is important to emphasize that Iran's reaction to international shaming went beyond mere "denial" in the sense discussed by Risse, Ropp, and Sikkink in their "spiral model" and rather resembled the proactive tactics of what IR scholars describe as "rival networks" or "norm antipreneurs."[103] In many ways, Iran's countershaming strategy mirrored the "Save Sakineh" campaign, complete with propaganda films, media outreach, and other coordinated PR material.

OUTCOME AND AFTERMATH

As chapter 3 explained, deflection provides a way to ameliorate both compliance and defiance pressures. Indeed, Iran's response appeared effective in assuaging Brazilian leadership, at least temporarily.[104] For shaming coun-

---

98. Vision of the Islamic Republic of Iran 2010.

99. Fletcher 2010b.

100. Press TV 2011.

101. Press TV 2010.

102. Fletcher 2010c; *Islamic Republic News Agency* 2010.

103. Bob 2012; Bloomfield and Scott 2016.

104. Once Dilma Rousseff took over from Lula as president, Iran-Brazil relations cooled, partly over human rights (Gómez 2012).

tries, leaders tend to be more lenient when pressuring a friend; they lower the bar for what constitutes adequate compliance. Iran's counterargument that Sakineh was merely a criminal awaiting punishment for murdering her husband provided rhetorical cover for Lula to defend against metanorm pressures from the Brazilian public. And the fact that Iranian officials ultimately decided not to execute Sakineh could be viewed as a capitulation to allies like Brazil (as well as Turkey, which reportedly engaged in substantial private diplomacy behind the scenes).[105]

At the same time, by counterattacking, Iranian officials satisfied internal forces that refused to cave to Western pressure. Not only were Western shamers not assuaged by Iran's response, but they grew more indignant and intensified their efforts. A perverse dynamic evolved in which Iran's resistance outraged Western activists, fueling more intense shaming efforts, which in turn generated more resistance.

In some ways, the Western reaction is puzzling. If Western pressure only fueled Iran's resistance to releasing Sakineh, why did it continue after Iran's stance became clear? Certainly, many activists believed that what they were doing was effective in making progress toward the goal of Iran releasing Sakineh. However, as I explained in chapter 2, shaming can be rational even if it is not expected to result in the desired change of behavior. When actors are motivated primarily by stigma imposition, resistance to shaming is welcome insofar as it serves the ultimate purpose of tarnishing the target's legitimacy. Similarly, when metanorms are the primary concern, the target's continued deviance provides additional opportunities for shamers to showcase their identity as human rights defenders. This was probably the case for Sakineh's Western advocates, for whom resistance provided all the more reason to shame Iran.

At times, the incentives to vilify Iran (stigma imposition) and satisfy local audiences (metanorms) appeared to outweigh the goal of protecting Sakineh and her closest associates (behavioral interests). In one instance, two German journalists, Marcus Hellwig and Jens Koch, entered Iran illegally on tourist visas, hoping to interview Sakineh's son Sajjad and lawyer Houtan Kian, who replaced Mohammad Mostafaie after he fled to Norway to escape persecution from the Iranian government. The reporters worked for *Bild am Sonntag*, the largest-selling German national Sunday tabloid,

---

105. Facing domestic pressure, Turkish prime minister Recep Tayyip Erdoğan asked his foreign minister, Ahmet Davutoğlu, to try to stop the execution of Sakineh. Following Erdoğan's instructions, Davutoğlu launched an intensive diplomatic effort by phone with his Iranian counterpart, Manohucher Mottaki (Haberturk 2010).

described as "notorious for its mix of gossip, inflammatory language, and sensationalism."[106] To plan their trip, the journalists consulted heavily with Ahadi, who put them in contact with Sajjad and Kian and arranged the interview. Ahadi also volunteered to serve as a remote interpreter by phone, despite knowing as early as August 20 that Kian was under surveillance by Iranian intelligence, including the monitoring of his phone calls. Shortly after the interview started on October 10, 2010, security forces raided Kian's office and arrested all four individuals. Mehmanparast later said that the two journalists "were arrested because they had a link to a foreign anti-revolution network" in Germany. Hellwig and Koch were released after four months in detention as part of a deal whereby Germany aided the transfer of up to $1.5 billion from past sanctions to reach Iran.[107] Sajjad was eventually released on bail and began cooperating with Iranian officials. Kian spent three years in detention, during which he was starved and tortured.

Ahadi told me that she does not regret getting on the telephone that day. When I asked her if she ever felt responsible for the arrest of Sajjad and Kian, she said no, explaining: "Anyone who says I was responsible doesn't understand the nature of dictatorships."[108] For Western campaigners, any negative development in Sakineh's case could be divorced from their actions and instead attributed to the barbarity of the Islamic regime, thus advancing the stigma operation. In this sense, the suffering of Sakineh and her closest associates was beneficial insofar as it reinforced the cruelty of the regime and provided fresh content on a high-demand story.

Ahadi and other activists never officially ended the campaign to save Sakineh. However, once Sajjad and Kian were arrested—and presumably stopped cooperating with Ahadi—news coverage and activism slowed to a trickle. Sakineh was eventually released on March 19, 2014, nearly four years after the campaign started and three years since it dissolved completely. She served a total of nine years in prison, four more than her original sentence.

After some debate, the 2013 Islamic Penal Code removed stoning as the prescribed punishment for adultery, but it made no other specific provision on how to punish this crime. Instead, it now refers such cases to valid Islamic sources and fatwas, but these sources mandate that adultery be punished by stoning. By inserting ambiguity into the Code, Iranian officials could mislead international audiences into thinking that the punishment has been

---

106. Steininger 2012.
107. Boyes 2011; *Indian Express* 2011; Marquart et al. 2011.
108. Mina Ahadi, interview with the author, April 30, 2015.

eradicated while in reality stoning remains in Iran's legal framework. As one commentator put it, stoning has "merely been moved to a more obscure position so as not to attract the attention of critics."[109]

Indeed, if the international uproar around Sakineh achieved anything, it was not the reform of Iran's stoning laws but their obfuscation in order to avoid the global spotlight. For some theorists, Iranian officials' "denial" is progress in itself, but this is not exactly the case: they never said that stoning had been abolished or was a violation of human rights but simply took measures to prevent international criticisms of it.

DISCUSSION

The Sakineh case presents an intriguing puzzle for conventional theories of international shaming. Despite intense compliance pressures, Iran resisted in bombastic ways. Typical explanations for norm resistance, particularly those centering on material interests or ideological commitments, come up short.

A relational framework enables a more satisfying explanation for both the causes and consequences of the "Save Sakineh" campaign. For shamers, a combination of behavioral motives (deeply felt repugnance for stoning), metanorms (a cacophony of fervent activism, media publicity, and public outrage), and stigma imposition (a desire to vilify the Islamic regime) produced enormous international pressures on Iran. For Iranian officials, international shaming unleashed domestic political forces that constrained policymakers' ability to respond to foreign demands, not by reminding them of some material interest or ideological commitment to stoning *per se* but rather by invoking an imperative to defy foreign, especially Western, demands. At the same time, the unexpected involvement of Brazil and other allies imposed relational costs on Iran. To manage the resulting dilemma of crosscutting incentives, Iranian leadership turned to an overall strategy akin to deflection.

The case also illustrates how international shaming and resistance reinforce one another, with each side acting in ways that advance their own goals while galvanizing the opposition. This "shame-defiance spiral" fueled the political escalation of a seemingly apolitical case, ultimately (re)victimizing Sakineh and her closest advocates. To clarify, I categorize the Sakineh case as one of deflection, not full-on defiance, because stonings did not increase following the international shaming of Iran. If Iranian officials were

109. Nayyeri 2011.

dissuaded from stoning Sakineh or others, it was probably owing to interference from Iran's allies (Brazil and Turkey), not the efforts of European
advocates. Of course, leaders in Brazil and Turkey were clearly pressured
by domestic publics and other audiences who were energized by Ahadi's
campaign. Thus, the "Save Sakineh" campaign demonstrates the dilemma
at the heart of naming and shaming: the kind of rhetoric that successfully
demands media attention, sparks public outrage, and mobilizes international
pressure is the same rhetoric that flares up indignation and defiance. I return
to the "shamer's dilemma" in the concluding chapter.

7

Conclusion

In the last four decades, scholars and activists have argued that international "naming and shaming" can improve human rights conditions around the world. When a repressive government violates the rights of its citizens, the so-called international community—states, advocacy groups, media outlets, international organizations—can respond by exerting moral pressure on that government from the outside: shining the global spotlight, condemning abuses, and urging reform. More and more, however, the faith in the power of shaming has come under challenge. Many of the most egregious violations of human rights seem to go unpunished. When punishment does occur, not only is shaming often ineffective, but it can also backfire by provoking resistance and worsening human rights practices. How can international actors effectively enforce human rights commitments? When does shaming lead to an improvement in rights conditions, and when does it backfire?

This book has examined human rights enforcement between states. I have argued that shaming human rights enforcement is a fundamentally relational interaction: *deployed by* particular actors, it *targets* specific actors, *in front of* particular audiences. If we want to know when international shaming promotes compliance with human rights standards and when it backfires in defiance, we must attend to the relational context in which it occurs. Geopolitical relations shape both the causes and consequences of this process.

I first addressed the behavior of potential shamers. States have multiple reasons to punish perceived human rights abuse, even if they care little about human rights *per se*. Leaders are rewarded by third-party audiences, such as domestic publics, for punishing violators (metanorm pressures). They can also attempt to degrade the target's legitimacy and status, which can be beneficial in an adversarial relationship. Two key implications follow. First, shaming can be rational even when it is not expected to induce compliance. Second, states will shame their geopolitical rivals more often, and more harshly, than their partners.

Political relationships also moderate responses to international human rights pressure. Leaders in the target state are incentivized to comply with shaming that comes from friends and allies in order to avoid the relational costs associated with the disapproval of other countries. Accusations made by strategic partners are also broadly viewed as more credible and capable of inflicting greater reputational damage on target regimes. In contrast, leaders have few incentives to comply with shaming by adversaries, as there are no relational benefits at stake and their accusations are less credible. It can even be rational for leaders of a target state to defy the accusations by doubling down on violations, as doing so garners social rewards from audiences that associate shaming with international domination, particularly the domestic public. When pressure stems from both friends and adversaries, target states avoid outright compliance or defiance. Instead, they often opt for a strategy of deflection: denying accusations while stopping short of increasing violations or rejecting the norm altogether.

In short, shaming is a profoundly political exercise, mediated by the strategic relationship between the shamer and the target. In many ways, this argument may appear straightforward and even banal. After all, scholars have known for decades that international norms take a backseat to material power and self-interests in world politics. What, then, is new or different about the current study? In this final chapter, I flesh out my contributions to at least four areas in IR: the motivations behind international shaming, NGOs and transnational advocacy, resistance to international norms, and the relationship between norms and power politics. Despite their initial familiarity, my findings intercede in these debates in ways that break from conventional wisdom. I close the book by providing practical guidance to those wanting to promote human rights abroad, including state actors and civil society.

Contributions and Implications

SHAMING MOTIVATIONS

One of the most pervasive assumptions in the literature on international human rights has to do with why actors punish perceived abuses. The idea is straightforward: actors value norm-compliant behavior and attempt to sanction defectors in order to deter future violations. In chapter 2, I described this logic as "behavioral motives" but also argued that there is more to the story. Actors publicly enforce norms not only out of an interest in the behavior of others but also to obtain social rewards for themselves. First, they may be responding to metanorms: norms that demand the enforcement of norms. Leaders often want to showcase their identity as human rights promoters in order to please audiences, especially in their own domestic context. One way they can do this is by punishing perceived violators abroad. Second, leaders may shame certain countries or their leaders in order to stigmatize them. Stigmatizing a state could degrade its status, with significant implications for other conventional geopolitical interests.

To be certain, many scholars have recognized something akin to metanorms and stigma motives in international human rights dynamics. But the full implications have yet to be appreciated. For instance, one insight stemming from this discussion is that some actors engage in shaming regardless of its expected effect on future violations. Even those scholars who acknowledge shaming's adverse consequences nonetheless assume that such consequences are unwanted. "Human rights activists," Jack Snyder writes, "do not desire or intend pushback from perpetrators," although they often anticipate it.[1] Snyder's account assumes that activists and other shamers would choose different tactics if only they fully internalized his argument about shaming's harmful consequences. What this view overlooks is the fact that advancing compliance is not the only goal of shaming actors; indeed, it is often not the primary goal. For those actors who are moved primarily by metanorms, the target's response to shaming is largely irrelevant. The point is not to change the target's behavior (although that may be a welcome side effect), but to collect social rewards through the very act of enforcement. For those motivated by stigma imposition, backlash is *welcomed* insofar as it brands the target as a human rights abuser, thus advancing the interests of the stigmatizer.

It is also important to note that stigma imposition and metanorms are not exclusive to state actors. Although we tend to think of NGOs as altruistic, driven solely by a moral commitment to human rights, scholars recognize that these organizations also have their own interests and priorities, such as survival, funding, or access. These interests may sometimes conflict with the goal of advancing human rights or democracy.[2] Less work has been done, however, on the ways in which stigma promotion and metanorms shape the work of

1. Snyder 2020a, 124–25.
2. Bush 2017; Cooley and Ron 2002; Hill, Moore, and Mukherjee 2013.

NGOs. Some activists may want to overthrow a foreign regime or showcase their involvement in a widely publicized case—desires that may or may not work to improve the actual human rights situation on the ground.

For example, in the "Save Sakineh" case presented in chapter 6, many of Sakineh's Western advocates clearly had an interest in stigmatizing the Islamic Republic. Many of the most outspoken activists were Iranian expatriates who fled their homeland during or shortly after the Islamic Revolution. Some, like Mina Ahadi, were quite open about their desire to overthrow the Islamic Republic and were involved in political organizations oriented toward this goal (see chapter 6). These activists employed shaming tactics and rhetoric that were particularly effective in stirring up Western hostility toward the regime, but not necessarily in protecting Sakineh or her family's well-being. This book has focused mainly on states, but extending the basic framework to nonstate actors could revise our understanding of NGOs and how they operate.

NGOs

My findings generate at least two other implications for the study of transnational human rights activism and organizations. First, I challenge widely held claims that international pressure empowers local human rights advocates. For many scholars, outside criticism is thought to extend legitimacy to local NGOs and advocates, broadening their basis of support and raising the likelihood of their success in mobilizing social movements (see chapter 1). Local groups, it is thought, seek connections within transnational networks and market their cause to foreign audiences precisely because they anticipate that global attention will bolster their cause at home.[3]

However, as I argue, international pressure can also delegitimize and disempower local activists, hindering their efforts. The results from the survey experiments in chapter 4 reveal that external shaming can backfire by suppressing popular support for human rights activism. When individuals respond defensively to foreign criticism of their country, they become less willing to contribute to human rights causes. Contrary to the view that international pressure widens the coalition for human rights, the evidence suggests a *narrowing* of support for mobilization.

International shaming can also delegitimize local activists by associating them with hostile foreign influences, leaving them vulnerable to state

3. Bob 2005.

repression. In chapter 6, I provided an example in the Sakineh case, where external involvement directly harmed Sakineh's closest advocates. Her first lawyer was forced to flee Iran, and her second lawyer was arrested and imprisoned for years owing to his associations with Mina Ahadi and other foreign agitators. Thus, the "boomerang" analogy is misleading inasmuch as international attention and transnational connections may become significant liabilities for domestic activists. Together, these two insights challenge the expectation that international shaming generates compliance pressures "from below."

The second implication has to do with international NGOs (INGOs). INGOs play a crucial role as mobilizers of metanorms as they pressure leaders to shame alleged violations abroad. For example, in Khashoggi's case, international human rights activists—as well as journalists, intellectuals, and other public figures—stirred up outrage among Western audiences and lobbied government officials to take action against Saudi Arabia, though these leaders were hesitant to do so. In the Sakineh case, international advocacy generated metanorm pressure on the Brazilian president, leading him to shame Iran when he probably would not have interfered otherwise. Pressure from Brazil was influential, as Brazil was a credible enforcer and capable of inflicting direct and indirect relational costs on Iran.

However, the actions of INGOs do not always have positive effects. In the same case, Western-based activists may have contributed to interventions by European and North American governments in ways that were unhelpful and even counterproductive. Western advocates' often sensationalist rhetoric to fuel massive public awareness and outrage over Sakineh's case was ultimately appropriated by Iranian officials to stir up a defensive, negative reaction. Put differently, INGOs mobilize metanorms in ways that are both helpful, in that they encourage states to pressure their friends and allies when they otherwise would not, and unhelpful when they fuel the kind of international shaming that is likely to catalyze a defiant reaction from the target state.

These two implications generate several avenues for future research on transnational advocacy. Scholars have long been interested in the conditions under which transnational advocacy is effective, and this book advances some additional hypotheses. For example, the identity and location of NGOs may matter for their ability to promote human rights. Western-based NGOs such as Amnesty International and Human Rights Watch are perhaps more likely to be perceived as surrogates for Western powers. NGOs embedded in the Global South, in contrast, might be perceived differently. This book has not explored this possibility in depth, but future research can test this hypothesis and extend the framework developed here.

ENDOGENOUS RESISTANCE OF NORMS

The theory also generates novel insights about normative conflict and contestation in world affairs. Much of the existing literature locates the roots of norm resistance in pre-established beliefs or preferences that override the desire for international approval.[4] In chapter 3, I described these preferences as "behavioral interests," because they correspond to the value or utility that actors gain from behaviors that happen to violate international norms. For example, leaders may resist international pressure to comply with the anti-torture norm because torture is an effective tactic to stay in power. Or they may resist norms promoting LGBT rights because they conflict with local traditions and beliefs. Simply put, leaders may resist compliance pressures because they prefer noncompliant practices.

In contrast, my theory demonstrates that it can be rational for leaders to resist norms regardless of their preferences regarding the content of the norm—indeed, even if they would have adopted the norm in the absence of overt pressure to do so—because international shaming alters the domestic political playing field in ways that reward resistance to outside demands. By provoking a defensive reaction in target audiences, foreign criticism can drive perceptual, attitudinal, and behavioral shifts vis-à-vis the norm in question. Not only do citizens in the target country dismiss foreign criticism as illegitimate, but they begin to value norm violation *qua* violation as a form of in-group solidarity and identity expression. A prominent defensive reaction introduces political resources and incentives that penalize policymakers for complying and reward those who outwardly resist. Thus, shaming is not merely irrelevant but counterproductive as it edges leaders away from compliance and toward defiance as a way to accrue legitimacy.

Although I am certainly not the first to acknowledge that shaming can stimulate resistance to international norms, my theory differs from others in emphasizing relational over substantive driving factors. For example, one prominent substantialist argument is the "norm congruence thesis," which looks to whether there is a "match" between an international norm and the target state's domestic environment.[5] Adler-Nissen, for instance, explains state responses to international stigmatization in part by highlighting "the

---

4. For a review see Cardenas 2004. Exceptions include Adler-Nissen 2014; Epstein 2012; Zarakol 2014.

5. Cloward 2016; Cortell and Davis 1996. For a critique of the norm congruence thesis, see Acharya 2004.

degree to which the norms underpinning the stigma are shared."[6] When they are not shared, states are more likely to reject and rebel against international normative pressures. Likewise, Fernando Nuñez-Mietz and Lucrecia Garcia Iommi argue that norm backlash is more likely when "the advocated norm clashes with prominent elements of the local culture"; in fact, they explicitly take this possibility as exogenous in their model of international advocacy.[7] Uganda resists recognizing LGBT rights, they argue, partly because the content of the underlying norm—acceptance of homosexuality—conflicts with the content of its local culture, which rejects homosexuality. Thus, the story fundamentally rests on what I call "behavioral interests": Uganda maintains preexisting preferences opposing LGBT rights that are derived from its local culture and exist *ex ante* any transnational advocacy. Transnational advocacy might energize these preferences, but it does not create them.

My purpose in this book has not been to disprove the norm congruence thesis or any other substantive theory. Clearly the substantive properties of norms and target states are important. Rather, what I wish to suggest is that responses to international shaming—as well as resistance and backlash to norms more generally—hinge not only on the *content* of norms but also on the relational *context* in which they are invoked. This aspect of the argument is most clearly demonstrated in chapter 4's analysis of the Universal Periodic Review, whose empirical design was able to differentiate norm content from relational context by controlling for the issue area in individual recommendations. Even when comparing recommendations addressing identical concerns—for example, torture—I found that normative pressure varies considerably (in both its causes and its consequences) depending on the relationship between the source and the target.

Similarly, in chapter 5, I found that American survey respondents were largely supportive of international human rights criticism—that is, until their own country was targeted. Even when shaming changed people's private views in a positive direction, it nonetheless inflamed nationalist sentiments and reduced support for advocacy efforts, thus undermining the potential for political mobilization. Importantly, these adverse effects can be found even among Democrats and those who are ideologically predisposed to support human rights or criminal justice reform. These patterns suggest that responses to human rights shaming hinge to an important extent on

6. Adler-Nissen 2014, 154.
7. Nuñez-Mietz and Garcia Iommi 2017, 6–7.

relational context, regardless of preexisting ideological beliefs or interests in human rights *per se.*

In brief, I argue that norm resistance is *endogenous* to the process of international shaming. That is, I move away from attributing noncompliance to autonomous forces that originate prior to or outside international interactions—such as the regime type or fixed local culture in the target state. Instead, I highlight the ways in which international shaming compels governments to resist norms, not out of an intrinsic desire to violate but because doing so confers legitimacy and social rewards within the domestic sphere.

I have focused on the target state's immediate response, but these insights have implications for more structural, long-term dynamics, including the evolution of norms and state identity. In the "spiral model" of normative change (see chapter 1), states may initially comply with human rights norms for tactical reasons but then internalize these norms over time as part of their own identity, institutionalizing and habituating them into their domestic structures. Defiance may exhibit a similar dynamic, in that shaming may encourage norm breaking as a strategic move that leads to the construction of oppositional domestic institutions, which eventually become internalized as constitutive of a state's political culture and identity. The Sakineh case is suggestive of this mechanism. Before her sentencing, stoning was hardly a pillar of Iranian identity. And yet it was their encounter with global shaming that led Iranian officials to defend the stoning law as critical to their religious authenticity and political autonomy. This endogenous, reiterative process could operate to entrench norm opposition in both the domestic and international spheres.[8]

THE POLITICIZATION PARADOX

Finally, this book opens new avenues for theorizing the relationship between norms and power in international relations. I have argued that shaming is an inherently political exercise, mediated by the preexisting relationship between shamer and target. When it comes to human rights violations, the need to protect important strategic relationships makes states hesitant to shame their friends and allies, but not to condemn rivals in order to inflict political damage. At the same time, strategic ties provide a critical source of leverage when pushing compliance. In a politicized environment, governments expect to be shamed by their rivals and can easily brush off such

---

8. For more on the long-term dynamics of stigma and shaming, see Zarakol 2010 2013.

commentary as a cynical attempt to sully their country's reputation. That is not so easy when allies offer scrutiny.

That human rights are politicized in this way is hardly surprising to many IR scholars. As E. H. Carr taught us, because states act primarily to further their own interests under anarchy, "supposedly absolute and universal principles [are] not principles at all," but rather "the transparent disguises of selfish vested interests."[9] Since Carr, IR scholars of all theoretical stripes have affirmed this intuition, finding that states use and manipulate human rights ideals for instrumental purposes, while documenting rampant politicization within the human rights regime. Indeed, some readers may view my argument as simply another iteration on this familiar argument: norms are weapons in the arsenal of power politics.

But this familiarity masks an underappreciated, yet foundational, theoretical puzzle: many of the same scholars who characterize human rights shaming as hopelessly politicized also underscore its inability to impose meaningful costs on violators. Shaming, in their view, is toothless "cheap talk": too weak and frivolous to impose a meaningful coercive effect.[10] It is important to clarify that politicization and toothlessness reflect two distinct problems: the former relates to the distribution of penalties, the latter to the strength of those penalties. Yet many observers lament both in the same breath, such as when US congresswoman Illeana Ros-Lehtinen characterized the UN Human Rights Council as "a weak voice subject to gross political manipulation."[11] But if shaming is uniformly irrelevant to its targets, then it is unclear why states would bother discriminating between geopolitical partners and adversaries at all. What exactly do leaders think they are sparing their friends from—and inflicting on their adversaries—if shaming imposes negligible political costs on the target?

A similar puzzle appears in recent constructivist thinking. A burgeoning literature highlights the ways in which states use and manipulate international norms (as well as laws, rules, and organizations) instrumentally in pursuit of their strategic interests.[12] Although this literature offers an important corrective to the liberal-constructivist approach to norms as an antidote to naked power, it also runs the risk of evacuating norms of any independent substantive content or regulatory purchase that might resist appropriation. In doing so, it ultimately accedes to the realist view of

9. Carr 2001, 80.
10. Krasner 1999; Mearsheimer 1994; Simmons 2009, chap. 4.
11. Gedda 2007.
12. Bob 2019; Búzás 2018; Dixon 2017; Hurd 2017.

international institutions as nothing more than power politics in disguise.[13] Thus, the same problem presents itself: Why would states bother to use and manipulate norms if they have no ability to influence political outcomes? In other words, both realists and constructivists underspecify the mechanisms that drive states to inject their political interests into the human rights arena in the first place.

I call this general puzzle the "politicization paradox." On the one hand, the fact that human rights norms are so easily manipulated, politicized, and selectively enforced is thought to reveal their fundamental *weakness* (that is, an inability to exert independent influence) and thus their *irrelevance*. And yet the fact that these norms remain ubiquitous as weapons in high-stakes geopolitical struggles presupposes their potential *strength* (that is, their ability to exert independent influence) and thus *importance*. Put differently, states supposedly go to great lengths to politicize something that supposedly has no political irrelevance.

My theory resolves the politicization paradox by emphasizing both the causal powers of norms and their use and manipulation in the service of state interests. Contrary to realist intuition, the politicization of international human rights shaming is a direct consequence of its ability to affect behavior and influence outcomes. Because human rights have broad moral appeal, accusations of human rights abuse have the potential to inflict considerable damage on target regimes. When states view certain criticisms as particularly embarrassing or threatening to a target state, they are less likely to impose those criticisms on their geopolitical friends and more likely to impose them on adversaries. For targeted actors, it is precisely this perception of threat and animosity that sparks a defensive reaction, which ironically motivates resistance and yet more norm violations. Thus, traditional realists underestimate the power of norms in both positive and negative directions, eliding their ability to constrain violations and promote compliance, on the one hand, and to enable violations and promote defiance, on the other. In brief, it is their *normative* powers that make human rights subject to *political* manipulation.

Furthermore, politicization—that is, the selective enforcement of human rights standards based on strategic interests—is not an inherently corrupting influence on these normative powers, as is typically thought. For many observers, international human rights institutions rely on a certain legitimacy gained through rational-legal authority, an "ability to present themselves as

13. Peters 2018.

impersonal and neutral."[14] And yet, to the extent that international shaming promotes compliance some of the time, it hinges on the strategic leverage afforded by a politicized system. In the UPR, for instance, strategic ties constitute the very mechanism by which social pressure drives behavioral outcomes, in both positive and negative directions. Thus, the very forces that undermine the impartiality of the human rights regime—strategic partnerships and rivalries—are the same forces that underlie its ability to secure compliance.

In sum, this book both affirms and radically diverges from the received wisdom about the politicization of human rights. Human rights institutions are politicized by virtue of their normative powers, and they remain powerful to an important extent because they are politicized. Acknowledging this mutual reliance invites us to reexamine the link between norms and politics in global affairs.

The Shamer's Dilemma

Despite being thought of as one of the most powerful antidotes to atrocities abroad, naming and shaming poses a serious conundrum for human rights promoters. On the one hand, human rights abuses demand some kind of condemnation; simply allowing violations to take place is morally and politically impossible. On the other hand, shaming is a risky business. Punishing rights violators can harm the shamer's interests by undermining valuable political relationships. Shaming can even motivate further abuse. I close this volume by sketching how this "shamer's dilemma" affects various actors, including governments and activists, before offering some practical yet modest suggestions for navigating this dilemma and promoting human rights more effectively.

FOR GOVERNMENTS

Most political leaders seem intuitively aware of the shamer's dilemma. That's why they take careful steps and use delicate language when criticizing other states, especially their friends and allies. They also realize that, when it comes to human rights diplomacy, the messenger is just as important as the message. This basic principle can be found in all areas of human rights diplomacy. For instance, the promoters of the controversial Human Rights Council

---

14. Barnett and Finnemore 2004, 21.

resolution on "human rights, sexual orientation, and gender identity" placed great importance on having South Africa present the final text, knowing that it would not bode well to have Western states lecture their former colonies on such matters.[15]

On the other hand, governments wanting to prioritize human rights in their foreign policy must reckon with their own domestic constraints and pressures, including a potentially outraged public demanding unequivocal condemnation of a perceived atrocity abroad. American leaders, for instance, are under constant pressure by societal groups for going "too soft" on certain countries that violate human rights. For example, President Barack Obama came under intense scrutiny for "abandoning" Iranian protesters during the disputed 2009 presidential elections.[16] Even when shaming is ineffective or counterproductive, a leader's desire to effectively advance human rights may be compromised by other political imperatives, such as assuaging relevant audiences and interest groups at home.

Despite the political liabilities involved, the evidence presented in this book suggests that governments are in a better position to influence states with which they share political or economic ties. If they really want to secure human rights, leaders must summon the political will to overcome the potential enforcement costs involved in shaming a strategic friend or ally. They must be willing to put relational benefits—including security or economic benefits—on the line.

When it comes to adversaries, the arguments detailed in this book suggest that a strategy of engagement, not isolation, provides the best chance for promoting human rights in the long term. Practically speaking, this could mean cooperating with human rights violators. If a government is incapable of taking that route, it may attempt to work through other countries, ones that have friendlier relations with the violating state. For example, when Iran arrested and imprisoned the Canadian-Iranian academic Homa Hoodfar in 2016, Canada, which did not have a diplomatic presence in Iran, turned to Oman, which served as a critical intermediary.[17] A government might also consider private diplomacy, which some studies suggest is a more effective means to promote human rights.[18] In any case, attempting to isolate an abuser is likely to backfire. Insofar as shaming relies on incentivizing actors to change their behavior in order to maintain social

15. Symons and Altman 2015.
16. See, for example, Xiyue 2021.
17. Erdbrink 2016.
18. Myrick and Weinstein 2021.

relationships, stigmatizing a norm violator or calling for their removal from the "community of civilized nations" only serves to break the ties on which effective shaming depends.

FOR CIVIL SOCIETY

The arguments in this book also have tremendous salience for civil society actors working to promote human rights. Shaming is now the preferred strategy of human rights activists worldwide. Human Rights Watch, in the words of its executive director, Kenneth Roth, "rel[ies] foremost on shaming and the generation of public pressure to defend rights."[19] Amnesty International publishes upwards of ten thousand "urgent actions" a year with the expressed purpose of mobilizing public outrage. Shaming is also performed by news outlets and journalists when they publish stories about atrocities around the world, which are then shared on social media along with petitions and open letters.

This book challenges international NGOs and other human rights promoters to reconsider their strategic prioritization of shaming and its attendant tactics, including publicity, petitions, letter-writing campaigns, and urgent actions. These tactics wield a double-edged sword when it comes to human rights promotion: the kind of rhetoric that is most effective in captivating public attention and mobilizing international pressure is often the same rhetoric that sparks defiance and backlash. Thus, what initially appears to be a "successful" campaign to address human rights violations could engender adverse consequences.

In the Sakineh case, for instance, widespread publicity of the case was both constructive, in that it influenced important parties such as Brazil and Turkey, and destructive as it propagated misleading information, stigmatized the Iranian government, and provoked a defensive response. Sakineh's lawyer, Mohammad Mostafaie, spoke to this point when reflecting on the role of international human rights organizations in the affair:

> Frankly, I have a lot of criticisms. I have worked for years against the death penalty and have met 300 people who were condemned to death. I give myself the right to be very angry at these organizations' performance. . . . The only thing that they do is to issue statements and write letters, without doing anything useful. Every time that I read a report by a news agency or a political party that describes the conditions of a condemned prisoner

19. Roth 2004.

as told by his family, I become depressed because I think they are using it as a tool against the Islamic Republic. It is stupid and inhuman to abuse a human life.[20]

Here, Mostafaie laments the widespread use of shaming and stigmatization in the Sakineh case and human rights advocacy more broadly. While such tactics clearly helped fuel massive public awareness and outrage over Sakineh's plight, it is not at all clear that they improved her welfare or advanced her position.

When they do engage in public shaming, INGOs should take time to critically evaluate the costs and benefits of doing so and attempt to anticipate any unintended consequences, such as those described here. They may also consider shifting their resources to other activities that might be more helpful. Other tactics besides shaming, Mostafaie suggests, include "work[ing] on individual defendants, analyzing the specific case and supporting the accused from the time of arrest [instead of shortly before execution]."[21] Indeed, one of the most powerful actions that NGOs can take is to provide credible information on human rights violations to both local and international advocates. But they can do so only if they devote resources to monitoring and fact-finding, embed themselves in the local context, and create partnerships with on-the-ground actors. Research indicates INGOs have the greatest impact when they maintain a domestic presence in the target country.[22] Donors can aid these efforts by supporting the NGOs that are doing the greatest good on the ground, not necessarily those that are the loudest shamers.

When NGOs do engage in the strategy of shaming, they should focus their efforts on actors that hold political or economic leverage against a violating government. That is, instead of shaming the government accused of abuse, NGOs should pressure that government's strategic allies and partners—including both state and nonstate actors with ties to the abusing government—to intervene. The Jamal Khashoggi case discussed in chapter 6 provides an illustrative example. The massive public outrage in countries with ties to Saudi Arabia that was mobilized by civil society organizations, including human rights groups and media outlets, put significant metanorm pressures on policymakers and businesses. The talent firm Endeavor, for instance, returned a $400 million investment out of protest over Khashoggi's

20. *Iran Wire* 2014.
21. Ibid.
22. Barry et al. 2014; Murdie and Davis 2012b.

assassination.[23] Such tactics were ultimately insufficient to push the US government to intervene in a meaningful way. But to the extent that Saudi Arabia suffered *any* costs, it was likely due to these metanorm pressures.

———

The goal of this book was not to summon a normative argument against human rights shaming but to provide an empirical examination of its role in international life. This process needs to be understood for the incentives it generates and the conditions it manifests, which in turn drive political changes that may or may not be normatively desirable. It is also important to consider that shaming may hold value beyond impelling states to reform their human rights practices; moreover, it may defy instrumental logic altogether. It is my hope that, by elucidating the micro- and macrostructures that shape the work of human rights defenders, they can use this book as a resource as they continue to fight for freedom and justice across borders.

23. Kelly and Hubbard 2019; Stokel-Walker 2018.

WORKS CITED

Abbasgholizadeh, Mahboubeh. 2007. "Nazam-e ghazayi dar tangena: Tahlili bar arayesh niruha-ye movafegh va mokhalef-e sangsar" (The Judicial System in Crisis: An Analysis of the Formation of Pro- and Anti-Stoning Forces). *Zanan,* Tir 86.

Abebe, Allehone Mulugeta. 2009. "Of Shaming and Bargaining: African States and the Universal Periodic Review of the United Nations Human Rights Council." *Human Rights Law Review* 9 (1): 1–35.

Acharya, Amitav. 2004. "How Ideas Spread: Whose Norms Matter? Norm Localization and Institutional Change in Asian Regionalism." *International Organization* 58 (2): 239–75.

Adkins, Karen. 2019. "When Shaming Is Shameful: Double Standards in Online Shame Backlashes." *Hypatia* 34 (1): 76–97.

Adler-Nissen, Rebecca. 2014. "Stigma Management in International Relations: Transgressive Identities, Norms, and Order in International Society." *International Organization* 68 (1): 143–76.

———. 2015. "Conclusion: Relationalism: Why Diplomats Find International Relations Theory Strange." In *Diplomacy and the Making of World Politics,* edited by Ole Jacob Sending, Vincent Pouliot, and Iver B. Neumann, 284–308. Cambridge: Cambridge University Press.

———. 2016. "The Social Self in International Relations: Identity, Power, and the Symbolic Interactionist Roots of Constructivism." *European Review of International Security* 3 (3): 27–39.

Agence France-Presse. 2010. "Britain Condemns Planned Stoning in Iran as 'Medieval.'" *Agence France-Presse,* August 7.

Ahadi, Mina. 2010. "A Reply to Ahmadinejad's Denial of Sakineh Mohammadi Ashtiani's Stoning Verdict." International Committee against Stoning, September 19. https://web.archive.org/web/20111225085622/http://stopstonningnow.com/wpress/4097 (accessed April 30, 2015).

Akin, David. 2010. "PM's Wife Opposes Iranian Woman's Death Sentence." *Toronto Sun,* July 10.

Al Arabiya. 2010. "Iran Suspends Woman's Stoning: Foreign Ministry." *Al Arabiya* (Dubai, Jordan), September 7. http://search.proquest.com/docview/749948242/1DCB4944426A4851PQ/519?accountid=14496 (accessed April 23, 2015).

Al Arabiya Staff Writer. 2018. "Saudi Official Source: Action against Kingdom Will Be Met with Greater Reaction." *Al Arabiya English,* October 14. https://english.alarabiya.net/News/gulf/2018/10/14/Saudi-Arabia-renews-its-rejection-of-any-threats-and-attempts-to-undermine-it- (accessed November 10, 2021).

Aldakhil, Turki. 2018. "US Sanctions on Riyadh Would Mean Washington Is Stabbing Itself." *Al Arabiya English,* October 14. https://english.alarabiya.net/features/2018/10/14/US-sanctions-on-Riyadh-would-mean-Washington-is-stabbing-itself (accessed November 3, 2021).

Alesina, Alberto, and David Dollar. 2000. "Who Gives Foreign Aid to Whom and Why?" *Journal of Economic Growth* 5 (1): 33–63.

Allen, Elizabeth Palchik. 2014. "Unintended Consequences." *Foreign Policy,* February 26. http://www.foreignpolicy.com/articles/2014/02/26/unintended_consequences_uganda_gay_law (accessed August 3, 2014).

Al-Mujahed, Ali, and Karen DeYoung. 2015. "Saudi Arabia Launches Air Attacks in Yemen." *Washington Post*, March 25. https://www.washingtonpost.com/world/middle_east/report-yemens-embattled-president-flees-stronghold-as-rebels-advance/2015/03/25/e0913ae2-d2d5-11e4-a62f-ee745911a4ff_story.html (accessed October 26, 2021).

Alter, Karen J. 2014. *The New Terrain of International Law: Courts, Politics, Rights*. Princeton, NJ: Princeton University Press.

Amnesty International. 2010. "Iran: Sakineh Mohammadi Ashtiani: A Life in the Balance." July 8. https://www.amnesty.org/en/documents/mde13/066/2011/en/.

———. 2021. "Saudi Arabia 2021." https://www.amnesty.org/en/location/middle-east-and-north-africa/saudi-arabia/report-saudi-arabia/.

Ariyanto, Amarina, Matthew J. Hornsey, and Cindy Gallois. 2009. "United We Stand: Intergroup Conflict Moderates the Intergroup Sensitivity Effect." *European Journal of Social Psychology* 40 (1): 169–77.

Arnson, Cynthia, Hālāh Esfandiari, and Adam Stubits, eds. 2010. *Iran in Latin America: Threat or "Axis of Annoyance"?* Woodrow Wilson Center Reports on the Americas 23. Washington, DC: Woodrow Wilson International Center for Scholars. https://www.wilsoncenter.org/sites/default/files/media/documents/publication/Iran_in_LA.pdf.

Associated Press. 2010. "Iran Snubs Brazilian Asylum Offer for Stoning Woman." *Associated Press*, August 3. http://www.theguardian.com/world/2010/aug/03/iran-stoning-woman-brazil-asylum (accessed March 30, 2015).

Ausderan, Jacob. 2014. "How Naming and Shaming Affects Human Rights Perceptions in the Shamed Country." *Journal of Peace Research* 51 (1): 81–95.

Axelrod, Robert. 1986. "An Evolutionary Approach to Norms." *American Political Science Review* 80 (4): 1095–1111.

Ayoub, Phillip M. 2014. "With Arms Wide Shut: Threat Perception, Norm Reception, and Mobilized Resistance to LGBT Rights." *Journal of Human Rights* 13 (3): 337–62.

Baghdasaryan, Meri. 2022. "Indonesia's New Draft Criminal Code Restrains Political Dissent." Electronic Frontier Foundation, August 23. https://www.eff.org/deeplinks/2022/08/indonesias-new-draft-criminal-code-cracks-down-political-dissent (accessed August 29, 2022).

Bailey, Jennifer. 2008. "Arrested Development: The Fight to End Commercial Whaling as a Case of Failed Norm Change." *European Journal of International Relations* 14 (2): 289–318.

Bailey, Michael, Anton Strezhnev, and Erik Voeten. 2015. "Estimating Dynamic State Preferences from United Nations Voting Data." *Journal of Conflict Resolution* 61 (2). https://doi.org/10.1177/0022002715595700.

BAOBAB for Women's Human Rights. 2003. "Please Stop the International Amina Lawal Protest Letter Campaigns." May 1. https://www.africa.upenn.edu/Urgent_Action/apic-050203.html (accessed February 14, 2019).

Barnett, Michael, and Martha Finnemore. 2004. *Rules for the World: International Organizations in Global Politics*. Ithaca, NY: Cornell University Press.

Barrionuevo, Alexei. 2010. "Brazil's President Offers Asylum to Woman Facing Stoning in Iran." *New York Times*, August 1. http://www.nytimes.com/2010/08/02/world/americas/02brazil.html (accessed March 31, 2015).

Barry, Colin M., Sam Bell, K. Chad Clay, Michael E. Flynn, and Amanda Murdie. 2014. "Choosing the Best House in a Bad Neighborhood: Location Strategies of Human Rights INGOs in the Non-Western World." *International Studies Quarterly* 59 (1): 86–98.

Bassan-Nygate, Lotem. 2022. "The Micro-Foundations of Naming and Shaming: Evidence from the Proposed Annexation of the West Bank." Working paper. https://www.lotembassanygate.com/_files/ugd/c6c686_27a1741c51364d799d4acbf387062dd0.pdf.

Bayoumi, Moustafa. 2018. "Mohammed bin Salman's Talk of Reform Is a Smokescreen." *Guardian*, March 22. http://www.theguardian.com/commentisfree/2018/mar/22/mohammed-bin-salmans-talk-reform-smokescreen (accessed April 9, 2021).

Becker, Howard S. 2008. *Outsiders: Studies in the Sociology of Deviance*. New York: Simon & Schuster.

Belmonte, Laura A. 2013. *Selling the American Way: US Propaganda and the Cold War*. Philadelphia: University of Pennsylvania Press.

Bendor, Jonathan, and Piotr Swistak. 2001. "The Evolution of Norms." *American Journal of Sociology* 106 (6): 1493–1545.

Benner, Katie, Mark Mazzetti, Ben Hubbard, and Mike Isaac. 2018. "Saudis' Image Makers: A Troll Army and a Twitter Insider." *New York Times*, October 20. https://www.nytimes.com/2018/10/20/us/politics/saudi-image-campaign-twitter.html (accessed January 25, 2022).

Blanton, Shannon Lindsey. 2005. "Foreign Policy in Transition? Human Rights, Democracy, and US Arms Exports." *International Studies Quarterly* 49 (4): 647–67.

Bloomfield, Alan, and Shirley V. Scott, eds. 2016. *Norm Antipreneurs and the Politics of Resistance to Global Normative Change*. New York: Routledge.

Bob, Clifford. 2005. *The Marketing of Rebellion: Insurgents, Media, and International Activism*. Cambridge: Cambridge University Press.

———. 2012. *The Global Right Wing and the Clash of World Politics*. New York: Cambridge University Press.

———. 2019. *Rights as Weapons: Instruments of Conflict, Tools of Power*. Princeton, NJ: Princeton University Press.

Bonikowski, Bart. 2015. "The Promise of Bourdieusian Political Sociology." *Theory and Society* 44 (4): 385–91.

Boockmann, Bernhard, and Axel Dreher. 2011. "Do Human Rights Offenders Oppose Human Rights Resolutions in the United Nations?" *Public Choice* 146 (3/4): 443–67.

Boyes, Roger. 2011. "Release of Ashtiani Journalists Linked with Pounds 1bn Tehran Deal." *The Times* (London), April 4. http://search.proquest.com/internationalnews/docview/859726590/6F6AB859390B46F1PQ/292?accountid=14496 (accessed June 22, 2015).

Braithwaite, John. 1989. *Crime, Shame, and Reintegration*. Cambridge: Cambridge University Press.

Branscombe, Nyla R., Naomi Ellemers, Russell Spears, and Bertjan Doosje. 1999. "The Context and Content of Social Identity Threat." In *Social Identity: Context, Commitment, Content*, edited by Naomi Ellemers, Russell Spears, and Bertjan Doosje, 35–58. Oxford: Blackwell Science.

Brewer, Marilynn B. 1999. "The Psychology of Prejudice: In-group Love or Out-group Hate." *Journal of Social Issues* 55 (3): 429–44.

Brutger, Ryan, and Anton Strezhnev. 2022. "International Investment Disputes, Media Coverage, and Backlash against International Law." *Journal of Conflict Resolution* 66 (6): 983–1009.

Brysk, Alison. 1993. "From Above and Below: Social Movements, the International System, and Human Rights in Argentina." *Comparative Political Studies* 26 (3): 259–85.

Burt, Alistair. 2010. "Statement on Iran Stoning." GOV.UK, Foreign and Commonwealth Office, July 7. https://www.gov.uk/government/news/statement-on-iran-stoning (accessed April 20, 2015).

Busby, Joshua W., and Kelly M. Greenhill. 2015. "Ain't That a Shame? Hypocrisy, Punishment, and Weak Actor Influence in International Politics." In *The Politics of Leverage in International Relations: Name, Shame, and Sanction*, edited by H. Richard Friman, 105–22. London: Palgrave Macmillan.

Bush, Sarah Sunn. 2015. *The Taming of Democracy Assistance: Why Democracy Promotion Does Not Confront Dictators*. New York: Cambridge University Press.

Bush, Sarah Sunn. 2017. "The Politics of Rating Freedom: Ideological Affinity, Private Authority, and the Freedom in the World Ratings." *Perspectives on Politics* 15 (3): 711–31.

Bush, Sarah Sunn, and Amaney A. Jamal. 2015. "Anti-Americanism, Authoritarian Politics, and Attitudes about Women's Representation: Evidence from a Survey Experiment in Jordan." *International Studies Quarterly* 59 (1): 34–45.

Búzás, Zoltán I. 2017. "Evading International Law: How Agents Comply with the Letter of the Law but Violate Its Purpose." *European Journal of International Relations* 23 (4): 857–83.

———. 2018. "Is the Good News about Law Compliance Good News about Norm Compliance? The Case of Racial Equality." *International Organization* 72 (2): 351–85.

Camarena, Rodrigo. 2010. "2010 Brazil Election Update: Dilma Advances in the Polls and Foreign Policy Takes Center Stage." *Foreign Policy*, August 2. http://foreignpolicyblogs.com/2010/08/02/election-update-dilma-advances-in-the-polls-and-foreign-policy-takes-center-stage/ (accessed April 22, 2015).

Cardenas, Sonia. 2004. "Norm Collision: Explaining the Effects of International Human Rights Pressure on State Behavior." *International Studies Review* 6 (2): 213–32.

———. 2006. "Violators' Accounts: Hypocrisy and Human Rights Rhetoric in the Southern Cone." *Journal of Human Rights* 5 (4): 439–51.

———. 2011. *Conflict and Compliance: State Responses to International Human Rights Pressure.* Philadelphia: University of Pennsylvania Press.

Carothers, Thomas. 2006. "The Backlash against Democracy Promotion." *Foreign Affairs* 85: 55.

Carpenter, Charli. 2007a. "Setting the Advocacy Agenda: Theorizing Issue Emergence and Non-emergence in Transnational Advocacy Networks." *International Studies Quarterly* 51 (1): 99–120.

———. 2007b. "Studying Issue (Non)-Adoption in Transnational Advocacy Networks." *International Organization* 61 (3): 643–67.

———. 2011. "Vetting the Advocacy Agenda: Network Centrality and the Paradox of Weapons Norms." *International Organization* 65 (1): 69–102.

Carr, Edward Hallett. 2001. *The Twenty Years' Crisis, 1919–1939: An Introduction to the Study of International Relations.* Basingstoke, UK: Harper Perennial.

Carraro, Valentina. 2017. "The United Nations Treaty Bodies and Universal Periodic Review: Advancing Human Rights by Preventing Politicization?" *Human Rights Quarterly* 39 (4): 943–70.

———. 2019. "Promoting Compliance with Human Rights: The Performance of the United Nations' Universal Periodic Review and Treaty Bodies." *International Studies Quarterly* 63 (4): 1079–93.

Carraro, Valentina, Thomas Conzelmann, and Hortense Jongen. 2019. "Fears of Peers? Explaining Peer and Public Shaming in Global Governance." *Cooperation and Conflict* 54 (3): 335–55.

Carter, Brett L. 2016. "How International Pressure Can Help." *Journal of Democracy* 27 (3): 36–50.

Cengiz, Hatice. 2018. "Please, President Trump, Shed Light on My Fiance's Disappearance." *Washington Post*, October 9. https://www.washingtonpost.com/news/global-opinions/wp/2018/10/09/please-president-trump-shed-light-on-my-fiances-disappearance/ (accessed November 2, 2021).

Chapman, Terrence L., and Stephen Chaudoin. 2020. "Public Reactions to International Legal Institutions: The International Criminal Court in a Developing Democracy." *Journal of Politics* 82 (4): 1305–20.

Chaudhry, Suparna. 2022. "The Assault on Civil Society: Explaining State Crackdown on NGOs." *International Organization* 76 (3): 549–90.

Chaudoin, Stephen. 2016. "How Contestation Moderates the Effects of International Institutions: The International Criminal Court and Kenya." *Journal of Politics* 78 (2): 557–71.

Checkel, Jeffrey. 1997. "International Norms and Domestic Politics: Bridging the Rationalist—Constructivist Divide." *European Journal of International Relations* 3 (4): 473.

———. 2001. "Why Comply? Social Learning and European Identity Change." *International Organization* 55 (3): 553–88.

Chekroun, Peggy, and Armelle Nugier. 2011. "'I'm Ashamed Because of You, so Please, Don't Do That!': Reactions to Deviance as a Protection against a Threat to Social Image." *European Journal of Social Psychology* 41 (4): 479–88.

Cialdini, Robert B., and Noah J. Goldstein. 2004. "Social Influence: Compliance and Conformity." *Annual Review of Psychology* 55: 591–621.

Cloward, Karisa. 2016. *When Norms Collide: Local Responses to Activism against Female Genital Mutilation and Early Marriage*. New York: Oxford University Press.

CNN Wire Staff. 2010. "Human Rights Activist Tries to Stop Death by Stoning for Iranian Woman." *CNN*, July 5. https://www.cnn.com/2010/WORLD/meast/07/05/iran.stoning/index.html.

Cohen, Albert K. 1955. *Delinquent Boys: The Culture of the Gang*. New York: Free Press.

———. 1970. "A General Theory of Subcultures." In *The Sociology of Subcultures*, edited by David O. Arnold. Berkeley, CA: Glendessary Press.

Cohen, Stanley. 2001. *States of Denial: Knowing about Atrocities and Suffering*. Cambridge: Polity Press.

Cohen, Zachary, and Betsy Klein. 2019. "Trump Vetoes 3 Bills Prohibiting Arms Sales to Saudi Arabia." *CNN*, July 24. https://www.cnn.com/2019/07/24/politics/saudi-arms-sale-resolutions-trump-veto/index.html (accessed November 2, 2021).

Cole, Wade M. 2010. "No News Is Good News: Human Rights Coverage in the American Print Media, 1980–2000." *Journal of Human Rights* 9 (3): 303–25.

———. 2012. "Institutionalizing Shame: The Effect of Human Rights Committee Rulings on Abuse, 1981–2007." *Social Science Research* 41 (3): 539–54.

Coleman, James S. 1994. *Foundations of Social Theory*. Cambridge, MA: Harvard University Press.

Cooley, Alexander, and James Ron. 2002. "The NGO Scramble: Organizational Insecurity and the Political Economy of Transnational Action." *International Security* 27 (1): 5–39.

Cooley, Charles Horton. 1992. *Human Nature and the Social Order*. Piscataway, NJ: Transaction Publishers.

Coppock, Alexander, and Oliver A. McClellan. 2019. "Validating the Demographic, Political, Psychological, and Experimental Results Obtained from a New Source of Online Survey Respondents." *Research and Politics* 6 (1). https://doi.org/10.1177/2053168018822174.

Cordelli, Chiara. 2015. "Justice as Fairness and Relational Resources." *Journal of Political Philosophy* 23 (1): 86–110.

Cortell, Andrew P., and James W. Davis Jr. 1996. "How Do International Institutions Matter? The Domestic Impact of International Rules and Norms." *International Studies Quarterly* 40 (4): 451–78.

Council on Foreign Relations. 2019. "The Presidential Candidates on Saudi Arabia." July 30. https://www.cfr.org/article/presidential-candidates-saudi-arabia (accessed November 15, 2021).

Dafoe, Allan, Samuel Liu, Brian O'Keefe, and Jessica Chen Weiss. 2022. "Provocation, Public Opinion, and International Crises: Evidence from China." *International Studies Quarterly* 66 (2): sqac006. https://doi.org/10.1093/isq/sqac006.

Dafoe, Allan, Jonathan Renshon, and Paul Huth. 2014. "Reputation and Status as Motives for War." *Annual Review of Political Science* 17 (1): 371–93.

Dafoe, Allan, and Jessica Chen Weiss. 2017. "Authoritarian Audiences and Elite Rhetoric in International Crises: Evidence from China." *International Organization* 63 (4): 963–73.

Dai, Xinyuan. 2005. "Why Comply? The Domestic Constituency Mechanism." *International Organization* 59 (2): 363–98.

Davenport, Christian. 1999. "Human Rights and the Democratic Proposition." *Journal of Conflict Resolution* 43 (1): 92–116.

Davis, David R., Amanda Murdie, and Coty Garnett Steinmetz. 2012. "'Makers and Shapers': Human Rights INGOs and Public Opinion." *Human Rights Quarterly* 34 (1): 199–224.

Davis, Julie Hirschfeld, and Eric Schmitt. 2018. "Senate Votes to End Aid for Yemen Fight over Khashoggi Killing and Saudis' War Aims." *New York Times*, December 13. https://www.nytimes.com/2018/12/13/us/politics/yemen-saudi-war-pompeo-mattis.html (accessed November 8, 2021).

Dehghan, Saeed Kamali, and Ian Black. 2010. "Sakineh Mohammadi Ashtiani 'at Home' Pictures Trigger Confusion over Her Fate." *Guardian*, December 9. http://www.theguardian.com/world/2010/dec/09/sakineh-mohammadi-ashtiani-freed-iran-stoning (accessed April 29, 2015).

DeMeritt, Jacqueline H. R. 2012. "International Organizations and Government Killing: Does Naming and Shaming Save Lives?" *International Interactions* 38 (5): 597–621.

DeYoung, Karen, and Kareem Fahim. 2018. "US, Saudi Steps in Khashoggi Case Don't Go Far Enough, Lawmakers Say." *Washington Post*, November 15. https://www.washingtonpost.com/world/national-security/2018/11/15/4385a472-e8e8-11e8-a939-9469f1166f9d_story.html (accessed November 18, 2021).

Dixon, Jennifer M. 2017. "Rhetorical Adaptation and Resistance to International Norms." *Perspectives on Politics* 15 (1): 83–99.

———. 2018. *Dark Pasts: Changing the State's Story in Turkey and Japan.* Ithaca, NY: Cornell University Press.

Donnelly, Jack. 1986. "International Human Rights: A Regime Analysis." *International Organization* 40 (3): 599–642.

———. 1998. "Human Rights: A New Standard of Civilization?" *International Affairs* 74 (1): 1–23.

Donno, Daniela. 2010. "Who Is Punished? Regional Intergovernmental Organizations and the Enforcement of Democratic Norms." *International Organization* 64 (4): 593–625.

———. 2013. *Defending Democratic Norms: International Actors and the Politics of Electoral Misconduct.* New York: Oxford University Press.

Downes, David, Paul Elliott Rock, and Eugene McLaughlin. 2016. *Understanding Deviance: A Guide to the Sociology of Crime and Rule-Breaking.* Oxford: Oxford University Press.

Downs, George W. 1998. "Enforcement and the Evolution of Cooperation." *Michigan Journal of International Law* 19 (2).

Dreier, Sarah K. 2018. "Resisting Rights to Renounce Imperialism: East African Churches' Strategic Symbolic Resistance to LGBTQ Inclusion." *International Studies Quarterly* 62 (2): 423–36.

Drezner, Daniel W. 1999. *The Sanctions Paradox: Economic Statecraft and International Relations.* Cambridge: Cambridge University Press.

Druckman, James N., Erik Peterson, and Rune Slothuus. 2013. "How Elite Partisan Polarization Affects Public Opinion Formation." *American Political Science Review* 107 (1): 57–79.

Dupuy, Kendra, James Ron, and Aseem Prakash. 2015. "Stop Meddling in My Country! Governments' Restrictions on Foreign Aid to NGOs." *Academy of Management Annual Meeting Proceedings* 2015 (1): 14437.

Duque, Marina G. 2018. "Recognizing International Status: A Relational Approach." *International Studies Quarterly* 62 (3): 577–92.

Earthjustice. 2020. "Australia's Climate Inaction Is a Human Rights Violation." Earthjustice, July 9. https://earthjustice.org/news/press/2020/australias-climate-inaction-is-a-human-rights-violation (accessed August 29, 2022).

The Economist. 2010. "Payback Time." *The Economist*, August 2. http://www.economist.com/blogs/newsbook/2010/08/brazils_relationship_iran (accessed January 28, 2015).

EFE News Service. 2010. "Spain Asks Iran to Overturn Woman's Death Sentence: SPAIN-IRAN." *EFE News Service*, July 12. http://search.proquest.com/docview/734774483/1DCB4944426A4851PQ/117?accountid=14496 (accessed April 22, 2015).

Ellemers, Naomi, Russell Spears, and Bertjan Doosje. 2002. "Self and Social Identity." *Annual Review of Psychology* 53 (1): 161–86.

Ellickson, Robert C. 1994. *Order without Law: How Neighbors Settle Disputes.* Cambridge, MA: Harvard University Press.

Emirates 24/7. 2010. "West Using Stoning Woman Case as 'Pressure': Iran." *Emirates 24/7*, November 3. http://www.emirates247.com/news/world/west-using-stoning-woman-case-as-pressure-iran-2010-11-03-1.313000 (accessed June 21, 2015).

Epstein, Charlotte. 2012. "Stop Telling Us How to Behave: Socialization or Infantilization?" *International Studies Perspectives* 13 (2): 135–45.

Erdbrink, Thomas. 2016. "Iran Releases Homa Hoodfar, a Canadian-Iranian Professor Held since June." *New York Times*, September 26. https://www.nytimes.com/2016/09/27/world/canada/iran-prisoner-release-homa-hoodfar.html (accessed September 6, 2022).

Esarey, Justin, and Jacqueline H. R. DeMeritt. 2017. "Political Context and the Consequences of Naming and Shaming for Human Rights Abuse." *International Interactions* 43 (4): 1–30.

Esfandiari, Haleh. 2010. "Case of Sakineh Ashtiani Reflects Iran's Internal Divisions." PBS, *Frontline*, November 18. http://www.pbs.org/wgbh/pages/frontline/tehranbureau/2010/11/case-of-sakineh-ashtiani-reflects-irans-internal-divisions.html (accessed March 31, 2015).

Esposo, Sarah R., Matthew J. Hornsey, and Jennifer R. Spoor. 2013. "Shooting the Messenger: Outsiders Critical of Your Group Are Rejected Regardless of Argument Quality." *British Journal of Social Psychology* 52 (2): 386–95.

Europe 1. 2010. "Les pays nordiques interviennent pour Sakineh" (Nordic Countries Intervene for Sakineh). *Europe 1*, November 4. http://www.europe1.fr/international/les-pays-nordiques-interviennent-pour-sakineh-303118 (accessed April 23, 2015).

European Parliament. 2010. "Resolution on the Human Rights Situation in Iran, in Particular the Cases of Sakineh Mohammadi Ashtiani and Zahra Bahrami." September 8. http://www.europarl.europa.eu/sides/getDoc.do?type=TA&reference=P7-TA-2010-0310&language=EN.

Evers, Miles M. 2017. "On Transgression." *International Studies Quarterly* 61 (4): 786–94.

Fariss, Christopher. 2014. "Respect for Human Rights Has Improved over Time: Modeling the Changing Standard of Accountability." *American Political Science Review* 108 (2): 297–318.

Fattah, Khaled, and K. M. Fierke. 2009. "A Clash of Emotions: The Politics of Humiliation and Political Violence in the Middle East." *European Journal of International Relations* 15 (1): 67–93.

Fearon, James D. 1994. "Domestic Political Audiences and the Escalation of International Disputes." *American Political Science Review* 88 (3): 577–92.

Fehr, Ernst, and Simon Gächter. 2002. "Altruistic Punishment in Humans." *Nature* 415 (6868): 137–40.

Feng, Zhaoyin. 2020. "George Floyd Death: China Takes a Victory Lap over US Protests." *BBC News*, June 5. https://www.bbc.com/news/world-us-canada-52912241 (accessed July 27, 2021).

Finnemore, Martha, and Kathryn Sikkink. 1998. "International Norm Dynamics and Political Change." *International Organization* 52 (4): 887–917.

Fletcher, Martin. 2010a. "'I Lost My Usefulness,' Says Stoning Lawyer's Wife Freed after He Escaped Iran's Clutches." *The Times* (London), August 9.

———. 2010b. "Outcry over Stoning 'Is a Western Plot': Campaigners Playing Rigged Game, Regime Says." *The Times* (London), August 31. https://www.thetimes.co.uk/article/iran-dismisses-outcry-over-stoning-sentence-as-western-plot-r2qpbn6n3qx.

Fletcher, Martin. 2010c. "Ahmadinejad Attacks 'Hypocrisy' of West on Eve of US Woman's Execution." *The Times* (London), September 22. http://search.proquest.com/docview/751962982 /EFC428CF53704775PQ/695?accountid=14496 (accessed April 24, 2015).

Flockhart, Trine. 2006. "'Complex Socialization': A Framework for the Study of State Socialization." *European Journal of International Relations* 12 (1): 89–118.

Franklin, James C. 2008. "Shame on You: The Impact of Human Rights Criticism on Political Repression in Latin America." *International Studies Quarterly* 52 (1): 187–211.

Freedom House. 2014. "The Democratic Leadership Gap: Freedom in the World 2014." https:// freedomhouse.org/sites/default/files/2020-02/Freedom_in_the_World_2014_Booklet.pdf.

Friedman, Thomas L. 2017. "Saudi Arabia's Arab Spring, at Last." *New York Times*, November 23. https://www.nytimes.com/2017/11/23/opinion/saudi-prince-mbs-arab-spring.html (accessed April 10, 2021).

Frye, Harrison. 2021. "The Problem of Public Shaming." *Journal of Political Philosophy* 30 (2): 188–208. https://onlinelibrary.wiley.com/doi/abs/10.1111/jopp.12252 (accessed September 28, 2021).

Gall, Carlotta. 2018. "Erdogan Presses for Answers from Saudi Prince in Khashoggi Killing." *New York Times*, November 13. https://www.nytimes.com/2018/11/13/world/europe/erdogan -khashoggi-crown-prince-mohammed.html (accessed November 8, 2021).

Gedda, George. 2007. "US Criticizes UN Human Rights Body for Anti-Israel Bias." *Associated Press*, March 7. http://www.dailyalert.org/rss/Mainissues.php?id=6345 (accessed September 7, 2020).

Gibler, Douglas M. 2008. *International Military Alliances, 1648–2008.* Washington, DC: CQ Press.

Global Times. 2021. "Human Rights Used by West Countries as Tool of Political Manipulation: Chinese Ambassador to UN." *Global Times*, February 25. https://www.globaltimes.cn/page /202102/1216523.shtml (accessed February 11, 2022).

Goddard, Stacie E. 2018. *When Right Makes Might: Rising Powers and World Order.* Ithaca, NY: Cornell University Press.

Goertz, Gary, and Paul F. Diehl. 1992. "Toward a Theory of International Norms." *Journal of Conflict Resolution* 36 (4): 634.

Goffman, Erving. 1951. "Symbols of Class Status." *British Journal of Sociology* 2 (4): 294.

———. 2009. *Stigma: Notes on the Management of Spoiled Identity.* New York: Simon & Schuster.

Gómez, Eduardo J. 2012. "Why Iran-Brazil Friendship Has Gone Cold." *CNN*, April 5. https://www .cnn.com/2012/04/05/opinion/gomez-iran-brazil-chill/index.html (accessed April 9, 2020).

Goode, Erich, and George Ritzer. 2007. "Deviance." In *The Blackwell Encyclopedia of Sociology*, edited by George Ritzer. Hoboken, NJ: Wiley-Blackwell.

Goodliffe, Jay, and Darren Hawkins. 2009a. "A Funny Thing Happened on the Way to Rome: Explaining International Criminal Court Negotiations." *Journal of Politics* 71 (3): 977–97.

———. 2009b. "A Funny Thing Happened on the Way to Rome: Explaining International Criminal Court Negotiations." *Journal of Politics* 71 (3): 977–97.

Goodliffe, Jay, Darren Hawkins, Christine Horne, and Daniel L. Nielson. 2012. "Dependence Networks and the International Criminal Court." *International Studies Quarterly* 56 (1): 131–47.

Goodman, Ryan, and Derek Jinks. 2013. *Socializing States: Promoting Human Rights through International Law.* Oxford: Oxford University Press.

Gordon, Michael R., and David D. Kirkpatrick. 2015. "Kerry Warns Egypt Human Rights Abuses Can Hurt Fight against Terrorism." *New York Times*, August 2. http://www.nytimes.com/2015 /08/03/world/middleeast/kerry-in-egypt-discusses-balancing-human-rights-and-terror -fight.html (accessed January 14, 2016).

Gould, Joe, and Aaron Mehta. 2021. "Boeing, Raytheon Missile Sales to Saudi Arabia Paused by Biden Administration." *Defense News*, February 5. https://www.defensenews.com/global

/mideast-africa/2021/02/05/boeing-raytheon-missile-sales-to-saudi-arabia-canceled-by -biden-administration/ (accessed November 16, 2021).

Greenhill, Brian. 2010. "The Company You Keep: International Socialization and the Diffusion of Human Rights Norms." *International Studies Quarterly* 54 (1): 127–45.

Greenhill, Brian, and Dan Reiter. 2022. "Naming and Shaming, Government Messaging, and Backlash Effects: Experimental Evidence from the Convention against Torture." *Journal of Human Rights* 21 (4): 399–418.

Greenwald, Glenn. 2015. "US Government Celebrates Its Arming of the Egyptian Regime with a YouTube Video." *Intercept*, August 3. https://theintercept.com/2015/08/03/u-s -government-celebrates-arming-egyptian-regime-youtube-video/ (accessed January 14, 2016).

Greenwald, Glenn, and Murtaza Hussain. 2014. "The NSA's New Partner in Spying: Saudi Arabia's Brutal State Police." *Intercept*, July 25. https://theintercept.com/2014/07/25/nsas-new -partner-spying-saudi-arabias-brutal-state-police/ (accessed October 26, 2021).

Grossman, Guy, Devorah Manekin, and Yotam Margalit. 2018. "How Sanctions Affect Public Opinion in Target Countries: Experimental Evidence from Israel." *Comparative Political Studies* 51 (4). https://doi.org/10.1177/0010414018774370.

Gruffydd-Jones, Jamie J. 2018. "Citizens and Condemnation: Strategic Uses of Human Rights Pressure in Authoritarian States." *Comparative Political Studies* 52 (4). https://doi.org/10.1177 /0010414018784066.

Guardian Staff and Agencies. 2021. "Biden Defends Move Not to Punish Saudi Crown Prince over Khashoggi Killing." *Guardian*, March 17. https://www.theguardian.com/world/2021/mar/17 /joe-biden-saudi-arabia-crown-prince-mohammed-bin-salman-jamal-khashoggi (accessed October 28, 2021).

Gurowitz, Amy. 1999. "Mobilizing International Norms: Domestic Actors, Immigrants, and the Japanese State." *World Politics* 51 (3): 413–45.

Guzman, Andrew T. 2007. *How International Law Works: A Rational Choice Theory*. Oxford: Oxford University Press.

Haber Türk. 2010. "Turkey's Erdoğan Responds [to] World Outcry for Sakineh Ashtiani." *Haber Türk*, August 18. http://www.haberturk.com/general/haber/543463-turkeys-erdogan -responds-world-outcry-for-sakineh-ashtiani (accessed April 22, 2015).

Hafner-Burton, Emilie M. 2005. "Trading Human Rights: How Preferential Trade Agreements Influence Government Repression." *International Organization* 59 (3): 593–629.

———. 2008. "Sticks and Stones: Naming and Shaming the Human Rights Enforcement Problem." *International Organization* 62 (4): 689–716.

———. 2014. "A Social Science of Human Rights." *Journal of Peace Research* 51 (2): 273–86.

Hafner-Burton, Emilie M., and James Ron. 2013. "The Latin Bias: Regions, the Anglo-American Media, and Human Rights." *International Studies Quarterly* 57 (3): 474–91.

Hafner-Burton, Emilie M., and Kiyoteru Tsutsui. 2005. "Human Rights in a Globalizing World: The Paradox of Empty Promises." *American Journal of Sociology* 110 (5): 1373–1411.

Hafner-Burton, Emilie M., Kiyoteru Tsutsui, and John W. Meyer. 2008. "International Human Rights Law and the Politics of Legitimation: Repressive States and Human Rights Treaties." *International Sociology* 23 (1): 115–41.

Hahl, Oliver, Minjae Kim, and Ezra W. Zuckerman Sivan. 2018. "The Authentic Appeal of the Lying Demagogue: Proclaiming the Deeper Truth about Political Illegitimacy." *American Sociological Review* 83 (1): 1–33.

Hall, Todd H. 2017. "On Provocation: Outrage, International Relations, and the Franco–Prussian War." *Security Studies* 26 (1): 1–29.

Harris, Shane, Greg Miller, and Josh Dawsey. 2018. "CIA Concludes Saudi Crown Prince Ordered Jamal Khashoggi's Assassination." *Washington Post*, November 16. https://www.washingtonpost .com/world/national-security/cia-concludes-saudi-crown-prince-ordered-jamal-khashoggis -assassination/2018/11/16/98c89fe6-e9b2-11e8-a939-9469f1166f9d_story.html (accessed October 26, 2021).

Hendrix, Cullen, and Wendy Wong. 2013. "When Is the Pen Truly Mighty? Regime Type and the Efficacy of Naming and Shaming in Curbing Human Rights Abuses." *British Journal of Political Science* 43 (3): 651–72.

———. 2014. "Knowing Your Audience: How the Structure of International Relations and Organizational Choices Affect Amnesty International's Advocacy." *Review of International Organizations* 9 (1): 29–58.

Hernández, Javier C., and Benjamin Mueller. 2020. "Global Anger Grows over George Floyd Death, and Becomes an Anti-Trump Cudgel." *New York Times*, June 1. https://www .nytimes.com/2020/06/01/world/asia/george-floyd-protest-global.html (accessed July 27, 2021).

Herrmann, Richard K. 2017. "How Attachments to the Nation Shape Beliefs about the World: A Theory of Motivated Reasoning." *International Organization* 71 (S1): S61–84.

Hertel, Shareen. 2006. *Unexpected Power: Conflict and Change among Transnational Activists.* Ithaca, NY: Cornell University Press.

Hill, Daniel W., Will H. Moore, and Bumba Mukherjee. 2013. "Information Politics versus Organizational Incentives: When Are Amnesty International's 'Naming and Shaming' Reports Biased?" *International Studies Quarterly* 57 (2): 219–32.

Hokayem, Emile. 2012. "Syria and Its Neighbours." *Survival* 54 (2): 7–14.

Hopgood, Stephen, Jack Snyder, and Leslie Vinjamuri, eds. 2017. *Human Rights Futures.* Cambridge: Cambridge University Press.

Horne, Christine. 2001. "The Enforcement of Norms: Group Cohesion and Meta-norms." *Social Psychology Quarterly* 64 (3): 253–66.

———. 2004. "Collective Benefits, Exchange Interests, and Norm Enforcement." *Social Forces* 82 (3): 1037–62.

———. 2007. "Explaining Norm Enforcement." *Rationality and Society* 19 (2): 139–70.

———. 2009. *The Rewards of Punishment: A Relational Theory of Norm Enforcement.* Stanford, CA: Stanford University Press.

Hornsey, Matthew J. 2005. "Why Being Right Is Not Enough: Predicting Defensiveness in the Face of Group Criticism." *European Review of Social Psychology* 16 (1): 301–34.

Hornsey, Matthew J., and Armin Imani. 2004. "Criticizing Groups from the Inside and the Outside: An Identity Perspective on the Intergroup Sensitivity Effect." *Personality and Social Psychology Bulletin* 30 (3): 365–83.

Hornsey, Matthew J., Tina Oppes, and Alicia Svensson. 2002. "'It's OK if We Say It, but You Can't': Responses to Intergroup and Intragroup Criticism." *European Journal of Social Psychology* 32 (3): 293–307.

Hornsey, Matthew J., Mark Trembath, and Sasha Gunthorpe. 2004. "'You Can Criticize Because You Care': Identity Attachment, Constructiveness, and the Intergroup Sensitivity Effect." *European Journal of Social Psychology* 34 (5): 499–518.

Hubbard, Ben. 2018. "Saudi Arabia Says Jamal Khashoggi Was Killed in Consulate Fight." *New York Times*, October 19. https://www.nytimes.com/2018/10/19/world/middleeast/jamal -khashoggi-dead-saudi-arabia.html (accessed October 26, 2021).

———. 2020. "Saudi Arabia Abolishes Flogging as a Punishment for Crime." *New York Times*, April 25. https://www.nytimes.com/2020/04/25/world/middleeast/saudi-arabia-abolishes -flogging.html.

Huddy, Leonie, and Alexa Bankert. 2017. "Political Partisanship as a Social Identity." *Oxford Research Encyclopedia of Politics*, May 24. https://doi.org/10.1093/acrefore/9780190228637 .013.250.

Huddy, Leonie, and Nadia Khatib. 2007. "American Patriotism, National Identity, and Political Involvement." *American Journal of Political Science* 51 (1): 63–77.

Hug, Simon, and Richard Lukács. 2014. "Preferences or Blocs? Voting in the United Nations Human Rights Council." *Review of International Organizations* 9 (1): 83–106.

Human Rights Watch. 2019. "Human Rights Watch Submission to the United Nations Human Rights Council's Universal Periodic Review of the United States of America." Human Rights Watch, October 3. https://www.hrw.org/news/2019/10/03/human-rights-watch-submission -united-nations-human-rights-councils-universal (accessed August 29, 2022).

———. 2021. "Saudi Arabia: Events of 2020." https://www.hrw.org/world-report/2021/country -chapters/saudi-arabia (accessed September 1, 2021).

Hurd, Ian. 1999. "Legitimacy and Authority in International Politics." *International Organization* 53 (2): 379–408.

———. 2005. "The Strategic Use of Liberal Internationalism: Libya and the UN Sanctions, 1992– 2003." *International Organization* 59 (3): 495–526.

———. 2007. "Breaking and Making Norms: American Revisionism and Crises of Legitimacy." *International Politics* 44 (2/3): 194–213.

———. 2017. *How to Do Things with International Law*. Princeton, NJ: Princeton University Press.

Hyde, Susan D. 2011. *The Pseudo-Democrat's Dilemma: Why Election Observation Became an International Norm*. Ithaca, NY: Cornell University Press.

Ignatieff, Michael. 2009. *American Exceptionalism and Human Rights*. Princeton, NJ: Princeton University Press.

Ilgit, Asli, and Deepa Prakash. 2019. "Making Human Rights Emotional: A Research Agenda to Recover Shame in 'Naming and Shaming.'" *Political Psychology* 40 (6).

Indian Express. 2011. "To Free Two Reporters, Germany Helped India Pay Iran." *Indian Express* (Mumbai), April 1. http://search.proquest.com/internationalnews/docview/859581484 /6F6AB859390B46F1PQ/290?accountid=14496 (accessed June 22, 2015).

International Committee against Stoning. 2010. "Italy Rises to Sakineh's Defence." September 1, press release 59. https://web.archive.org/web/20110303000110/http://stopstonningnow.com /wpress/3653 (accessed April 23, 2015).

Iran Solidarity. 2010. "Mostafaei's Prejudicial Statements and Ashtiani's Children's Counter!" August 20, press release 47. http://iransolidarity.blogspot.com/2010/08/mostafaeis-prejudicial -statements-and.html (accessed April 17, 2015).

Iran Wire. 2014. "The Value of Human Life: An Interview with Mohammad Mostafaei." *Iran Wire*, February 14. https://iranwire.com/en/society/60253/.

Isenberg, Daniel J. 1986. "Group Polarization: A Critical Review and Meta-Analysis." *Journal of Personality and Social Psychology* 50 (6): 1141.

Islamic Republic News Agency. 2010. "West's 'Slogan' of Human Rights 'Unreal,' Iran President." *Islamic Republic News Agency* (Tehran), September 21. http://search.proquest.com/docview /751839930/EFC428CF53704775PQ/682?accountid=14496 (accessed April 24, 2015).

Islamic Republic of Iran News Network. 2010a. "French First Lady Said Angered by 'Immoral Acts' Charges in Iran Media." *Islamic Republic of Iran News Network* (Tehran), August 30. http://search.proquest.com/docview/748162953/1DCB4944426A4851PQ/422?accountid =14496 (accessed April 22, 2015).

———. 2010b. "Iran President Accuses West of 'Making Hue and Cry' over Convicted Woman." *Islamic Republic of Iran News Network* (London), October 5. http://search.proquest.com/docview /756270726/EFC428CF53704775PQ/758?accountid=14496 (accessed April 24, 2015).

Iyengar, Shanto, Gaurav Sood, and Yphtach Lelkes. 2012. "Affect, Not Ideology: A Social Identity Perspective on Polarization." *Public Opinion Quarterly* 76 (3): 405–31.

Jackson, Patrick. 2006. *Civilizing the Enemy: German Reconstruction and the Invention of the West.* Ann Arbor: University of Michigan Press.

Jackson, Patrick Thaddeus, and Daniel H. Nexon. 1999. "Relations before States: Substance, Process, and the Study of World Politics." *European Journal of International Relations* 5 (3): 291–332.

———. 2019. "Reclaiming the Social: Relationalism in Anglophone International Studies." *Cambridge Review of International Affairs* 32 (5): 582–600.

Jacquet, Jennifer. 2016. *Is Shame Necessary? New Uses for an Old Tool.* New York: Vintage.

Jardina, Ashley. 2019. *White Identity Politics.* Cambridge: Cambridge University Press.

Jeffries, Carla H., Matthew J. Hornsey, Robbie M. Sutton, Karen M. Douglas, and Paul G. Bain. 2012. "The David and Goliath Principle: Cultural, Ideological, and Attitudinal Underpinnings of the Normative Protection of Low-Status Groups from Criticism." *Personality and Social Psychology Bulletin* 38 (8): 1053–65.

Johns, Leslie. 2022. *Politics and International Law.* Cambridge: Cambridge University Press.

Johnson, Tana. 2011. "Guilt by Association: The Link between States' Influence and the Legitimacy of Intergovernmental Organizations." *Review of International Organizations* 6 (1): 57–84.

Johnston, Alastair Iain. 2001. "Treating International Institutions as Social Environments." *International Studies Quarterly* 45 (4): 487–515.

Jordan, Jillian J., Moshe Hoffman, Paul Bloom, and David G. Rand. 2016. "Third-Party Punishment as a Costly Signal of Trustworthiness." *Nature* 530 (7591): 473–76.

Jordan, Jillian J., and David G. Rand. 2020. "Signaling When No One Is Watching: A Reputation Heuristics Account of Outrage and Punishment in One-Shot Anonymous Interactions." *Journal of Personality and Social Psychology* 118 (1): 57–88.

Joseph, Pat. 2014. "'Victims Can Lie as Much as Other People.'" *Atlantic*, June 5. http://www.theatlantic.com/international/archive/2014/06/somaly-mam-scandal-victims-can-lie/372188/ (accessed August 19, 2014).

Joseph, Sarah. 2015. "Global Media Coverage of the Universal Periodic Review Process." In *Human Rights and the Universal Periodic Review: Rituals and Ritualism*, edited by Emma Larking and Hilary Charlesworth, 147–66. Cambridge: Cambridge University Press.

Kahan, Dan M. 1996. "What Do Alternative Sanctions Mean?" *University of Chicago Law Review* 63: 591–653.

Kahan, Dan M., and Eric A. Posner. 1999. "Shaming White-Collar Criminals: A Proposal for Reform of the Federal Sentencing Guidelines." *Journal of Law and Economics* 42 (S1): 365–92.

Kaplan, Lennie, Mark Milke, and Germain Belzile. 2020. "Foreign Oil Imports to Canada: $477 Billion between 1988 and 2019." Canadian Energy Centre, September 14. https://www.canadianenergycentre.ca/foreign-oil-imports-to-canada-477-billion-between-1988-and-2019/ (accessed March 11, 2021).

Katzenstein, Peter, ed. 1996. *The Culture of National Security: Norms and Identity in World Politics.* New York: Columbia University Press.

Kaufmann, Chaim D., and Robert A. Pape. 1999. "Explaining Costly International Moral Action: Britain's Sixty-Year Campaign against the Atlantic Slave Trade." *International Organization* 53 (4): 631–68.

Keck, Margaret E., and Kathryn Sikkink. 1998. *Activists beyond Borders: Advocacy Networks in International Politics.* New York: Cambridge University Press.

Kelley, Judith G., and Beth A. Simmons. 2015. "Politics by Number: Indicators as Social Pressure in International Relations." *American Journal of Political Science* 59 (1): 55–70.

Kelly, Kate, and Ben Hubbard. 2019. "Endeavor Returns Money to Saudi Arabia, Protesting Khashoggi Murder." *New York Times*, March 8. https://www.nytimes.com/2019/03/08/business/endeavor-saudi-arabia.html (accessed September 7, 2022).

Kelly, Laura. 2021. "Biden Struggles to Rein in Saudi Arabia amid Human Rights Concerns." *The Hill*, October 17. https://thehill.com/policy/international/576987-biden-struggles-to-rein-in-saudi-arabia-amid-human-rights-concerns (accessed October 28, 2021).

Khashoggi, Jamal. 2018. "Read Jamal Khashoggi's columns for The Washington Post." *Washington Post*, October 6. https://www.washingtonpost.com/news/global-opinions/wp/2018/10/06/read-jamal-khashoggis-columns-for-the-washington-post/ (accessed October 18, 2021).

Kirchgaessner, Stephanie, and Bethan McKernan. 2021. "Biden's $500m Saudi Deal Contradicts Policy on 'Offensive' Weapons, Critics Say." *Guardian*, October 27. https://www.theguardian.com/us-news/2021/oct/27/joe-biden-saudi-arabia-arms-weapons-deal (accessed October 28, 2021).

Kirkpatrick, David D., Ben Hubbard, Mark Landler, and Mark Mazzetti. 2018. "The Wooing of Jared Kushner: How the Saudis Got a Friend in the White House." *New York Times*, December 8. https://www.nytimes.com/2018/12/08/world/middleeast/saudi-mbs-jared-kushner.html (accessed October 27, 2021).

Klotz, Audie. 1999. *Norms in International Relations: The Struggle against Apartheid*. Ithaca, NY: Cornell University Press.

Knickmeyer, Ellen. 2021. "Analysis: Biden Retreats from Vow to Make Pariah of Saudis." *AP News*, https://apnews.com/article/biden-retreats-saudi-arabia-sanctions-khashoggi-killing-d91d31edece5db07112d1c2d4dd3be33 (accessed November 16, 2021).

Knutson, Brian. 2004. "Sweet Revenge?" *Science* 305 (5688): 1246–47.

Koliev, Faradj. 2020. "Shaming and Democracy: Explaining Inter-state Shaming in International Organizations." *International Political Science Review* 41 (4): 538–53.

Koliev, Faradj, and James H. Lebovic. 2018. "Selecting for Shame: The Monitoring of Workers' Rights by the International Labour Organization, 1989 to 2011." *International Studies Quarterly* 62 (2): 437–52.

Koschut, Simon. 2022. "Reintegrative Shaming in International Relations: NATO's Military Intervention in Libya." *Journal of International Relations and Development* 25 (2): 497–522.

Krain, Matthew. 2012. "J'accuse! Does Naming and Shaming Perpetrators Reduce the Severity of Genocides or Politicides?" *International Studies Quarterly* 56 (3): 574–89.

Krasner, Stephen D. 1993. "Sovereignty, Regimes, and Human Rights." In *Regime Theory and International Relations*, edited by Volker Rittberger, 139–67. New York: Oxford University Press.

———. 1999. *Sovereignty: Organized Hypocrisy*. Princeton, NJ: Princeton University Press.

Krebs, Ronald R. 2015. *Narrative and the Making of US National Security*. Cambridge: Cambridge University Press.

Krebs, Ronald R., and Patrick Thaddeus Jackson. 2007. "Twisting Tongues and Twisting Arms: The Power of Political Rhetoric." *European Journal of International Relations* 13 (1): 35–66.

Kuo, Lily. 2018. "China Says UN Criticism of Human Rights Record Is 'Politically Driven.'" *Guardian*, November 6. https://www.theguardian.com/world/2018/nov/06/china-un-criticism-human-rights-record (accessed August 29, 2022).

Kuo, Lily, and Emily Rauhala. 2022. "China Slams UN 'Farce' on Xinjiang as Uyghur Exiles Praise Report." *Washington Post*, September 1. https://www.washingtonpost.com/world/2022/09/01/china-united-nations-xinjiang-uyghur-human-rights/ (accessed September 1, 2022).

Lamont, Michèle, and Virág Molnár. 2002. "The Study of Boundaries in the Social Sciences." *Annual Review of Sociology* 28 (1): 167–95.

Landler, Mark. 2018. "In Extraordinary Statement, Trump Stands with Saudis Despite Khashoggi Killing." *New York Times*, November 20. https://www.nytimes.com/2018/11/20/world /middleeast/trump-saudi-khashoggi.html (accessed November 8, 2021).

Landler, Mark, and Peter Baker. 2019. "Trump Vetoes Measure to Force End to US Involvement in Yemen War." *New York Times*, April 16. https://www.nytimes.com/2019/04/16/us/politics /trump-veto-yemen.html (accessed November 15, 2021).

Lebovic, James H. 1988. "National Interests and US Foreign Aid: The Carter and Reagan Years." *Journal of Peace Research* 25 (2): 115–35.

———. 2005. "Donor Positioning: Development Assistance from the US, Japan, France, Germany, and Britain." *Political Research Quarterly* 58 (1): 119–26.

Lebovic, James H., and Erik Voeten. 2006. "The Politics of Shame: The Condemnation of Country Human Rights Practices in the UNHCR." *International Studies Quarterly* 50 (4): 861–88.

———. 2009. "The Cost of Shame: International Organizations and Foreign Aid in the Punishing of Human Rights Violators." *Journal of Peace Research* 46 (1): 79–97.

Lee, Melissa M., and Lauren Prather. 2020. "Selling International Law Enforcement: Elite Justifications and Public Values." *Research and Politics* 7 (3).

Leigh, David. 2011. "US Put Pressure on Saudi Arabia to Let Women Drive, Leaked Cables Reveal." *Guardian*, May 27. https://www.theguardian.com/world/2011/may/27/us-pressurised-saudis -let-women-drive (accessed September 5, 2020).

Lemert, Edwin McCarthy. 1972. *Human Deviance, Social Problems, and Social Control.* Englewood Cliffs, NJ: Prentice-Hall.

Lévy, Bernard-Henri. 2010. "Interview: Sakineh's Attorney Speaks from Exile." *HuffPost*, August 15. http://www.huffingtonpost.com/bernardhenri-levy/sakinehs-attorney-speaks _b_682721.html (accessed March 24, 2015).

Leyne, Jon. 2010. "Stoning Furore Gives Iran Foreign Policy Problems." *BBC News*, September 6. http://www.bbc.com/news/world-middle-east-11208458 (accessed March 30, 2015).

Lind, Jennifer. 2008. *Sorry States: Apologies in International Politics.* Ithaca, NY: Cornell University Press.

Lindemann, Thomas. 2011. *Causes of War: The Struggle for Recognition.* Colchester, UK: ECPR Press.

Link, Bruce G., and Jo C. Phelan. 2001. "Conceptualizing Stigma." *Annual Review of Sociology* 27 (1): 363–85.

Little, Andrew T. 2019. "The Distortion of Related Beliefs." *American Journal of Political Science* 63 (3): 675–89. https://onlinelibrary.wiley.com/doi/abs/10.1111/ajps.12435 (accessed June 5, 2019).

Lüders, Adrian, Eva Jonas, Immo Fritsche, and Dimitrij Agroskin. 2016. "Between the Lines of Us and Them: Identity Threat, Anxious Uncertainty, and Reactive In-group Affirmation: How Can Antisocial Outcomes Be Prevented?" In *Understanding Peace and Conflict through Social Identity Theory*, edited by Shelley McKeown, Reeshma Haji, and Neil Ferguson, 33–53. Cham, Switzerland: Springer International Publishing.

Lutz, Ellen L., and Kathryn Sikkink. 2000. "International Human Rights Law and Practice in Latin America." *International Organization* 54 (3): 633–59.

Madsen, Mikael Rask, Juan A. Mayoral, Anton Strezhnev, and Erik Voeten. 2022. "Sovereignty, Substance, and Public Support for European Courts' Human Rights Rulings." *American Political Science Review* 116 (2): 419–38.

Mahdawi, Arwa. 2018. "Saudi Arabia Is Not Driving Change—It Is Trying to Hoodwink the West." *Guardian*, June 26. http://www.theguardian.com/world/2018/jun/26/saudi-arabia-is-not -driving-change-it-is-trying-to-hoodwink-the-west (accessed April 9, 2021).

Maibom, Heidi L. 2010. "The Descent of Shame." *Philosophy and Phenomenological Research* 80 (3): 566–94.

Major, Brenda, and Laurie T. O'Brien. 2005. "The Social Psychology of Stigma." *Annual Review of Psychology* 56 (1): 393–421.

Mantesso, Sean. 2021. "'The Biggest Lie of the Century': China Hits Back at Human Rights Criticism." *ABC News*, July 19. https://www.abc.net.au/news/2021-07-20/china-responds-to-western-criticism-of-human-rights-record/100295550 (accessed August 26, 2022).

Marquart, Maria, Veit Medick, Roland Nelles, Severin Weiland, and Philipp Wittrock. 2011. "Two Journalists and an Oil Transaction: Germany's Role in a Business Deal with Iran." *Spiegel Online*, April 1. http://www.spiegel.de/international/germany/two-journalists-and-an-oil-transaction-germany-s-role-in-a-business-deal-with-iran-a-754571.html (accessed June 29, 2015).

Massaro, Toni M. 1997. "The Meanings of Shame: Implications for Legal Reform." *Psychology, Public Policy, and Law* 3 (4): 645.

McAuliffe, Katherine, Jillian J. Jordan, and Felix Warneken. 2015. "Costly Third-Party Punishment in Young Children." *Cognition* 134 (January): 1–10.

McCourt, David M. 2016. "Practice Theory and Relationalism as the New Constructivism." *International Studies Quarterly* 60 (3): 475–85.

McEntire, Kyla Jo, Michele Leiby, and Matthew Krain. 2015. "Human Rights Organizations as Agents of Change: An Experimental Examination of Framing and Micromobilization." *American Political Science Review* 109 (3): 407–26.

McKeown, Ryder. 2009. "Norm Regress: US Revisionism and the Slow Death of the Torture Norm." *International Relations* 23 (1): 5–25.

Mearsheimer, John J. 1994. "The False Promise of International Institutions." *International Security* 19 (3): 5–49.

Meernik, James, Rosa Aloisi, Marsha Sowell, and Angela Nichols. 2012. "The Impact of Human Rights Organizations on Naming and Shaming Campaigns." *Journal of Conflict Resolution* 56 (2): 233–56.

Menéndez, Valeria Reyes. 2022. *Beyond Reporting: Transformational Changes on the Ground.* Geneva: UPR Info (June). https://www.upr-info.org/sites/default/files/general-document/2022-07/Beyond%20Reporting-EN-Web.pdf (accessed August 30, 2022).

Mercer, Jonathan. 1995. "Anarchy and Identity." *International Organization* 49 (2): 229–52.

Merry, Sally Engle. 2006. "Transnational Human Rights and Local Activism: Mapping the Middle." *American Anthropologist* 108 (1): 38–51.

Meyer, John W., John Boli, George M. Thomas, and Francisco O. Ramirez. 1997. "World Society and the Nation-State." *American Journal of Sociology* 103 (1): 144–81.

Moallem, Minoo. 2005. *Between Warrior Brother and Veiled Sister: Islamic Fundamentalism and the Politics of Patriarchy in Iran.* Berkeley: University of California Press.

Monin, Benoît, and Kieran O'Connor. 2011. "Reactions to Defiant Deviants: Deliverance or Defensiveness?" In *Rebels in Groups: Dissent, Deviance, Difference, and Defiance*, edited by Jolanda Jetten and Matthew J Hornsey, 261–80. Malden, MA: Wiley Blackwell.

Moravcsik, Andrew. 2000. "The Origins of Human Rights Regimes: Democratic Delegation in Postwar Europe." *International Organization* 54 (2): 217–52.

Morris, Loveday, Souad Mekhennet, and Kareem Fahim. 2018. "Saudis Are Said to Have Lain in Wait for Jamal Khashoggi." *Washington Post*, October 9. https://www.washingtonpost.com/world/saudis-lay-in-wait-for-jamal-khashoggi-and-left-turkey-quickly-sources-say/2018/10/09/0e283e2e-cbc5-11e8-ad0a-0e01efba3cc1_story.html (accessed October 20, 2021).

Murdie, Amanda. 2009. "The Impact of Human Rights NGO Activity on Human Right Practices." *International NGO Journal* 4 (10): 421–40.

———. 2013. "Scrambling for Contact: The Determinants of Inter-NGO Cooperation in Non-Western Countries." *Review of International Organizations* 9: 309–31.

Murdie, Amanda. 2014. *Help or Harm: The Human Security Effects of International NGOs*. Stanford, CA: Stanford University Press.

Murdie, Amanda, and Tavishi Bhasin. 2011. "Aiding and Abetting: Human Rights INGOs and Domestic Protest." *Journal of Conflict Resolution* 55 (2): 163.

Murdie, Amanda, and David Davis. 2012a. "Looking in the Mirror: Comparing INGO Networks across Issue Areas." *Review of International Organizations* 7 (2): 177–202.

———. 2012b. "Shaming and Blaming: Using Events Data to Assess the Impact of Human Rights INGOs." *International Studies Quarterly* 56 (1): 1–16.

Murdie, Amanda, and Dursun Peksen. 2013. "The Impact of Human Rights INGO Activities on Economic Sanctions." *Review of International Organizations* 8 (1): 33–53.

———. 2014. "The Impact of Human Rights INGO Shaming on Humanitarian Interventions." *Journal of Politics* 76 (1): 215–228.

———. 2015. "Women's Rights INGO Shaming and the Government Respect for Women's Rights." *Review of International Organizations* 10 (1): 1–22.

Murdie, Amanda, and Johannes Urpelainen. 2015. "Why Pick on Us? Environmental INGOs and State Shaming as a Strategic Substitute." *Political Studies* 63 (2): 353–72.

Myers, David G., and Helmut Lamm. 1976. "The Group Polarization Phenomenon." *Psychological Bulletin* 83 (4): 602–27.

Myrick, Rachel, and Jeremy M. Weinstein. 2021. "Making Sense of Human Rights Diplomacy: Evidence from a US Campaign to Free Political Prisoners." *International Organization*. https://doi.org/10.1017/S0020818321000424.

Nayyeri, Mohammad Hossein. 2011. "The Question of 'Stoning to Death' in the New Penal Code of the IRI." Abdorrahman Boroumand Center for Human Rights in Iran, November 30. http://www.iranrights.org/library/document/2072/the-question-of-stoning-to-death-in-the-new-penal-code-of-the-iri (accessed April 23, 2015).

Neumayer, Eric. 2003a. "Do Human Rights Matter in Bilateral Aid Allocation? A Quantitative Analysis of 21 Donor Countries." *Social Science Quarterly* 84 (3): 650–66.

———. 2003b. "Is Respect for Human Rights Rewarded? An Analysis of Total Bilateral and Multilateral Aid Flows." *Human Rights Quarterly* 25 (2): 510–27.

New York Times. 2010. "Iran Lifts Sentence of Stoning for Woman." *New York Times*, September 8. http://www.nytimes.com/2010/09/09/world/middleeast/09stoning.html (accessed April 24, 2015).

Nicholson, Stephen P. 2012. "Polarizing Cues." *American Journal of Political Science* 56 (1): 52–66.

Nielsen, Richard A. 2013. "Rewarding Human Rights? Selective Aid Sanctions against Repressive States." *International Studies Quarterly* 57 (4): 791–803.

Nincic, Miroslav. 2005. *Renegade Regimes: Confronting Deviant Behavior in World Politics*. New York: Columbia University Press.

Nugent, Elizabeth R. 2020. "The Psychology of Repression and Polarization." *World Politics* 72 (2): 1–44.

Nuñez-Mietz, Fernando, and Lucrecia Garcia Iommi. 2017. "Can Transnational Norm Advocacy Undermine Internalization? Explaining Immunization against LGBT Rights in Uganda." *International Studies Quarterly* 61 (1): 196–209.

Nussbaum, Martha C. 2005. "Inscribing the Face: Shame, Stigma, and Punishment." *Nomos* 46: 259–302.

Nyhan, Brendan, and Jason Reifler. 2010. "When Corrections Fail: The Persistence of Political Misperceptions." *Political Behavior* 32 (2): 303–30.

O'Donnell, Norah. 2018. "Saudi Arabia's Heir to the Throne Talks to 60 Minutes." *CBS News: 60 Minutes*. https://www.cbsnews.com/news/saudi-crown-prince-talks-to-60-minutes/ (accessed April 10, 2021).

Olsen, Johan P., and James G. March. 1989. *Rediscovering Institutions: The Organizational Basis of Politics*. New York: Free Press.

Olson, Mancur. 1965. *The Logic of Collective Action: Public Goods and the Theory of Groups*, 2nd ed., with a new preface and appendix. Cambridge, MA: Harvard University Press.

Onion, Rebecca. 2013. "How the Soviets Used Our Civil Rights Conflicts against Us." *Slate*, July 9. https://slate.com/human-interest/2013/07/civil-rights-coverage-how-the-soviets-used-evidence-of-racial-strife-against-us-in-the-world-press.html (accessed February 2, 2019).

Onishi, Norimitsu. 2015. "US Support of Gay Rights in Africa May Have Done More Harm than Good." *New York Times*, December 20. http://www.nytimes.com/2015/12/21/world/africa/us-support-of-gay-rights-in-africa-may-have-done-more-harm-than-good.html (accessed December 20, 2015).

Ovsiovitch, Jay S. 1993. "News Coverage of Human Rights." *Political Research Quarterly* 46 (3): 671–89.

Paidar, Parvin. 1997. *Women and the Political Process in Twentieth-Century Iran*. Cambridge: Cambridge University Press.

Pappas, Alex. 2018. "GOP Senators Urge Consequences for Saudi Arabia, as Trump Warns against Rush to Judgment." *Fox News*, October 17. https://www.foxnews.com/politics/trump-u-s-wants-audio-and-video-related-to-khashoggi-disappearance-if-it-exists.amp (accessed November 2, 2021).

Paul, Thaza Varkey, Deborah Welch Larson, and William C. Wohlforth. 2014. *Status in World Politics*. Cambridge: Cambridge University Press.

Perkins, Richard, and Eric Neumayer. 2010. "The Organized Hypocrisy of Ethical Foreign Policy: Human Rights, Democracy, and Western Arms Sales." *Geoforum* 41 (2): 247–56.

Perlez, Jane. 2019. "China Wants the World to Stay Silent on Muslim Camps. It's Succeeding." *New York Times*, September 25. https://www.nytimes.com/2019/09/25/world/asia/china-xinjiang-muslim-camps.html (accessed October 12, 2019).

Peters, Anne. 2018. "How Not to Do Things with International Law." *Ethics and International Affairs* 32 (4): 483–91.

Piccone, Ted. 2018. *China's Long Game on Human Rights at the United Nations*. Washington, DC: Brookings Institution.

Poe, Steven C., and C. Neal Tate. 1994. "Repression of Human Rights to Personal Integrity in the 1980s: A Global Analysis." *American Political Science Review* 88 (4): 853–72.

Poe, Steven C., C. Neal Tate, and Linda Camp Keith. 1999. "Repression of the Human Right to Personal Integrity Revisited: A Global Cross-National Study Covering the Years 1976–1993." *International Studies Quarterly* 43 (2): 291–313.

Posner, Eric. 2000. *Law and Social Norms*. Cambridge, MA: Harvard University Press.

Pratt, Simon Frankel. 2016. "A Relational View of Ontological Security in International Relations." *International Studies Quarterly* 61 (1): 78–85. https://academic.oup.com/isq/article-abstract/doi/10.1093/isq/sqw038/2742035/A-Relational-View-of-Ontological-Security-in (accessed February 28, 2017).

———. 2019. "From Norms to Normative Configurations: A Pragmatist and Relational Approach to Theorizing Normativity in IR." *International Theory* 12 (1): 1–24.

Press TV. 2010. "Iran Refutes Propaganda about Ashtiani." *Press TV*, November 4.

———. 2011. "West Politicizing Ashtiani Case." *Press TV*, January 12.

Radio Zamaneh. 2010. "Iran Says Brazil Offer of Asylum a Western Ruse." *Radio Zamaneh*, December 17. http://www.zamaaneh.com/enzam/2010/08/iran-says-brazils-offer-o.html (accessed April 22, 2015).

Rafi, Mohammad, and A.M.R. Chowdhury. 2000. "Human Rights and Religious Backlash: The Experience of a Bangladeshi NGO." *Development in Practice* 10 (1): 19–30.

Ramos, Howard, James Ron, and Oskar N. T. Thoms. 2007. "Shaping the Northern Media's Human Rights Coverage, 1986–2000." *Journal of Peace Research* 44 (4): 385–406.

Rao, Rahul. 2014. "The Locations of Homophobia." *London Review of International Law* 2 (2): 169–99.

Renshon, Jonathan. 2016. "Status Deficits and War." *International Organization* 70 (3): 513–50.

Repucci, Sarah. 2020. "Freedom in the World 2020: A Leaderless Struggle for Democracy." Freedom House. https://freedomhouse.org/sites/default/files/2020-02/FIW_2020_REPORT_BOOKLET_Final.pdf (accessed October 18, 2021).

Rescher, Nicholas. 1996. *Process Metaphysics: An Introduction to Process Philosophy.* Albany: State University of New York Press.

Reus-Smit, Christian. 2007. "International Crises of Legitimacy." *International Politics* 44 (2/3): 157–74.

Reynolds, Emma. 2018. "How Saudis Are Getting Away with Khashoggi Murder." *news.com.au* (Australia), October 28. https://www.news.com.au/world/middle-east/how-saudis-are-getting-away-with-khashoggi-murder/news-story/4632ff5a196d9013a2b1b8e3e7139175 (accessed November 3, 2021).

RFI. 2010. "Carla Bruni-Sarkozy's Letter to Iranian Woman Sentenced to Death." *RFI*, August 24. http://www.english.rfi.fr/france/20100824-carla-bruni-s-letter-iranian-woman-sentenced-stoning (accessed April 22, 2015).

Riedel, Bruce. 2021. "It's Time to Stop US Arms Sales to Saudi Arabia." Brookings Institution, February 4. https://www.brookings.edu/blog/order-from-chaos/2021/02/04/its-time-to-stop-us-arms-sales-to-saudi-arabia/ (accessed October 28, 2021).

Riotta, Chris. 2018. "Lindsey Graham Warns of 'Hell to Pay' for Saudi Arabia in Jamal Khashoggi Disappearance." *Independent*, October 10. https://www.independent.co.uk/news/world/americas/jamal-khashoggi-missing-saudi-arabia-turkey-istanbul-consulate-dismembered-lindsey-graham-us-a8578266.html (accessed November 3, 2021).

Risse, Thomas. 2000. "Let's Argue! Communicative Action in World Politics." *International Organization* 54 (1): 1–39.

Risse, Thomas, and Stephen C. Ropp. 1999. "International Human Rights Norms and Domestic Change: Conclusions." In *The Power of Human Rights: International Norms and Domestic Change,* 234–78. Cambridge: Cambridge University Press.

Risse, Thomas, Stephen C. Ropp, and Kathryn Sikkink, eds. 1999. *The Power of Human Rights: International Norms and Domestic Change.* New York: Cambridge University Press.

———, eds. 2013. *The Persistent Power of Human Rights: From Commitment to Compliance.* Cambridge: Cambridge University Press.

Rodogno, Raffaele. 2009. "Shame, Guilt, and Punishment." *Law and Philosophy* 28 (5): 429–64.

Ron, James, Howard Ramos, and Kathleen Rodgers. 2005. "Transnational Information Politics: NGO Human Rights Reporting, 1986–2000." *International Studies Quarterly* 49 (3): 557–88.

Ropp, Stephen C., and Kathryn Sikkink. 1999. "The Socialization of International Human Rights Norms into Domestic Practices: Introduction." In *The Power of Human Rights: International Norms and Domestic Change,* 1–39. Cambridge: Cambridge University Press.

Roth, Kenneth. 2004. "Defending Economic, Social, and Cultural Rights: Practical Issues Faced by an International Human Rights Organization." *Human Rights Quarterly* 26 (1): 63–73.

Russell, George. 2015. "UN Human Rights Council Takes Aim at New Target: United States." *Fox News*, December 9. https://www.foxnews.com/world/u-n-human-rights-council-takes-aim-at-new-target-united-states (accessed August 29, 2022).

Sadr, Shadi. 2010. "Stones Aimed at Us: An Overview of the Stop Stoning Forever Campaign." Project. Association for Women's Rights in Development (AWID). http://www.iran-women-solidarity.net/IMG/pdf/Shadi-1.pdf.

Salama, Vivian, and Margherita Stancati. 2018. "Trump, Saudis Escalate Threats." *Wall Street Journal*, October 14. https://www.wsj.com/articles/saudi-arabia-threatens-to-retaliate-after -u-s-pressure-over-journalists-disappearance-1539522239 (accessed January 25, 2019).

Salem, Mostafa. 2020. "Iran Criticizes 'Oppressive' US Reaction to Protests." *CNN*, June 2. https:// www.cnn.com/us/live-news/george-floyd-protests-06-02-20/h_81fe8d03234c4e03540ada 77c99a009a (accessed July 27, 2021).

Sanders, Rebecca. 2016. "Norm Proxy War and Resistance through Outsourcing: The Dynamics of Transnational Human Rights Contestation." *Human Rights Review* 17 (2): 165–91.

Sanger, David E. 2021a. "Candidate Biden Called Saudi Arabia a 'Pariah.' He Now Has to Deal with It." *New York Times*, February 24. https://www.nytimes.com/2021/02/24/us/politics/biden -jamal-khashoggi-saudi-arabia.html (accessed November 16, 2021).

———. 2021b. "Biden Won't Penalize Saudi Crown Prince over Khashoggi's Killing, Fearing Relations Breach." *New York Times*, February 26. https://www.nytimes.com/2021/02/26 /us/politics/biden-mbs-khashoggi.html (accessed March 7, 2021).

Scheff, Thomas J. 2000. "Shame and the Social Bond: A Sociological Theory." *Sociological Theory* 18 (1): 84–99.

Schimmelfennig, Frank. 2000. "International Socialization in the New Europe: Rational Action in an Institutional Environment." *European Journal of International Relations* 6 (1): 109–39.

———. 2001. "The Community Trap: Liberal Norms, Rhetorical Action, and the Eastern Enlarge- ment of the European Union." *International Organization* 55 (1): 47–80.

Schmitt, Eric, and Nicholas Fandos. 2018. "Saudi Prince 'Complicit' in Khashoggi's Murder, Sena- tors Say after CIA Briefing." *New York Times*, December 4. https://www.nytimes.com/2018 /12/04/us/politics/cia-senate-khashoggi-.html (accessed October 26, 2021).

Sengupta, Somini. 2003. "The World: When Do-Gooders Don't Know What They're Doing." *New York Times*, May 11. http://www.nytimes.com/2003/05/11/weekinreview/the-world-when-do -gooders-don-t-know-what-they-re-doing.html (Accessed August 19, 2014).

Shalaby, Sondos. 2018. "Spain U-turns on Ending Bomb Contract with Saudi after Jobs Threat." *Middle East Eye*, September 13. http://www.middleeasteye.net/news/spain-u-turns-ending -bomb-contract-saudi-after-jobs-threat (accessed November 3, 2021).

Shannon, Vaughn P. 2000. "Norms Are What States Make of Them: The Political Psychology of Norm Violation." *International Studies Quarterly* 44 (2): 293–316.

Sherman, David K., Zoe Kinias, Brenda Major, Heejung S. Kim, and Mary Prenovost. 2007. "The Group as a Resource: Reducing Biased Attributions for Group Success and Failure via Group Affirmation." *Personality and Social Psychology Bulletin* 33 (8): 1100–12.

Sherman, Lawrence W. 1993. "Defiance, Deterrence, and Irrelevance: A Theory of the Criminal Sanction." *Journal of Research in Crime and Delinquency* 30 (4): 445–73.

Sheth, Sonam, and John Haltiwanger. 2020. "'I Saved His A—': Trump Boasted That He Pro- tected Saudi Crown Prince Mohammed bin Salman after Jamal Khashoggi's Brutal Murder, Woodward's New Book Says." *Business Insider*, September 10. https://www.businessinsider .com/trump-woodward-i-saved-his-ass-mbs-khashoggi-rage-2020-9 (accessed November 16, 2021).

Sikkink, Kathryn. 1993. "Human Rights, Principled Issue-Networks, and Sovereignty in Latin America." *International Organization* 47 (3): 411–41.

Simmons, Beth A. 2009. *Mobilizing for Human Rights: International Law in Domestic Politics*. New York: Cambridge University Press.

Snyder, Jack. 2020a. "Backlash against Human Rights Shaming: Emotions in Groups." *Interna- tional Theory* 12 (1): 109–32.

———. 2020b. "Backlash against Naming and Shaming: The Politics of Status and Emotion." *British Journal of Politics and International Relations* 22 (4): 644–53.

Spencer-Rodgers, Julie, Brenda Major, Daniel E. Forster, and Kaiping Peng. 2016. "The Power of Affirming Group Values: Group Affirmation Buffers the Self-Esteem of Women Exposed to Blatant Sexism." *Self and Identity* 15 (4): 413–31.

Spivak, Rhonda. 2010. "Over 137,000 Sign Petition Initiated by Reisman to Free Sakineh." *Behind the News in Israel*, July 27. http://israelbehindthenews.com/over-137000-sign-petition -initiated-by-reisman-to-free-sakineh/6575/ (accessed March 31, 2015).

Squatrito, Theresa, Magnus Lundgren, and Thomas Sommerer. 2019. "Shaming by International Organizations: Mapping Condemnatory Speech Acts across 27 International Organizations, 1980–2015." *Cooperation and Conflict* 54 (3): 356–77.

Steele, Claude M., Steven J. Spencer, and Joshua Aronson. 2002. "Contending with Group Image: The Psychology of Stereotype and Social Identity Threat." In *Advances in Experimental Social Psychology* 34: 379–440.

Steininger, Michael. 2012. "German Tabloid Bild Takes Down Politicians with Its Unmatched Megaphone." *Christian Science Monitor*, January 18. http://www.csmonitor.com/World /Europe/2012/0118/German-tabloid-Bild-takes-down-politicians-with-its-unmatched -megaphone (accessed June 26, 2015).

Stockholm International Peace Research Institute (SIPRI). 2019. "SIPRI Arms Transfers Data- base." https://www.sipri.org/databases/armstransfers (accessed August 31, 2022).

———. 2020. "USA and France Dramatically Increase Major Arms Exports; Saudi Arabia Is Largest Arms Importer, Says SIPRI." March 9. https://www.sipri.org/media/press-release /2020/usa-and-france-dramatically-increase-major-arms-exports-saudi-arabia-largest-arms -importer-says (accessed October 28, 2021).

Stokel-Walker, Chris. 2018. "Khashoggi's Death Is Forcing UK Tech to Reckon with Its Saudi Links." *Wired UK*, October 23. https://www.wired.co.uk/article/saudi-arabia-khashoggi -murder-tech-conference (accessed September 7, 2022).

Strezhnev, Anton, Judith G. Kelley, and Beth A. Simmons. 2021. "Testing for Negative Spillovers: Is Pro- moting Human Rights Really Part of the 'Problem'?" *International Organization* 75 (1) 1–32.

Sunstein, Cass R. 2002. "The Law of Group Polarization." *Journal of Political Philosophy* 10 (2): 175–95.

Symons, Jonathan, and Dennis Altman. 2015. "International Norm Polarization: Sexuality as a Subject of Human Rights Protection." *International Theory* 7 (1): 61–95.

Tajfel, Henri, and John C. Turner. 1986. "The Social Identity Theory of Intergroup Behavior." In *Psychology of Intergroup Relations*, edited by Stephen Worchel and William Austin, 7–24. Chicago: Nelson-Hall.

Terman, Rochelle. 2017. "Islamophobia and Media Portrayals of Muslim Women: A Computa- tional Text Analysis of US News Coverage." *International Studies Quarterly* 61 (3): 489–502.

Terman, Rochelle, and Joshua Byun. 2022. "Punishment and Politicization in the International Human Rights Regime." *American Political Science Review* 116 (2): 385–402.

Terman, Rochelle, and Mufuliat Fijabi. 2010. "Stoning Is Not Our Culture: A Comparative Analysis of Human Rights and Religious Discourses in Iran and Nigeria." Violence Is Not Our Culture, March. https://www.oursplatform.org/wp-content/uploads/VNC-Stoning-Comparative -Analysis-of-HR-and-Religious-Discourses-in-Iran-and-Nigeria.pdf.

Terman, Rochelle, and Erik Voeten. 2018. "The Relational Politics of Shame: Evidence from the Universal Periodic Review." *Review of International Organizations* 13 (1): 1–23.

The Times. 2010. "Stone Cold Shame." *The Times* (London), July 8. https://www.thetimes.co.uk /article/stone-cold-shame-cvk67dchl7t.

Tingley, Dustin, and Michael Tomz. 2022. "The Effects of Naming and Shaming on Public Sup- port for Compliance with International Agreements: An Experimental Analysis of the Paris Agreement." *International Organization* 76 (2): 445–68.

Tomz, Michael R., and Jessica L. P. Weeks. 2020. "Human Rights and Public Support for War." *Journal of Politics* 82 (1): 182–94.

Toosi, Nahal. 2017. "Leaked Memo Schooled Tillerson on Human Rights." *Politico*, December 19. https://www.politico.com/story/2017/12/19/tillerson-state-human-rights-304118 (accessed August 24, 2022).

Towns, Ann. 2009. "The Status of Women as a Standard of 'Civilization.'" *European Journal of International Relations* 15 (4): 681–706.

———. 2010. *Women and States: Norms and Hierarchies in International Society.* Cambridge University Press.

———. 2012. "Norms and Social Hierarchies: Understanding International Policy Diffusion 'From Below.'" *International Organization* 66 (2): 179–209.

Towns, Ann, and Bahar Rumelili. 2017. "Taking the Pressure: Unpacking the Relation between Norms, Social Hierarchies, and Social Pressures on States." *European Journal of International Relations* 23 (4). https://doi.org/10.1177/1354066116682070.

Traven, David, and Marcus Holmes. 2021. "Measuring without a Ruler: Assessing Compliance with Calculative International Norms." *Journal of Global Security Studies* 6 (1). https://doi.org/10.1093/jogss/ogz061.

Tsutsui, Kiyoteru, Claire Whitlinger, and Alwyn Lim. 2012. "International Human Rights Law and Social Movements: States' Resistance and Civil Society's Insistence." *Annual Review of Law and Social Science* 8 (1): 367–96.

United Nations General Assembly. 2005a. *In Larger Freedom: Towards Development, Security, and Human Rights for All: Report of the Secretary-General.* March 21, A/59/2005. https://www.refworld.org/docid/4a54bbfa0.html.

———. Human Rights Council. 2005b. "Explanatory Note by the Secretary-General." In *In Larger Freedom: Toward Development, Security and Human Rights for All.* May 23, A/59/2005/Add.1. http://www.preventionweb.net/files/resolutions/N0535601.pdf.

———. Human Rights Council. 2006. Resolution 60/251. April 3, A/RES/60/251. http://www2.ohchr.org/english/bodies/hrcouncil/docs/A.RES.60.251_En.pdf (accessed July 29, 2015).

———. Human Rights Council. 2011. "Report of the Working Group on the Universal Periodic Review: United States of America." January 4, A/HRC/16/11. http://undocs.org/en/A/HRC/16/11 (accessed September 8, 2021).

———. Human Rights Council. 2013a. "Report of the Working Group on the Universal Periodic Review: Cuba." July 8, A/HRC/24/16. http://undocs.org/en/A/HRC/24/16 (accessed September 8, 2021).

———. Human Rights Council. 2013b. "Report of the Working Group on the Universal Periodic Review: Saudi Arabia." December 26, A/HRC/25/3. http://undocs.org/en/A/HRC/25/3 (accessed March 11, 2021).

———. Human Rights Council. 2014. "Report of the Working Group on the Universal Periodic Review: Islamic Republic of Iran." December 22, A/HRC/28/12. http://undocs.org/en/A/HRC/28/12 (accessed March 11, 2021).

———. Human Rights Council. 2019. *Annex to the Report of the Special Rapporteur on Extrajudicial, Summary or Arbitrary Executions: Investigation into the Unlawful Death of Mr. Jamal Khashoggi.* June 19, A/HRC/41/CRP.1. https://www.ohchr.org/EN/NewsEvents/Pages/DisplayNews.aspx?NewsID=24713&LangID=E (accessed October 20, 2021).

UPR Info. 2014. *Beyond Promises: The Impact of the UPR on the Ground.* Geneva: UPR Info. https://www.upr-info.org/sites/default/files/documents/2014-10/2014_beyond_promises.pdf.

US Department of State. Bureau of Democracy, Human Rights, and Labor. 2021. *2020 Country Reports on Human Rights Practices: Saudi Arabia.* March 30. https://www.state.gov/reports/2020-country-reports-on-human-rights-practices/saudi-arabia/.

US Department of State. Bureau of Near Eastern Affairs. 2020. "US Relations with Saudi Arabia." Bilateral Relations Fact Sheet, May 11. https://www.state.gov/u-s-relations-with-saudi-arabia / (accessed October 26, 2021).

Vinjamuri, Leslie. 2017. "Human Rights Backlash." In *Human Rights Futures*, edited by Stephen Hopgood, Jack Snyder, and Leslie Vinjamuri, 114–34. Cambridge: Cambridge University Press.

Vision of the Islamic Republic of Iran. 2010. "Iran TV Airs Report on Woman Sentenced to Stoning Saying Deceived by Others." Network 1BBC Monitoring Middle East (London), November 15. http://search.proquest.com/docview/766746301/484FA12C6056481DPQ/26 ?accountid=14496 (accessed April 24, 2015).

Voeten, Erik. 2020. "Populism and Backlashes against International Courts." *Perspectives on Politics* 18 (2): 407–22.

Wachman, Alan M. 2001. "Does the Diplomacy of Shame Promote Human Rights in China?" *Third World Quarterly* 22 (2): 257–81.

Wagner, Wolfgang, Wouter Werner, and Michal Onderco. 2014. *Deviance in International Relations: "Rogue States" and International Security.* London: Palgrave Macmillan.

Ward, Steven. 2017. *Status and the Challenge of Rising Powers.* Cambridge: Cambridge University Press.

Washington Post Editorial Board. 2018. "The Saudi Explanation for Jamal Khashoggi's Death Is a Fable. Still Trump Plays Along." *Washington Post*, October 20. https://www.washingtonpost .com/opinions/global-opinions/the-saudi-explanation-for-jamal-khashoggis-death-is-a-fable -still-trump-plays-along/2018/10/20/1777e3b8-d457-11e8-8c22-fa2ef74bd6d6_story.html (accessed November 2, 2021).

Weeks, Jessica L. 2008. "Autocratic Audience Costs: Regime Type and Signaling Resolve." *International Organization* 62 (1): 35–64.

White House Office of the Press Secretary. 2018. "Statement from President Donald J. Trump on Standing with Saudi Arabia." November 20, press release. https://www.cnn.com/2018/11 /20/politics/trump-statement-saudi-khashoggi/index.html (accessed November 8, 2021).

Whitmore, Brian. 2013. "Vladimir Putin, Conservative Icon." *Atlantic*, December 20. http://www .theatlantic.com/international/archive/2013/12/vladimir-putin-conservative-icon/282572/ (accessed August 3, 2014).

Wiener, Antje. 2004. "Contested Compliance: Interventions on the Normative Structure of World Politics." *European Journal of International Relations* 10 (2): 189–234.

Williams, Michael C. 2003. "Words, Images, Enemies: Securitization and International Politics." *International Studies Quarterly* 47 (4): 511–31.

Winter, Bronwyn, Denise Thompson, and Sheila Jeffreys. 2002. "The UN Approach to Harmful Traditional Practices." *International Feminist Journal of Politics* 4 (1): 72–94.

Wohlforth, William C. 2009. "Unipolarity, Status Competition, and Great Power War." *World Politics* 61 (1): 28–57.

Wolf, Reinhard. 2011. "Respect and Disrespect in International Politics: The Significance of Status Recognition." *International Theory* 3 (1): 105–42.

Wong, Edward. 2020. "Trump Administration Is Bypassing Arms Control Pact to Sell Large Armed Drones." *New York Times*, July 24. https://www.nytimes.com/2020/07/24/us/politics /trump-arms-sales-drones.html (accessed November 16, 2021).

Wong, Scott. 2012. "Kony Captures Congress' Attention." *Politico*, March 22. https://www.politico .com/story/2012/03/kony-captures-congress-attention-074355 (accessed August 24, 2022).

Xiyue, Wang. 2021. "Don't Let Iran's Human Rights Be Sacrificed at the Altar of a Nuclear Deal." Hoover Institution, March 9. https://www.hoover.org/research/dont-let-irans-human-rights -be-sacrificed-altar-nuclear-deal (accessed September 20, 2022).

Yeganeh, Nahid. 1993. "Women, Nationalism, and Islam in Contemporary Political Discourse in Iran." *Feminist Review* 44 (Summer): 3–18.

Zarakol, Ayşe. 2010. *After Defeat: How the East Learned to Live with the West.* Cambridge: Cambridge University Press.

———. 2013. "Revisiting Second Image Reversed: Lessons from Turkey and Thailand." *International Studies Quarterly* 57 (1): 150–62.

———. 2014. "What Made the Modern World Hang Together: Socialisation or Stigmatisation?" *International Theory* 6 (2): 311–32.

———, ed. 2017. *Hierarchies in World Politics.* Cambridge: Cambridge University Press.

Zarpli, Omer, and Huseyin Zengin. 2022. "Shame, Endorse, or Remain Silent? State Response to Human Rights Violations in Other Countries." *Research and Politics* 9 (1). https://doi.org/10.1177/20531680211070344.

INDEX

A NOTE ON THE TYPE

This book has been composed in Adobe Text and Gotham. Adobe Text, designed by Robert Slimbach for Adobe, bridges the gap between fifteenth- and sixteenth-century calligraphic and eighteenth-century Modern styles. Gotham, inspired by New York street signs, was designed by Tobias Frere-Jones for Hoefler & Co.

Printed in the USA
CPSIA information can be obtained
at www.ICGtesting.com
JSHW081532170923
48425JS00003B/3